Against Security

· ·

Against Security

HOW WE GO WRONG AT AIRPORTS, SUBWAYS, AND OTHER SITES OF AMBIGUOUS DANGER

Harvey Molotch

with a new preface by the author

PRINCETON UNIVERSITY PRESS
PRINCETON AND OXFORD

Copyright © 2012 by Princeton University Press

Published by Princeton University Press,
41 William Street, Princeton, New Jersey 08540

In the United Kingdom: Princeton University Press,
6 Oxford Street, Woodstock, Oxfordshire OX20 1TW

press.princeton.edu

Second printing, and first paperback printing, with a new preface by the author, 2014

Paperback ISBN 978-0-691-16358-1

The Library of Congress has cataloged the cloth edition as follows

Molotch, Harvey Luskin.
Against security : how we go wrong at airports, subways,
and other sites of ambiguous danger / Harvey Molotch.
p. cm.
Includes bibliographical references and index.
ISBN 978-0-691-15581-4 (cloth : alk. paper)
1. Terrorism—Prevention—Government policy—United
States. 2. National security—United States. 3. Transportation—Security
measures—United States. I. Title.
HV6432.M645 2012
363.325'170973—dc23
2012012128

British Library Cataloging-in-Publication Data is available

This book has been composed in Electra

Printed on acid-free paper. ∞

Printed in the United States of America

3 5 7 9 10 8 6 4 2

．．．

For Christopher, Emma,
and
Darwin

Contents

● ●

Preface to the Paperback Edition

● ●

More than a decade beyond 9/11 and two years after this book was first published, we can see what still holds on the security front. More ambitiously still, we can examine the aftermath to learn how organizations respond to fear. We can see the way wars, like the so-called war on terror, are brought homeland and stay there. Here's the bottom-line of what to notice: the security apparatus, big or small, local or global, is costly, rude, and counter-productive. It hangs across the landscape and shapes, right down to the core, our ordinary life routines. Yet in ways I detail, it is doubtful that a single terrorist act has been thwarted through all the machinery and claptrap on our shores.

A brazen way of putting it: you can find our wars, domestic and foreign, in the laboratory of the U.S. public restroom. The war came out of the angst of attacks from the sky; life in the restroom churns with anxiety over who is around and what they may be up to. Both involve, as security systems do, anxious concealment. In the restroom it is not just a desire for privacy of the body, but a taboo of public discussion of the body's needs and how to provide for them. In regards to 9/11, official secrecy and silences sequester illegitimate actions from public critique.

In taking up places like the bathroom—but also the subway, the air-port, and emergency worksites in New Orleans and the Ground Zero rebuilding—I model the big story through the mundane and concrete elements mostly beyond the headlines. Odd as it may seem, taking up such diverse sites in a single lens is a route to discover the security essence common to them all. Useful for my purpose, it is also the strategy recommended by the illustrious sociological thinker, Howard Becker, for carrying out a social science inquiry on any topic, controversial or not, and no matter at what scale.[1] Look for some essence across what appear dissimilar cases.

A lot of what was behind the headlines when *Against Security* was first published has since burst into the open thanks to the works of Edward Snowden and Chelsea Manning. Troves of concealments now reveal, to a degree that I did not fully appreciate, the range of U.S. penetration of lives and governments—much of it against both domestic and international law. We are the snoopers of the world.

Unanticipated revelations are themselves a characteristic of security, especially in settings with a modicum of democracy. Large and complex concealment systems contain elements of their own demise. Too many people know too many things. All the scrutiny in the world won't weed them out, those so-called "bad apples." Some end up as whistle blowers because of conscience, others through a change of heart in the course of their work. Some may be at least a little nuts to begin with or go off program for whatever other idiosyncratic reason. Sometimes a great leak happens by sheer accident of machine, mouth, or fingers astray on a keyboard. Insider jobs have been with us since Brutus. The point is that revelations are an aspect of security itself, not simply an inadvertent failure of something that can be made to never fail.

Intelligence agencies have a dilemma: if they restrict access too much, their trusted operatives are not able to "connect the dots"—something held responsible for failure to detect the 9/11 plotters. On the scene at the World Trade Center disaster itself, a more naked blunder of disconnect: the police were alert to the impending building collapses, but couldn't warn fire department personnel because their radio systems were not interlinked. The fire fighters, following standard operating procedure, forged up the stairways. The result was that 343 of them died, compared to 23 members of the NYPD. Besides generally poor communication equipment, the two public safety agencies suffered from a long-standing interagency rivalry that blocked system alignment. It became a no-brainer to urge correction of the problem and put the police and fire operators on the same page. At the level of national intelligence, in contrast, erring on the side of access risks exposure of everything. Enter Mr. Snowden.

The Chancellor of Germany, Andrea Merkel, turned sour at the news that U.S. intelligence was eavesdropping on her cell phone. German authorities work closely with U.S. counterparts in fighting against terror. Whatever else that fight involves, it requires alert and real-time communication. Germany is crucial to global financial and trade agreements, matters on which U.S. interests are paramount. It is also an ally critical to outcomes in real politick contests of other sorts: nuclear armaments in Iran, civil war in the Middle East, disputes between China and Taiwan. Leaders of Brazil, France, and still other countries expressed more than casual displeasure. There is also a descent into "third party" effects. Indonesia is in discord with Australia because Australia was revealed as helping the U.S. to do its snooping on Indonesia.[2]

For the U.S., these are cumulating disadvantages, working against American "soft power." The counterproductive fall-out, as the chapters that follow repeatedly show, is commonplace—even within the narrow confines of the security worlds themselves and the limited logics of their operation. Like inspection points at airports that can ensnare a dignitary with an "Arab-sounding" name, spying on Merkel and other world leaders happens because it is possible to *do*. "This was colossally bad judgment—doing something because you can, instead of asking if you should," said an anonymous career American official who was spot-on.[3] A first suspicion should be that those so-called security gates happen not because they are effective, but because it is logistically feasible to set them up.

Back to the revelations. Hundreds of millions of people, maybe billions by now, rely on U.S. based internet systems and social media. The U.S. invented the Internet and its various digital outcomes have become the backbone of a vast economic workhorse. Now Facebook, Google, Twitter and the like must reassure the world that private lives are kept private, quite contrary to the evidence at hand. As put by a piece in the *Atlantic*, "The U.S. government, in its rush to spy on everybody, may end up killing our most productive golden goose."[4] Government officials around the world, including leaders of the EU, have called for investigations and relocation of data storage facilities to the confines of Europe itself (bypassing the U.S. where such data has been kept). Others have called for alternatives to U.S.-based networking operations, like Google and Facebook, in favor of indigenous European (and Asian) versions. Eric Schmidt, head of Google, called the NSA surveillance and related controls "a huge business risk."[5] At a more subtle level, national "branding" influences consumer behavior toward products associated with a given country. Image, whether in the garment business or digital economy, has some real fragility.

Perhaps still more profound, the transparency of U.S. markets may be under threat. Corporate actors who collude with U.S. intelligence agencies can be given immunity from testifying in criminal cases, something that could shield them more generally from questions that investors or regulators might have across any number of issues, including corporate asset content, the range of corporate activities around the world, and the persons with whom the firm does business. This unaccountability opens the way for abuses—likened to the kind of "state of lawlessness" that defeats not only democracy but also the possibility of markets. There are implications here for confidence in U.S. financial products and trustworthiness of the exchanges on which they are issued and traded.

At the other end of the risk spectrum are people identified as dangerous and hence put on watch lists. The U.S. terrorist version overflows with at least 700,000 names. That's a lot of people, but understates totals of those "of interest"—given the additional lists kept by other public agencies and private operatives of who is legitimate and who is not. Who, some have asked, "is watching the watch list?"[6] This is important within security itself since the rotten apple can be the official custodian supposed to be guarding the family jewels, as sophisticated spies have certainly sometimes been. They can also—the Soviets made a disease out of it—put hundreds, thousands, or even more in danger out of paranoia and power rivalries.

In the more routine U.S. procedural mode, hapless innocents get misidentified without the mayhem of a KGB purge. There is no doubt that guards and police profile at airports and subways, among other places.[7] There are also instances in which people try to nail a personal enemy by "saying something" to authorities to get revenge. In one grandiose instance, a Texas woman identified her estranged husband as the source of ricin poison mailed to President Obama and Mayor Bloomberg that she herself had sent. She got 18 years imprisonment.[8]

We do know that big databases can also store wrong information. It then migrates from one interlinked agency to another—"death by dossier" as sociologist Aaron Cicourel once called it.[9] A bad credit report, even if in error, can hinder life chances long into the future, perhaps without the victims knowing why they are not getting a loan or a job involving money handling (never mind the catastrophe of being listed as a sex offender). An appeal to authorities can take one into black holes of form letters, exasperating voicemail systems, and websites from hell.

In part to mitigate security excess at airports, federal agencies are expanding programs of "trusted traveler." These allow a subset of passengers—those who fly frequently, belong to elite airline categories, and have the money to pay the government-imposed fee—to bypass some of the inspections. They can leave their shoes on, for example. Presumably they are less subject to profiling and arbitrary interruption. Increasingly this will make the default into a category of *distrusted traveler*, immediately to be suspected of having failed the trust-tests. Once again, categorization creates error, and if misclassified, you may never get clear. Peril will set in should one become embroiled in an NSA-like apparatus whose very existence rests on the idea that bad people put up false fronts. And it has long been known about security (in the subways, for example) that various inspection systems lead to arrest for infractions, like marijuana possession, utterly unrelated to terrorist intent. Mission creep sets in. At the operational level, catching a "live one" helps overcome boredom. For those running things, pinching a culprit—any kind of culprit—shows "results" in an enforcement arena where results are few and far between.

Back again to the World Trade Center and the rebuild effort now reaching completion. There are indeed some positive design aspects including features to make the building green. Built heavily with public money, it is, however, the world's most expensive building,[10] in part because of security arrangements built into the construction. It has eroded revenues that otherwise could have, for example, improved the area's godforsaken airports (Vice President Biden recently called La Guardia "third world"). This repeats the pattern of diverting investment away from urban infrastructure and social programs into security systems. Indeed, in 2013 Department of Homeland Security [DHS] and its related security budgets amounted to almost $50 billion, which is more than all of the federal government's housing programs combined for that year. I had seen the same diversion work before in recovery efforts post-Katrina; instead of rescue boats, buses, and potable water, locals got troops and prohibitions against venturing out.

For the immediate World Trade Center neighborhood, plans have finally been unveiled for permanent security installations to replace the temporary roadblocks and security gates surrounding the site. Adjacent to the 16 acres of reconstruction, now dubbed a "campus" by the police, will be redesigned physical barriers, gates, and checkpoints. Locals will be eligible to enroll in a "Trusted Access Program" to ease their way in to the area, although specific operational details, say the police, will "not be released out of security concerns" (as the *New York Times* reported it[11]). But people have rebelled, calling it "fear's stockade."[12] A local group is suing the New York Police Department because its planning document, they say, "failed to explain and generally suppressed the NYPD's rationale for critical aspects of the plan based on a purported need for secrecy." In the affidavit against the project, a 30-year resident states her case: "I live in the City of New York—not 'on campus' or in a gated community. I do not want to prove who I am to come home to my own apartment."[13]

Hence the forces of security undermine the forces of amenity at the very location where "freedom" (as in "Freedom Tower") was supposed to be perpetuated. As a further sacrifice, the approximately 5 million people a year coming to the impressive World Trade Center Memorial—the two great cascading pools installed in front of the skyscraper—have no access to public toilets nor is such access to be provided in the future. This is a security loss of still another sort.

What's the good news here? The kind of moral panic that ensued after 9/11 has abated. Probably as a good outcome, the U.S. has lost its taste for entering foreign wars. It looks like no one wants to sacrifice a life, at least an American one, for security. And indeed the deal may be sealed with dramatic cutbacks in our standing Army as is being proposed, at this writing, by the U.S. Secretary of Defense. No such proposals have yet surfaced to lower allocations to the Department of Homeland Security. Joined by interested government operatives, corporate lobbying groups (based in military and intelligence industries) stay the course. The phrase "war on terror" has lost its frisson, but there will be no official ceremony to demobilize its civilian branches, no signatories on board a great ship to signal a war's end, no kisses on Times Square.

But time, I think, is on the side of easing off. Yes, the Boston Marathon led to a vast lock-down of the metropolis, most probably overdone. Alluding to the yellow police tape and overwhelming police presence at the New York Marathon that followed, one of the runners said the race "had morphed into a 26.2-mile crime scene." But at least until another big attack, the currents do run toward a relaxation. One thing to do is take advantage of the cool-headed interregnum and— fingers crossed it will last forever—build awareness of the dangers of security. Among those dangers, barely touched on in this preface, are the wholesale erosion of civil liberties and the establishment of martial law (recall the glimpse with Boston). Everything should be done as energetic precaution so that the fire next time will be controlled and less controlling, intelligent instead of intelligence-based, and as much as can be tolerated, decent, and law-abiding. This book tries to do its part.

Harvey Molotch
March 6, 2014

Notes

1. Howard Becker, *What About Mozart, What About Murder?* (Chicago: University of Chicago Press, forthcoming).

2. Joe Cochrane, "N.S.A. Spying Scandal Hurts Close Ties Between Australia and Indonesia," *New York Times*, Nov. 20, 2013, A11.

3. David E. Sanger and Mark Mazzetti, "Allegation of U.S. Spying on Merkel Puts Obama at Crossroads," *New York Times*, Oct. 24, 2013.

4. Christopher Jon Sprigman and Jennifer Granickjun, "U.S. Government Surveillance: Bad for Silicon Valley, Bad for Democracy Around the World," *The Atlantic*, June 28, 2013.

5. Cadie Thompson, "Google mulled ditching US after NSA scandal," CNBC.com, Nov. 22, 2013.

6. Susan Stellin "Who Is Watching the Watch Lists?" *New York Times*, Nov. 30, 2013.

7. Michael S. Schmidt, "Report Says T.S.A. Screening Is Not Objective," *New York Times*, June 4, 2013. http://www.nytimes.com/2013/06/05/us/report-says-tsa-screening-program-not-objective.html?_r=0.

8. Nomaan Merchant, "Texas Woman Admits To Sending Ricin To Obama," *Huffington Post*. Dec. 10, 2013.

9. Aaron Cicourel, *The Social Organization of Juvenile Justice*. (New Brunswick, NJ: Transaction Books, 1995).

10. Robert Sullivan, "A Look at the New One World Trade Center," *Architectural Digest*, http://www.architecturaldigest.com/architecture/2012–09/one-world-trade-center-new-york-david-childs-article.

11. David. D. Dunlap, "Residents Suing to Stop 'Fortresslike' Plan for World Trade Center," *New York Times*, Nov. 14, 2013, A31.

12. Michael Powell, "More Than a Decade After 9/11, A Bull Market for Barriers and Checkpoints," *New York Times*, Nov. 18, 2013.

13. David Dunlap, op. cit. A31.

Preface

• •

Although I mostly wander around to some very different places and topics, this book did begin with the events at Ground Zero. Living in downtown Manhattan and watching the towers collapse before my eyes, the bombing interrupted my day. There were less than two hours before the start time of my regular lecture at NYU, where I teach (Tuesday and Thursday mornings that semester). My mind was busy with preparations. The inertia of life—cleaning up the breakfast dishes, preparing class notes—was in full force. But planes into buildings? People jumping from ninety stories? What was I do with this extraordinary in my ordinary? Move forward in deference to the life I had been living or stop and—stop and what? That's a problem people face when disaster comes close by.

I also had some personal stakes. My partner of twenty-five years had set off that morning for a flight to Europe on United Airlines, and United, the news told us early on, was one of the airlines involved in the catastrophe. Was he on one of the planes? Was he stuck at Kennedy? Was he dead? Like the simultaneity of hot and cool breezes one can feel in coastal California when the Santa Ana winds blow hot desert air through the cool ocean breeze, things are oddly felt together. The private issue and public concern waft in and out, fear for a specific loved one and then back again to the public horror. Sometimes, and somehow, both at once.

This lived confusion is at least part of disaster response across the board and a basis for some of the investigations in this book. There is a need to do something, which is what being human is all about. We think and project forward. We rely on the sediments of past practice to make the next move. When something portending danger comes "out of the blue," we are at sea: we cannot just roll onward with our past. Mental practice continues as before; we have no cognitive choice. But consciousness, like a cartoon mouse running from the cat, flattens as it meets the wall of impossibility.

Maybe that is what I saw in faces when I went out to the street in front of my apartment building as my first attempt to "do something." We had television for only a short while because our reception depended on the broadcast antennae atop Tower One; when it got hit, we lost that connection. On the ground, I watched the early trickle of escapees make their way up through Washington Square from the Financial District, heading on foot to their own houses or some other haven farther up the island. All transit had been shut down and the streets were soon cordoned off. As the trickle thickened, I saw the perplexity of people who, in ways far deeper and harsher than in my own experience, did not know what had hit them. Their eyes seemed not to have the urbane go-ahead that is usually on the faces of city pedestrians. They reminded me more of gaunt models on a Milan fashion runway, seeming to be looking at nothing in particular, but deliberate indeed. Some of them moved in a shuffling kind of way, yet with intensity.

Among us bystanders, I felt the surge of the better angels. The lobby of the big apartment building adjacent to mine became a kind of rest stop for people to sit or lie down. Some women had given up on their high-heels and their bare feet endured shrapnel at the site or the ordinary streetscape fragments on route. A number of us went to the nearby grocery store to buy juice, water, and food to serve up. We competed a bit to pay for the stuff, like friends trying to buy a round of drinks. Then we had to contend with the shop owner's offer that it all be on him. As with the city's general gush of food, shelter, and volunteering, the samaritans were not just good but plentiful.

No matter what our identities of occupation, race, or social standing we did indeed come together. We did not have political discussions. World history was not on the menu. Ours was a consensus of sadness, something that would soon be reflected in spontaneous memorials all over the city—crèches for loved ones, alerts for the missing, candles of remembrance, murals of affection.

But at least for myself, I was indeed cooking up the larger vision, a sense of what needed to happen at the collective level. As the information started coming in of just who had done the dastardly acts and from how far away their plans had been hatched, I spontaneously came to the conclusion that we now had a clear demonstration of world interdependence. The security of U.S. citizens, it would now be clear to everyone, depended on the dignity of all peoples. I imagined a near-global Marshall Plan in which material aid, educational benefits, and cultural outreach would stretch from the United States to every hamlet: Pete Seeger's rainbow race, "one blue sky above us, one ocean lapping at our shore." We would all know it.

This did not happen. Bewilderment and the need to do something can go in different directions, I was to learn. Perhaps in atonement for having been so wrong about something so important, I came to follow up buying juice with trying to figure out how the grand security apparatus was taking shape on the blocks nearby and in the worlds far away. I wanted to see how it all functions in the concrete as well as the abstract. I had for a good while researched life in the mundane, including the material stuff through which we think and that facilitates the projects of our daily lives—roofs over our heads, the knives that slice our bread, and the toilets on which we depend. What had been added, again from direct observation if such directness were really needed, was that there were indeed threats to our stuff and our lives and that some form of defense was indeed reasonable. How then does threat work itself out in life practices, artifacts, and city building? How could it work out better? I look in the here and now for the right path. Some results of the search are what follow.

Acknowledgments

My indispensible accomplice in much of the work has been Noah Mc-Clain, first as a Ph.D. student and then as my coinvestigator of the New York City subways. His dedicated effort, insights, and nose for news inflect all the chapters, even on matters he has no idea he helped me access. My debt to him, continuing as he moves forward with his own academic career, is fulsome and a great pleasure to acknowledge.

Several others played key roles. Lee (aka "Chip") Clarke, sociologist at Rutgers University, worked both harder and with greater expertise that did I as we conducted our research in New Orleans, now only very partially represented by materials in chapter 6 on the Katrina disaster. In addition to walking me through the bayous of risk, technology, and ways to generate interviews, he read every chapter of this book and offered constructive suggestions, large and small. He is a model coworker.

Christina Nippert-Eng did the unheard of thing: she came to Manhattan and devoted several days to teaching Noah McClain and myself how to look closely in the subways—the details of work being done, objects in interaction with passengers, sounds and sights all around. She is an empiricist's empiricist; she got down and dirty with us— literally. When I was readying this manuscript for publication, she read the whole thing, making countless suggestions, always helping to make my points more convincing to others. Wow, what a colleague. Another close reader of it all was my friend Howard Rubinstein, a renegade New York banker, whose acerbic commentaries caused me to take a harder line against idiocy, "what a bunch of jerks," as he would put it.

With their own hands deep in the realm of disaster studies, especially of the Gulf region, Shirley Laska and Robert Gramling lent unique support. Both were generous with their time and with details, answering my often naive questions. Shirley read the New Orleans chapter, correcting errors and helping me figure out the dynamics of the winds, waters, and social currents. She also played the major role in generating interview subjects for Chip Clarke and me to contact in the Gulf region.

Here in the north, my New York colleague James Jasper read and critiqued the lion's share of the manuscript, interrupting his own projects to make way for mine. Also at the New York end, my steadfast friend Michael Schwartz read the concluding chapter, expanding my thinking, as he always does, toward the larger politics of crises—outward, in this case, to the great catastrophes of Iraq and Afghanistan. At NYU, my dedicated urbanist colleague Eric Klinenberg critiqued the chapter on the rebuilding of the World Trade Center and worried with me about titles. Jörg Potthast, of the Berlin Technical University provided useful comments on the airport chapter, just as his own prior work helped point the way. Susan Sibley, at a timely last-minute opportunity, read and discussed the final chapter at a meeting of the Eastern Sociological Society and gave me excellent suggestions.

Not around to know how much I appreciate him, William Freudenburg died after his wisdom and wit had left their mark on this project, as they did on so many others. He had been my jovial and decisive partner on past researches and some of his spirit, I hope, lives on in these pages. I also acknowledge the person who was Bill's beloved mentor, Kai Ericson. Kai facilitated many people's work in the Gulf, not just my own, and was so generous—in ways only he can be—in characterizing my book for Princeton University Press. His graciousness is boundless, and I am so fortunate, at long last in my career, to have gained directly from it. At the other end of the demographic line, the youngest of my professional facilitators is Max Besbris. Max edited and reedited the text, chased down alleged facts, and acted as my all-round support. I grabbed him up as a first-year Ph.D. student at NYU; by the time this book is published, he will be well beyond such exploitation. He is smart, talented, and headed for the big time.

Still other debts: My late friend Leigh Star was so dignified and brilliant; she remains on my mind and I miss the chance to know what might be on hers. Howard Saul Becker, a great moving force in both Leigh's work and much of my own, is in every sentence—heading off pretension (I hope), the passive voice, and most importantly giving me the continuous impression that I can do the craft. He is also incriminated through his influence on his one-time pupil Mitchell Duneier. Mitch and I share deep friendship and intellectual intimacy; he too is in the book. Finally I thank my partner of these many years, Glenn Wharton, a source of ideas, neatness, and love. Along with the great treasure of my children and grandchildren (to whom I dedicate this book), these are the people who move my earth, risks and all. "What a trip," as Howie might say.

• • •

A word about resources. I've had a lot of them and I wish to thank the funders in the timing of their provision: the Harry Frank Guggenheim and the National Science Foundation (SES 0542777) for supporting the subway research, the Russell Sage Foundation for giving me so fine an environment in which to work on all my projects through a salubrious one-year fellowship, and the Social Science Research Council that facilitated funding (through the Gates Foundation) for the Katrina research and writing. Finally, I thank my home-base institution, New York University, for taking me in and bestowing the pleasures and stimulation of its legendary milieu.

Against Security

• •

CHAPTER 1

Introduction: Colors of Security

How does anxiety travel into artifacts of life, people's ordinary practices, and public policies—policies that can sometimes engulf the
world? This book traces fear, from the soup of indistinct but keenly
felt worries over one's own body, to the hard nuts of bombs and bastions. In between, and connecting them up, are smaller-scale sites and
responses, like the hardware set up at airports or the barbed wire meant
to keep some out or others in. I examine strategies for security against
nature as well as against the machinations of human beings and their
organizations.

Through various intermediaries of institutions and physical implements, individual angst transmutes into the power of authorities who
themselves, of course, come to have an interest in stoking the fears
that feed them. Amidst the resulting confusions and ambiguities, we—
all of us—are stuck with the goal of distinguishing the sensible from
the non-sensible, the potentially constructive from the self-defeating.
Bad things do happen, and death is the final outcome no matter what;
but the routes to death can be more or less reasonable, more or less
decent—a guiding assumption in the chapters that follow. This book
is against security as officially practiced, favoring instead meaningful
ways to extend lives and provide people with decent experience.

My analytic strategy is threefold. First is the effort to understand this
massive social, moral, and political thing called "security," and what
goes on in its name. I try to explain where it all comes from, including
the shapes and procedures that greet us at a place like the airport. A
second goal emerges from the idea that, in the specific and sometimes
hell-bent responses to threats, we can see how a particular world works.
So studying security is a method, a way to learn how—through people's
scramble for survival, capacity, and position—"normal" life operates. A
third focus is practical: I assume the role of consultant, the kind who is

seldom if ever brought in because I am looking for the benign in a situation that is more often in hunt for the demonic. I recommend, in the form of concluding "what to do" sections in each chapter, alternatives to the command-and-control tactics that so often take hold as public policy. Instead of the resort to surveillance, walls, and hierarchy, I indicate what I take to be more effective—and happier—solutions. I try to be very concrete: I get practical, right to the kind of equipment that should be present and how it should be used. This is a book of analysis and also a book of directions.

I do not shrink from the mundane things, the public and private artifacts routinely consumed in everyday life. They cumulate as pleasures and punishments in the course of a day or lifetime, and they can facilitate safety or danger at critical and unexpected instances. I am drawn to the late Susan Leigh Star's call for an "ethnography of infrastructure."[1] A well-designed lever calls forth the right kind of pressure in just the right spot to make it work and with that a special human satisfaction as well as functional outcome.[2] We can see this by watching closely and talking to people. When a contraption frustrates, individuals will turn their displeasure into random bangs, pushes, and pulls that may well further derange an object's functioning. In happier outcomes, objects seduce with a "technology of enchantment," as the anthropologist Alfred Gell once called it.[3] In my own research of some years ago, I came to appreciate how utility and aesthetics, pleasure and practicality, are never separate spheres. Our lives are the sum total of our interactions with ensembles of artifacts and other people, including the people who are involved in managing the appliances. A misinterpretation of the machine, among workers overlooking telltale cues of malfunction at a nuclear plant, say, or system managers misreading calibrations for a space launch, can generate terrible trouble.[4] And sometimes it can be ordinary people who notice, if they are provided the opportunity, that something has gone awry.

As the micro and macro intertwine, I try to capture something of the meet-up at security. Nothing is more micro than existential threat, the fear that one may cease to be through biological demise, but also through social death by faux pas that goes beyond the pale. Fear of failure, abject failure like messing in one's pants, sticks on biography and sometimes on history. Nothing is more macro than the collective action that could result. As they form businesses, open plays, build cities, or make wars, humans carry their quotidian humblings as continuous companions. You don't have to be whole-hog Freudian to think that our early worries stay with us not only as private trouble but also as public forces. Life continues reinforcing our original vulnerability, with both ridicule and humiliation always in potential play.

The driving force behind all of it is fear that one's taken-for-granted world is being lost—in a fleeting moment or a longer *durée*. Security, for my purposes, means being able to assume that day-to-day, moment-to-moment human planning can go forward. When the whole welter of personal and collective projects can be thought about and acted on, succeeded in, and failed upon, the normalcy of the human condition is in play. I am not directed toward security in the sense of material satisfaction—a decent house or full belly—however righteous such goals may be. I'm thinking of security as the feeling and reality that such goals are even possible to pursue, that there is a sensible and reliable world in which to act. It is a more-or-less state; no individual and no community can be fully secure either in feeling or in reality, but some are closer than others. Places, offices, bureaucracies, and functionaries that explicitly use the word "security," as on their signs, uniforms, and mastheads, are working this idea as a professional and business practice. I am drawn to such designations in this book as relevant sites for thinking and further examination.

With so much at stake, there is a compulsion among those so charged with responsibility but also among many other people as well, to *do something*. Some individuals respond to disaster by fielding resources with imaginative generosity. Others may be mesmerized by routine and proceed as irrelevant bystanders. And still, as another alternative, there are scoundrels who revert to selfish power and reinforce their domination. All will be in evidence in the chapters that follow.

Although this book is overwhelmingly oriented to contemporary responses and from a U.S.-centric point of view, much of the basic repertoire is familiar enough to students of history and anthropology—particularly the darker sides that seem the most documented. In the cosmology of the Asmat people of southwest New Guinea, "Death was always caused by an enemy, either directly in war or by malevolent magic. Each death created an imbalance that had to be corrected through the death of an enemy."[5] The Black Death justified the search for witches or the demonization of Jews, the poor, the homeless, vagrants, or any Other who might have been locally available. "Moral panics"—as we now call them thanks to Stanley Cohen's studies of how publics cook up shared fears—are at the ready for crisis deployment. Lynchings in the U.S. South were, in this framework, events of exorcising fears of sexual threat and impending social upheaval. From the surviving photos, it appears that the white audiences enjoyed these scenes of strange fruit—an "ecstasy of bigotry," to use Christopher Lane's phrase in a somewhat different context.[6]

Anyone researching security, even in more placid places like the contemporary United States, runs into some unusual methodological problems. Authorities, and sometimes individual persons as well, fear that revealing details of what they do to enhance safety will, in the wrong hands, undo whatever protections are in place. If enemies know where New York's emergency headquarters are located (165 Cadman Plaza East, published on the city's website, replacing the agency's former headquarters, which were in the World Trade Center), they can zap it, bringing everything down. If access to emergency data is free and open, miscreants can get hold of that data. If bad guys know the locations of the pumping stations that keep water from inundating the city, they can disable them to create massive floods. The dilemma, instructive in itself, is that holding information secret also prevents people from knowing what to do when they might be of help. If you don't know where the fire station is, you can't run in and report the fire—especially salient when a big emergency knocks the phones out of commission. If those in charge become disabled, others can't take over if the communication system is password protected.

As with all decisions about risk, there is a distributional effect to keeping things close to the chest. Some people have easier access to the inside information and strategic materials than do others. For whatever reason, some end up with more security privilege than others. It was indeed women and children first as the *Titanic* went down, but social class also had played a role; first-class passengers were more likely to find a place on a lifeboat than were those in other classes. Second class came next, and third-class passengers had the least opportunity for survival. On airplanes, people in business and first class have special lines at security and when on board more toilet access when they need it. As Bridget Hutter and Michael Power remark, assigning risk and its trade-offs is a "moral technology."[7] Choices must be made about whose protection counts the most, what sources of danger will be most guarded against, and which types of remedies will come on board and at what stage of remediation.

Somewhat similar issues arose as a methodological problem for me: who would tell me what sorts of information, given the risks of sharing? I wanted access to information for my possible publications and to fulfill the mandate of my grants. Some officials were not sympathetic even if they themselves had access (and sometimes they did not). If, in interviewing an official, I mentioned the word "security," I risked a complete shutdown of what might already be a particularly closed bureaucracy, as was the case, for example, with the New York Metropolitan Transit Authority (MTA). Across the security world, outsiders have trouble learning from those who actually run the systems. Besides bother and more work for me, such knowledge barriers make it less likely that a nosy sociologist or someone else trying to be helpful might be of some use. All this, and more, contributes to what the sociologist Edward Shils, albeit referring to a different aspect of the problem, called "the torment of secrecy."[8]

Information in this book thus comes from wherever I could find it. In my research on the subways and also in regard to the mayhem of Hurricane Katrina, I—along with advanced graduate students and colleagues variously working with me—carried out extensive interviews with a large number of relevant individuals. We employed other commonplace social science techniques as well, including use of government documents, websites, and journalistic trails, and some archival investigations. I also gained from my NYU seminar students, primarily undergraduates, who did fieldwork projects related to some of the sites of concern. Dear friends trusted me with their own sometimes-intimate experiences of public spaces, particularly at airports and in the restroom (another site of consternation). At some sites, such as airport security gates, my close-in observation could only go up to the point where I would not be noticed as a suspicious character. Taking photos or video was a problem, something I wanted to do as a mnemonic assist when later reviewing my evidence and also for possible publication. At airport security, I received stern warnings to "put that thing away," despite the fact that Transportation Security Administration (TSA) rules explicitly permit picture taking and absolutely forbid confiscating cameras or film that may be used in the process.[9] Similarly in the subways, MTA personnel and especially the transit police, do not take kindly to picture taking even though the transit rule book is similarly explicit: "photography, filming or video recording in any facility or conveyance is permitted."[10] My coworker and I did take pictures but only surreptitiously. Officials' security concerns cause my data on airport security in particular to end up fragmented in general, although several former high-ranking officials at the TSA did provide me with more than five hours of detailed conversation. Some of the incompleteness in the various accounts provided—from whatever site—is due less, I think, to informants trying to obscure what goes on and due more to the troubled uncertainties they themselves experience.

FRAGILITY AND DISASTER

Uncertainty—for them, for me, for us all—is a very big deal, beginning with problems at the root of sense making and the deep need for a dependable world that more or less stays constant to our experience. Humans live, as Melvin Pollner and others have taught us, on the edge of deep quandary.[11] We agree to treat the world as "just there," regardless of the philosophical problems of relativism. Language itself, it is frequently enough observed, rests on "mere" social agreement. We use words under the convenience they mean more or less the same thing across individuals and regardless of situation. The "social construction of reality" is only the academic gloss on the more complete and profound fragility of experience. Call it common culture or call it a conspiracy to get by, but only benign lies provide the "ontological security" we have in our own self-identity and "the constancy of the surrounding social and material environments" we must take for granted.[12] We accomplish a normal, everyday existence by reassuring, through our constant and sometimes arduous mutual reinforcement, that things are indeed as we make them to seem. Or as the actor and commentator Lily Tomlin averred, "Reality is a collective hunch"— but, we need to add, an unstable and not fully believed one at that.[13] Absurdity beckons, threatening to upset all applecarts; we join together to ward off the "ontologically fatal insight," as Pollner again phrases it, that is always up for grabs.[14]

Enter Disaster

With reasons to be scared in general, we are sitting ducks for more concrete and substantive threats that we can identify and articulate through bad dreams and sometimes actual human experience. At least some of these crises in artifact, nature, or both scare "in new and special ways," and, writes Kai Erikson, "elicit an uncanny fear in us." "It involves," he says, "the destruction of sense" resulting in "epistemological confusion and ontological uncertainty."[15] At such moments, it almost follows logically, institutional and organizational routines lose their sufficiency for reassurance. So the arsenal of *reassurance* has to begin very soon and with gusto. The events of 9/11, of course, brought it home to the United States in a distinctive way—for Americans a "new species of trouble" indeed had been born.[16] As the buildings crumbled, so did the taken-for-granted idea that no such thing could happen. The need was to reconstruct the sense of reality that preceded the attack.

Such reconstruction is always necessary, but complicated by a context of uncertainty as to what actually to do. With regard to 9/11, it was especially ambiguous as to what it might mean to re-secure public life in the United States. The prior situation had, of course, its threats— crossing the street and getting cancer—but only those in our military were vulnerable to foreign enemies. The new trouble was given the word "terror." No one really knew of what the threat actually consisted, much less what it might mean to respond to it effectively.[17] Almost by definition, the inventory of techniques and locations of attack is practically infinite, but defense must be radically more focused. Only a few places can be fortified with walls and guns ("hardened" in the security lexicon), and there must be a selection of which types of people to be wary of—but from a huge population of candidates. This puts, as security experts sometimes point out, the opportunity for initiative always in the hands of the attacker, increasing both the level of anxiety and the uncertainty of proper defense. No permanent solution exists, making the war on terror ongoing, fueled by the continuing sense of being at risk against an agile (and "tricky") enemy.

We see in political and organizational life that the least viable stance is to express ignorance of cause or remedy. Not knowing is not an option for those charged with the collective well-being. Thus it happens that, in the words of a scholar who has examined responses up closely, "individuals and organizations sometimes act not because they understand risks, but because they feel they must act."[18] In her extraordinary and unique ethnography of Boston security planners' response to 9/11, Kerry Fosher (on the scene at the time) observes, "No local fire chief or emergency manager wants to be the first to turn in a plan that has sections saying 'we haven't figured out how to handle this yet.'"[19] It would not fit with the necessity, which, as Ulrich Beck states, is the more general necessity, of 'normalizing' non-calculable hazards."[20]

Normalizing can go in radically different directions. There was my own immediate sense of humanistic shared responsibility. It did not carry the day. Instead, as we all now know, there followed the campaign against the likes of al-Qaeda, as President Bush was to explain to the Prime Minister of Japan, "to smoke them out of their caves, to get them running so we can get them."[21] Those with a different attitude would be astonished by the absurdities of the aggression that found favor. Once again, it could have gone differently; it was not predetermined that I and those like me would be so far off the mark. A President Al Gore might well have used his bully pulpit to shape an alternative outcome. Our "allies," including some British officials, were outspoken in their reluctance to make war in Iraq, and the U.K. electorate was never on board. In dealing with the terror against their railroad trains post 9/11, the Spanish authorities pulled out of Iraq, rather than intensifying their military efforts there or anywhere else. Perhaps most famously, in another part of the world and after a different type of conflict, both sides in South Africa entered into post-apartheid reconciliation rather than follow up on settling scores.

The historian John Mueller sees the organization of the U.S. Department of Homeland Security as almost uniquely mired in old war models, unable to engage in any practical appraisal of the actual security dangers that face the country.[22] As evidence of this incapacity, he quotes James Woolsey, the CIA director in the early 1990s, testifying following the collapse of the Soviet Union: "We have slain a great dragon, but we now live in a jungle filled with a bewildering variety of poisonous snakes." Even though the danger posed by, say, "rogue states" was minimal, the hawks went at it. Or as Mueller says, "There seems to exist something that might be called a catastrophe quota . . . when big problems go away, smaller ones become magnified in importance to compensate."[23] Rather like the moral panics that Stanley Cohen describes which keep popping up in the domestic public realm, foreign threats also fill the vacuum of fear agendas. And they then take over other agendas as well, including the need to deal with much larger and genuine threats less amenable to a discourse of dragons and demons. So even though, at least according to a NASA Report issued by the Jet Propulsion Laboratory, global climate change is a "threat to global stability (that) vastly eclipses that of terrorism," individuals —and not just Americans but also conscientious citizens of even the most enlightened nations (Norway, for example)—have trouble taking it in.[24]

Scholars of risk often document the "irrationality" of risk judgment in everyday life. People underestimate the chance of death by car and overestimate the chance of death by plane. A key explanation given in the literature is that people worry less about things over which they sense potential control (the car wheel) versus things over which they lack control (airplane equipment).[25] Never mind that yearly U.S. highway fatalities are more than tenfold the number of deaths at the World Trade Center. The annual number of terror deaths worldwide since the late 1960s, when the State Department started record keeping, comes to the number of Americans annually lost in bathtub drowning. Rather than a war on terror, maybe we should have a war on baths. But tubs, with their helpful aura of hygiene and comfort, are not eligible. Terror carries *dread*, and dread, the risk literature tells us,[26] lowers the threshold for taking action. Or it enables authorities to take action on our behalf. As Mary Douglas argues,[27] and in ways to be specified in this book, they transfer decisions and dilemmas to institutions to take care of it—outsourcing, in effect, the imponderable dilemmas of what to do. The authorities then take license—indeed *must* do so—regardless of their own incapacities, the inherent ambiguities, and surrounding misperceptions of actual risk. The transfer of ambiguity to outside institutions and the bureaucratic layers of authority they represent can amplify and add further distortions along the way.

The key distortion is the insinuation of plausibility if not certainty that authorities have effective tools, when they are, in fact, operating from the seat of their pants. We will see a lot of that in this book. Among the more vaguely benign tools was the color code alert system that came after 9/11. Specific colors indicated level of danger and degree of precautions that should be exercised: red for "severe," orange for "high," yellow for "elevated," blue for "guarded," and green for "low risk." Blue and green were never used in the ten years of the system. Probably no one ever went to jail for doing something "yellow" under times of "orange." But the whole setup conveyed misinformation in its gross exaggeration of the degree to which there was a plan that made any real sense. Fosher notes, in regard to official changes in the colors of threat level, that "most planners and responders had little or no idea what was supposed to change about their activities" when color changes were issued.[28] There they were in front of her, the emergency managers from various and diverse agencies in the Boston area, trying to coordinate but with difficulties—that they were not eager to reveal—of "getting it together." Fosher adds, "There was also the difficulty that nobody quite knew what 'it' was supposed to look like when they got it 'together.'"[29] The problem was beyond color alerts.

MODELING TROUBLE

The misguided trust in the functioning of the institutions contrasts with suspicion about ordinary people and how they respond to disaster. It is not universal, by any means, but the trust in emergency officials is a frequent fallback in public opinion, often reinforced by those in power.

Political leaders, police authorities, and military commanders intone noble intentions and strong capacities, while casting suspicion on the ability of those below to cope with unexpected changes in the social or natural world. Not infrequently, they portray those further down, especially those well below, as disorderly and indeed on the verge of riot.

In striking contrast to the scenarios of crowds running amok, sociologists and other systematic observers document something closer to empathy and mutual assistance. Instead of acting crazy, people remain orderly and resourceful. As the pioneer disaster-researcher Enrico Quarantelli writes, "The research evidence indicates . . . it is the human beings and their informal groupings and linkages (rather than formal authorities) that typically rise to the daunting challenges that disasters pose." Quarantelli observes, "Formal, highly hierarchical, structured and bureaucratic organizations, whether pre-impact planned or post-impact imposed, are both the source and locus of most problems in community crises."[30]

Let us look at the collapse of the World Trade Center and how people behaved in real life and in real time. Thanks to extensive interviews of survivors by phone (eight hundred cases) and face-to-face (three hundred) carried out by a federal government–sponsored study, and augmented from other sources, we know a lot of what went on.[31] First are the mortality data: while about three thousand people died as a result of the tragedy about five times that many survived. A good number (in Tower Two especially, about 18 percent) were able to use elevators. But many had to make do with the stairs, quite ordinary ones (see figure 1). They encountered smoke, water spewing from sprinkler systems, and building debris.

Significant numbers of interviewees (17 percent) reported being helped by others. There are many anecdotes of individuals physically carrying the disabled in wheelchairs or lifting those too obese or otherwise unhealthy to make their way down (in some cases, two at a time took turns carrying somebody down). There is no indication of pushing or crushing of other human beings. As a survivor of Tower Two who walked down from the 78th floor described the situation, "People were having general conversations, seemed calm, and walked at a steady pace, no sense of panic."[32] Some of the stairways did become

Figure 1. Building occupants making their way down the shared stairway as a city firefighter (who did survive) makes his way up WTC1. © John Labriola, 2011.

very crowded but apparently remained orderly. A worker at Tower Two making her way down from a floor in the nineties explained,

> My coworker, who is a diabetic, hadn't eaten breakfast yet. We stopped on the stairs to rest for a minute. A lot of people seemed to be stopping, probably due to the heat and needing to catch their breath. On the 64th floor, another coworker turned to me and said (he or she) was getting tired and didn't feel well. I said "We will take a little break" and I gave (the occupant) mints.[33]

As the study authors concluded,

> The "first responders" were colleagues and regular building occupants. Actors of everyday heroism saved many people whom traditional emergency responders would have been unable to reach in time.[34]

Some firefighters and building personnel (guards, monitors, Port Authority staff—who indeed stayed on duty) also were singled out for their brave efforts. Rather in contrast, an impediment to survival was the request for occupants to go back up and return to their workspaces ("shelter in place" is the official lingo), which would have probably brought them death. An announcement urging people to return to their desks was heard, at one point, through the Tower Two intercom. In making their way down the stairs, some said they were delayed by firefighters trying to go up (likely to their own deaths, although not in the case of the firefighter pictured in figure 1, who did indeed make his way out safely). Although everyone involved had reasons for fear—the impacts of the planes, smoke, and physical disarray were in strong evidence—few possibly had a sense of the buildings' impending collapse. So, it must be said, the "orderliness" of the crowd and the mistakes made by authorities did not occur within the immediate eye of catastrophe—as in the immediate aftermath of the atomic explosion at Hiroshima, I would imagine, or in the early instants of a bursting dam. Compared to the slower demise of the *Titanic*, the rapid sinking of the *Lusitania*—accomplished within eighteen minutes of a strike by a German torpedo—led to more disorder (with no advantage going to social class; in this case, young men had the best chance of survival). But short of such utter and sudden upending of reality which is when no type of aid can make much difference, it appears that calm holds.[35]

The proclivity toward effective mundane response somewhat aligns with what security analysts now refer to as "resilience"—the capacity of organizations and infrastructure to rebound after assault. Particularly under conditions of uncertainty, it makes most sense to rely on strategies of resilience rather than trying to do an advance load-up of protections against particular but uncertain forms of threat. The doctrine of resilience is increasingly gaining favor in security circles. But resilience, too often a mere cliché of security argot, means honoring the ad hoc. It means building on the capacity of real human nature, social nature, to rise to the occasion. Performing well in complex and difficult conditions, according to an eminent student of the nuclear power industry, "depends upon deep historical and contextual knowledge of the worksite." There should be encouragement, the authority concludes, of "doubt, discovery, and interpretation rather than command and control."[36]

But after accepting such wisdoms as a generic key to the security issue, we do not have much by way of next steps—something this book tries to remedy. What we need is "a researchable concept of resilience in positive terms." In Jörg Potthast's words, we need "a more fine-grained empirical description" of what goes on in real-life activities that make up resilience.[37] For me, the places to look are the close-to-ground practices of which the 9/11 survivors are an example but that need to be expanded with what goes on in much more ordinary conditions. This is where, arguably, real security occurs, and it includes, most especially, the rehearsals people go through as they tend to more quotidian problems of danger and difficulty. In several of the case studies that make up this book, I try to show the remedy and social repair systems at work. I also sometimes trace, pace the warnings of Quarantelli, how misguided official efforts to establish order can throw things out of whack. In ways parallel to the way legal systems and police act to amplify and sustain criminality, the "ironies of social control," as Gary Marx explains, so it is that so-called solutions exacerbate problems in the security sphere.[38]

Official response can be so off the mark it might itself be viewed even as panic. Sociologist Lee Clarke thus uses the term "elite panic" to characterize what he sees as a common higher-circle reaction. Witnessing the social order they are supposed to maintain as under threat, elites field the artillery. Their fear of *others'* panic, especially of those lower down, justifies enhanced tools for command and control. The fear of riots is part of a broader panic model in which elites see the masses as emotional and ready to be unhinged, but view themselves as rational and "going by the book." It colors interpretations of protest movements as well as distinctions elites may make based on notions of class and "breeding."

People, and not just the elite, tolerate, and even encourage, instruments of emergency authority to pervade wider and wider zones of life—"mission creep" in organizational parlance. "Militarism," as used by political scientist Chalmers Johnson, means not that a country has a strong military, but that the military involves itself in activities that would otherwise be more appropriately considered civilian.[39] In his report on the great Chicago heat wave of 1995, Eric Klinenberg points out how replacing social workers with police as primary agents to deliver service—using the punishing branch of government to do what the giving branch had done before, as he puts it—led to more suffering and death than would have otherwise occurred.[40] More generally, as the shift takes place, soldiers and police replace ordinary people's civic engagement and the public offers deference toward the designated authorities. Resources go for the presence of military instead of rescue personnel or social service professionals. Police are put into the schools instead of counselors or therapists, as Kathleen Nolan describes.[41] Money goes toward border guards, along with walls and patrol cars, instead of information kiosks and welcome wagons. And in dealing with nature, authorities erect bastions of control instead of preserving soft paths of marsh and creating buildings that float.

The drug war is a well-known exhibit for the radical perversity of the fear/control model at work. Prior to a rather recent historic era, drug use was a private problem, if a problem at all in the United States. Families and churches handled it, with therapists later coming into the picture, sometimes like Doctor Freud, prescribing it for themselves. Before the late nineteenth century, there were no illegal drug substances in the United States (Coca Cola once contained cocaine); it was not until 1932 that a national control regime finally outlawed a range of what have become illicit substances. Thanks to the elite panic, terrible events now take place within the United States and various other parts of the world. To feed the illegal European and U.S. markets, gangs, sometimes murderous ones, infiltrate police regimes and corrupt large segments of societies far and wide. In the United States, drug-related incarceration has increased more than twelvefold since 1980, virtually turning young men of color into an incarcerated population—in jail, formerly in jail, headed for jail, or on the run to avoid jail.[42] It is not at all far-fetched to say, as indeed many have, that the war on drugs is a war on a people.[43] It is also, more indirectly, a cause of fiscal catastrophe at the state and local levels. It makes the country weaker, something ruefully acknowledged by former President Jimmy Carter, who urged, echoing sentiments from a growing number of the political and corporate elite, that the drug war be "called off."[44]

In other realms besides the fight against drugs, the cure can also be worse than the disease—indeed, it is part of the etiology of the disease itself. Intelligence units—snoopers, watchers, and investigators—create elements of the very troubles they "detect." In a way that is hardly even controversial, they profile and in so doing help constitute the nature of their criminals as well as the type of malfeasance they are out to find. Relying on stereotype, such as membership in social or religious groups, they choose where they will look, who they will ask about, and which dossiers they will examine. They immerse themselves in the locations and among the social types they think most likely lean toward nefarious behavior. So their targets are, if the intelligence officials have any skills at all, indeed those who most easily can be seduced into conspiring with an agent provocateur.

Besides whatever injustices this creates, and the American Civil Liberties Union thinks the privacy invasions are clear and present, the practice is sociologically suspect. Outside agents incubate bad thoughts into evil manifestations among those most susceptible. It is akin to what Ian Hacking calls "making up people," a complexly organized process of labeling and classification that creates a distinctive group.[45] Police agents egg their preselected individuals onward toward crimes that loom large on the security agenda. Putative wrongdoers can be nudged over the line into committing crimes, or at least become prepared to commit them. Their arrest through entrapment then can become the basis of still other resentments, from neighbors, kin, and acquaintances who believe their community has been inappropriately targeted and persecuted. There is a low legal threshold to prove conspiracy and even lower to generate charges and jail. As of September 2010, the entrapment defense has never been used successfully in a post-9/11 federal terrorism trial, helping sustain a conviction rate of about 90 percent in federal terrorist court cases.[46] Looked at from the other side of those in the fearful majority, the dynamic of court charges, pleas, or perhaps trials—regardless of merit (and sometimes there *is* merit)—gain strong media coverage and add fuel to anxieties of there being bad people out there.

No U.S. politician, left or right, can speak ill of the efforts to nail the bad guys. Compared to other public policies, questioning antiterrorist measures is less possible. In mundane spheres of life, there are energetic debates, for example, about what is the best health-care policy or about the relative advantages of iPad versus Kindle, paper versus plastic. But when it comes to security, despite enormous activity and financial expenditure, there is little debate on priorities relative to other goals. Security is thus a rather strange thing in the world, overwhelmingly myopic in its insistence that hardly anything else counts. The silencing of those who perceive the shortcomings of such an attitude, as will be displayed in this book, feeds irresponsibility.

Myopia is deviant in terms of common human practice. Normal people do not have just one goal; they have many. They do not search for one prize, but for numbers of them simultaneously. They can indeed dance and chew gum at the same time; they can screw in lightbulbs while they sing; they can write a thesis while watching a child. Duties and pleasures, local scenes and those farther away, priorities of the moment and those to come in the future—all are juggled in our blinks of thought and life practice. In statecraft as well as organizational administration, responsible individuals deal with the many things that count and try to figure out how to make them count together.

In settings where I have spent a good deal of time—among urban planners, architects, and especially product designers—dealing with more than one thing is a professional mandate as well as common practice. One sees this whether individuals are laying out a landscape or reconfiguring a can opener. The term often used is "lateral thinking." Designers (of whatever professional sort) have as point of departure how people actually function in the world, and their job is to facilitate as many aspects of that functioning as possible. As part of the research that they do, they strive—if they are good —to notice not just what is officially accomplished by a given artifact or facility (an appliance, a university building, a subway line) but also all the ways it operates in life practice.

We now often use the term "decentering" when such lateral think-ing is used as a political and intellectual practice, part of the postmod-ern turn in the academic world.[47] But it is also a more ancient practice of Zen, a focus on what is there as opposed to what is "supposed" to be there by dint of social convention or professional ideology. Out of such clarity, a designer can envision—if all goes well—new potentials for what can be brought into being. Light on academic logics or Buddhist principles, designers pitch and use laterality as the best way to respect and enhance human practice—and yes, usually for them, the profit bottom line along the way. Security, we can see, is boastfully the op-posite of all this. It is an extreme case of what Douglas says is a hazard for institutions more generally in how they "think": "it blocks personal curiosity, organizes public memory, and heroically imposes certainty upon uncertainty."[48]

What to do? It would be naive to suppose that there were zero threats "out there," and I readily acknowledge, as we so poignantly learned with the July 2011 massacre of eighty-four young people in a Norwe-gian summer camp, that even quiescent societies can be hit by horror. However an exaggeration in terms of actuarial statistics compared to other threats, attacks are likely. But even so, we spend absurdly too much and sacrifice beyond what makes sense as we enshrine the pos-sibility in national policy and local practice. But politically, if for no other reason, there is no choice but to do something.

The question is how can we act in a way that creates a better world and not an inferior one? Maybe there are tactics that, at least compared to the alternatives, really do enhance safety without having much, if any, effect on civil liberties or interfere with the pleasures of daily life. I am advocating a program, in effect, of civilianization—of a civilian invasion of what otherwise is thought properly military. I push reforms, many quite small scale and modest, but significant as they might gather force. And in some cases, the changes I advocate are not so small scale at all, but reach to the largest transformations of human identity and national stance. For each realm taken up in this book, I make sugges-tions for ways in the here and now to generate collateral benefits—to respond to the fear system in ways that add to rather than subtract from our well-being and that enhance the world, all round.

PLAN OF THE BOOK: ORDER OF SEARCH

To get to the plausible alternatives to end security as we know it, this book reaches across life settings, policy terrains, and urban infrastructures, lowly artifacts included. After this introduction I take up in the chapter that follows what might at first appear an unlikely setting for examining security dynamics: the public restroom. There are lessons to be taken from this venue, so often ignored in serious scholarship and indeed the usual basis only for jokes. Here we can see anxieties in play and all sorts of unsavory mechanisms, both at the micro and macro level, that come in response. One key element is taboo against speaking substantively; only the off-color and beating around the bush can speak at the site. This invites mischief as fear distracts from substantive conversation about real human need. In the vacuum of serious discourse, authorities create inconvenience, humiliation, and even—not so rare—death. God is again in the details, living, as William James taught us to suspect, "in the very dirt of private fact."[49] The toilet allows us to see the combination of factors that repress—the usual culprits of class, race, and gender discrimination—but also soulful anxieties that come with the more basic human territory. Some degree of capitalist plot is happening, but that is only part of the story—a larger lesson to be considered across other less intimate realms, whether market-based or not. Whatever the combination of sources, I point the way toward a safer and more pleasant toilet and one with the promise of ecological reform.

Moving up from the toilet, at least metaphorically, is the subway—the subject of chapter 3. Fellow sociologist Noah McClain and I spent numbers of months researching the New York subway system, stimulated by the post-9/11 campaigns to increase security for passengers. We focused on the way security interventions meshed—or failed to mesh—with existing procedures of subway work, much of it already oriented, as we learned, toward enhancing safety of riders. We found out a great deal we did not anticipate about the way subways operate. Because the system is already so thick with remedies, we learned, there is always a danger that new interventions will upset what is already in place. We can see, from the subway in particular, something of the way official provisioning of safety can indeed contradict safety as actual practice.

Rising further up still (literally as well as metaphorically this time) we come in chapter 4 to air travel, perhaps the most notorious venue of the security apparatus. We learn once again from the appliances and procedures, this time of the especially elaborate system of precautions in the post-9/11 world of flight, that much, in concept as well as in the detail, is quite beside the point. And some of it, as per pattern, runs counter to making things safe at all. The choices that have been made are just that, choices—explicable in the specifics of their moment in the United States' political and moral history. I offer up alternative ways to deal with the fear of others' flying, ways that at the same time enhance other human goals, simple ones like convenience and complex ones like contentment. The trick is to offer a response to fear of flying through less odious forms of intervention—and indeed enhancements of pleasure.

Nothing could be more directly linked to U.S. events of terror than Ground Zero and successive attempts to rebuild, the topic of chapter 5. I treat the replacement skyline of New York as a great mishap and wasted opportunity. Security measures display, on the ground, some rather new ways that political authority combines with market forces to shape the world. Although there were, as usual, varied aesthetic and moral visions of what should happen at the site, the pugilist instinct predominated. Post-9/11 measures to protect the downtown called for not just any sort of buildings, but those that would show the enemy that we could build tall and powerful. The result is a different kind of building in the form of One World Trade Center, a.k.a. "Freedom Tower." The "program" for the structure, still in another way, created vulnerabilities through misguided hardening up.

In a very different urban setting, that of New Orleans and the Gulf Coast, we see command and disarray in the way that city meets river— the topic of chapter 6. I describe how threats from nature become part of the social-political apparatus—with the Katrina disaster the unhappy result. It has become rather common to observe that "there is no such thing as a natural disaster,"[50] and Katrina is surely a poster child for that assertion. Much of the history of the New Orleans area was a kind of

Katrina in the making. Building levees, canals, and other infrastructural elements for the sake of safety yielded eventual mayhem. I trace out some of the details of the "downward precautionary spiral."[51] Each effort at a fix leads to a successive effort of the same sort, accumulating not as a series of individual safety features but as vulnerability to events of catastrophic proportion.

The book concludes by further drawing out some larger lessons. In anticipating danger, we learn, people rely on prior understandings and capacities—hardly a surprise. Extant goals and routines go at the danger, like chemicals on the surface of an oil slick. This includes forces of authority, more or less on standby, that come to bear. They do their thing. So do individuals struggling to stay on their feet and get families and communities back on course—in a word, to regain prior levels of security. It can be, like those chemicals on the slick and the remedial teams trudging across the beaches with their rakes and machines, that remediation creates more trouble than it solves—sometimes tragically. It is not always easy to know the difference, to be able to do something without making things worse. At the end of the book, thinking across the various sites and circumstances, I indicate how to know which is which. Indeed, as I argue, there are principles to follow, as local and national imperatives, for dealing with impending threat. The key is to exercise massive bias toward making life better all along the way.

● ●

CHAPTER 2

Bare Life: Restroom Anxiety and the Urge for Control

> I think avoiding humiliation is the core of tragedy and comedy
> and probably of our lives.
>
> —John Guare

Public restrooms are a first lab for examining how troubled anxiety transmutes into collective loss.[1]

With their link to human elimination, whatever anxieties that come from concerns about public misbehavior more generally are greatly intensified in this particular public place. Restrooms are imagined as locations of filth, theft, and rape. The special problem, however, is that they are difficult, if not impossible, to monitor. Rather than face the risk of disapproved behavior going on or meeting it headway with deep surveillance—like cameras in the stalls—authorities just close restrooms down. Human needs go unmet. The choice is often made without much discussion or sometimes even public knowledge. In a similarly tacit conspiracy of silence, authorities do not build them in the first place where new urban development occurs. Through taboo—that is, the absence of discussion—more constructive possibilities cannot arise. Security does its trick.

I first became aware of toilets as an analytic problem when interviewing a British product designer whose practice included bathroom fixtures. He had *no choice* but to examine toilets directly and figure out how they are used, how they function, and hence what could be done to make them better. He was frustrated by the fact that he was dealing with a "taboo product," a feature which enormously constrained opportunities for substantive improvement. If a product cannot be talked about in terms of its function, advertised accordingly, or demonstrated at the retail site, it becomes locked into its existing form. Much the same is true of a configuration of such appliances in a restroom; it is very hard to move discourse forward. Here, for the sake of a better security, I join in the limited toilet discourse that has taken place among a small band of colleagues.[2]

First to deal with the reality of the situation as opposed to its social construction: the "hard" perils of pee and shit. Pee is the easy stuff; it is sterile and indeed sometimes comes in handy. It historically has been used as an antiseptic. Rich in nitrogen as well as phosphates and potassium, it works as a fertilizer when diluted with eight parts water. On space ships, it transforms into potable water. Even in cases in which the urinator has an active bladder infection (something of a risk factor for those who might come into contact with tainted urine), it is highly unlikely that the infecting organism can survive long enough outside the body to damage another person. *Chlamydia*, a sexually transmitted infection, can pass in the urine of infected individuals, but, as with urinary tract infections caused by the more common *E. coli*, chlamydia would have a very difficult time finding its way from a hard surface to the mucosal membranes of another human being before its expiration.

On to Shit

Human feces are rich with potentially infectious elements. While it too has positive uses as fertilizer, it requires appropriate processing, often mixed with urine. Shit becomes fertilizer with heat treatment and proper aeration over time ("humanure" is the terminology for the benign combination). The technology has been incorporated into stand-alone composting toilets that do not require any hookups at all to public sewage systems. But short of such proper manipulation, the stink of the stuff appropriately signals its danger, perhaps indeed a relic of positive natural selection.

But how bad is it for those of us sharing a public bathroom? Not very. Germs would have to be transferred from the toilet seat to your urethral or genital tract, or through a cut or sore on the buttocks or thighs, which is possible but unlikely. "To my knowledge, no one has ever acquired an STD on the toilet seat—unless they were having sex on the toilet seat!" says Abigail Salyers, president of the American Society for Microbiology (ASM).[3] And even then, I would add, albeit as a sociologist, still improbable. Instead, as the microbiologist Charles Gerba—having in mind the rich microbiotic life on the household sponge—puts it, "Home is where the germs are."[4] The act of cleansing is what accumulates the nasty bits. Users of public restrooms, at least employees in restaurants, are instructed to wash their hands after every use and many others follow the same rule—no matter whether they have gone Number One or Number Two. Yet the sterility of pee means that contact with one's fresh urine creates no sanitary difficulty. Washing, however, brings the hands into contact with faucet handles that indeed may have been touched by another person whose fingers carry residue of feces. So we get a hint once again of how the moves to defend are not necessary and indeed may, if anything, create some danger.

Sitting down to eat is wildly riskier than using the public restroom, whether urinal or toilet seat. People ingest poisonous substances. Food and utensils readily spread dangerous microbes from one human being or animal to another. Although there are sometimes cautionary notices about washing up, the procedures (and pleasures) for food ingestion are far more often discussed, elaborated in unending detail, and made the foundation of celebrations and affections. Many people, from all levels of society and cultural groups, aestheticize—even fetishize—eating. Connoisseurs discern, rank, and reward food with graphic depictions of how to make it, present it, and roll it around the tongue. Politicians, foundation leaders, and entertainment celebrities call attention to hunger and famine as crises in the world. In the fullness of debate, there is also focus on the liabilities of excess, with attention to obesity and junk food ailments. Into her fourth year as First Lady, Michelle Obama presses an agenda of fresh produce to achieve a better country.

So much less focus, and little of it constructive, goes to the other end of the digestive process. But that's wrong. Lack of access to mechanisms of sanitary elimination harms people and indeed results, via bacteria and water-borne pollution, in mass death. Where it does not create large-scale disease, the silence regarding sanitation at least yields up personal distress. Not having our needs provided for and in an appropriate way generates an intense sense, as Douglas has taught us, of impurity and danger.[5] Without a way to properly relieve ourselves, we may lose confidence that we are in a civilized place at all—human elimination being a front line of decency and propriety as it evolves over the centuries.[6]

We do have some reasons, once again, for our anxiety. Waste elimination is a foundational starting point where we deal directly with our bodies and confront whatever it provides, demons included. It arises in our lives on a schedule not of our own making—an omen of insecurity in itself. The animal in us comes to the fore and we must accommodate to its tendencies and demands. The need for waste elimination reflects "bare life" meeting up with our civilization.[7] The bathroom is the "backstage" where we prepare the Goffmanian "presentation of self." And we often have only limited time for this process, either because we are squeezing it, often unexpectedly, between scheduled duties and events. Without the ability to take care of such basic needs, we are almost nothing in this world. Presenting oneself free from traces of waste is fundamental for any right to social membership.

No wonder fear of soiling occupies a great deal of conscious as well as unconscious thought. Based on his data set of people's dreams (16,000 in number),[8] the dream researcher (and also power analyst) G. William Domhoff reports, "People often have horrible dreams about the bathroom, and things that won't flush, and so on."[9] A little over one thousand of his collected dreams involve toilets or bathrooms. The terrors include being forced to eliminate in the wrong place or being subjected to violence, humiliations, or perversions in toilet settings.

It seems clear that the public nature of the public restroom creates its own special scenarios, some of which show up as Domhoff's collection of bad dreams. "Public" and "toilet" do not sit well together awake or asleep, but they must coexist as a practical matter. We have little control over with whom we share the restroom. School children know it as a place where bullies do mayhem, and such memories continue on in adult life. Compared to that in other places, surveillance from teachers or other authorities is constrained; in the restroom we may be on our own in the wrong way. There can also be pressure to observe a time limit out of deference to other users who need a turn. Unlike at home, where we have had some influence over the layout or specifics of equipment and provision—soap, paper, and so forth—in the public facility we must use goods we did not ourselves choose and whose presence we cannot anticipate with certainty.

Precisely because of the vulnerabilities, frisson, and potential for disgust, avant-garde artists use bathrooms, restrooms, and their appliances, as well as urine and feces, to establish themselves as on the edge. Duchamp's urinal (1917), Andres Serrano's depiction of a crucifix suspended in his own urine (1987), and Chris Ofili's animal dung—used notoriously in his Virgin Mary painting (1996) but in other of his works as well—were all sensations at their respective moments, in part because of the fear and loathing associated with the toilet. Waste is useful in the art world precisely because of all the heavy freight that comes with it.

Even the home bathroom can unleash embarrassment, shame, or criticism when family members detect by sight, sound, or scent what has been going on. Places like restaurants or shopping centers introduce some anonymity (often welcome) but also concerns about having to share near-intimate space with those who make us anxious and from whom we want to keep separate. The person in the next stall may be the boss or a rival coworker, a suitor, or one's student. The open-to-all facility, as in a public park or train station, invites its own range of anxieties. A person of filth or a stranger ready to attack may be only inches away. The stakes are high enough to ignore nature's call and just hold it in. Or people figure out a reason to delay going to work so they can use their bathroom at home rather than risk a colleague's hearing their sounds or smelling their odors. A person may call off a date, or end one early, to protect romance from elimination.

So here we have the problem at hand: the toilet involves doing the private in public and under conditions only loosely under the control of the actors directly involved. Something precious is at stake that must be urgently protected. At a level beyond the individual, it is neighborhoods, cities, cultures, and nations that organize the accomplishment or failure of waste elimination. In the process, they provide for some more than for others. As per the pattern, restroom security and its particulars are unevenly distributed. For those individuals put at a disadvantage there is no readily available means for expressing predicaments or demanding redress, the other common feature of security systems.

CLASS

On a massive scale, multitudes in poor countries of the world lack even rudimentary toilet access, a fact that points to the major class distinction of elimination security. Most must rely on communal facilities, and hence in many contexts virtually all toilets are public toilets. These can be substantial accommodations or as primitive as an uncovered ditch, open field, or corner of a camp. The better-off may build in-house bathrooms, but too frequently such toilets do not drain into proper sewerage, but instead connect to mere holes in the ground that do little to curtail spread of pollutants into local soil. A western appliance sits in a bathroom, but it is merely stylistic.

The toilet—or its absence—is the starting point in the network of elements through which excreta might find its way into more or less safe disposal locations rather than seeping into rivers, lakes, or water tables. It is a life-and-death topic, as Rose George points out in her remarkable book *The Big Necessity*.[10] About two and a half billion people live without basic sanitation.[11] U.N. estimates indicate that one and a half million children die each year from sanitation-related disease (primarily diarrhea), 90 percent of them under the age of five. It is not just the fixture, a minor matter in itself, but also the related infrastructure—including having clean water for wash-up—that makes the difference in preventing disease. The sink, or its functional equivalent, is part of a sanitation ensemble; it massively lessens the chance of spreading infection from feces.

The crisis of sanitation emerges and gains some special attention at moments of catastrophe. But the need for medical aid, famine relief, and even counseling more often occupy the world's newscasts and appeals for emergency assistance. Less explicit notice is taken of the dire problem of human waste. Indeed, soon after the 2010 Haiti earthquake, I heard the NPR news correspondent speak of the rainy season about to descend on the vast camps of tents and how the improvised cotton sheeting would not protect refugees during the deluge. And I thought, "It's the shit that will do them in" and create a health menace as the make-do infrastructure gives way to flood. The news does not get out. Two years earlier, in a sign of some headway, the U.N. General Assembly declared the year 2008 the International Year of Sanitation, proposing a multipronged plan to increase awareness among member states and generate reform on the ground. But it is safe to say that for most readers of this book, as well as for world leaders, the Year of Sanitation came and went with little notice. As always, inhibitions to full discourse — including what goes on and how — holds back progress.

Continuing into wealthier parts of the world, toilet conditions are, of course, much less dire. But problems happen. It often takes money to go, particularly I notice in countries outside the Untied States. Public authorities may charge enough to marginalize those without means, a dollar or more in some places. Different amounts are often charged for toilets versus urinals, with a ratio of as much as 4:1 in my experience — thus imposing heavy penalties for women, whose urinary needs require toilets. When facilities of the right sort are not proximate, trips to the loo require ever more costly trade-offs between work, domestic chores, and care giving. Removal of public restrooms changes the calculus of whether to use public transit, which is more attractive when stations have toilets. This then impacts the morphology of a city. Resort to commercial establishments puts a premium on being able to present the right combination of dress, age, deportment, and race.

Even with a good enough self-presentation, individuals in poor neighborhoods have fewer places to go, primarily due to a lower density of restaurants, bars, and shops. Besides picking and choosing to whom they will extend courtesy, commercial establishments are not always open for business, and indeed those in poor neighborhoods commonly have irregular and somewhat unpredictable hours.[12] Throughout the city, many can seek relief at the otherwise sometimes maligned chain stores like McDonald's and Starbucks. They function, in effect, as the city's bathroom. According to one study of New York Starbucks restroom use, the majority of people who go into the restroom are not customers; they come and go without buying anything.[13] Starbucks gives its managers, as per company policy, discretion over whom they will or will not allow to use the restroom.

Sometimes, especially if there is no Starbucks, individuals must fall back on a sense of privilege to demand access to a private establishment. Or they may use their special cunning to find a place —

something middle-class people have down to an art. Those with cause to fear official authorities, targeted immigrants for example, have special reasons to avoid anything that might be seen as confrontation or stepping out of place.

Decent establishments like Starbucks do not, in fact, saturate U.S. cities, being absent from many poor neighborhoods altogether. When it does occur, lack of access affects homeless people most directly—the public restroom being in many cases their last refuge for minimal human comforts. They are not always welcome at Starbucks or McDonald's or other chains.[14] This increases their risk of soiling themselves. Without a place to wash up, their smell or surface dirt gives offense. Despised by almost all, drug users in particular, are pushed to "the farthest margins of public space" and into "filthy nooks and crannies that are optimal for spreading infectious diseases."[15]

Again, different regions of the world give rise to particular notions of what an "available" restroom might be. From the modern European or North American point of view, there needs to be a toilet seat and not a squatting hole. Toilet paper must be present. Ideally, there will be paper covers to put on the seat. Anyone making contact with the various appliances needs some faith that cleaners were conscientious and effective (what did they really use?). The little displays of clean-up schedules posted near doorways help provide some assurance. If the facility is not thought clean, and clean in culturally specific ways, it will be avoided. If I am from a squatting part of the world, must I risk physical contact of my private parts with a public toilet seat? In many places in the world, water through a wash pipe that can be directed toward anus or vulva is utter necessity—the use of paper disgusts. While it may be universal to think that shit has a noxious smell, other perceptions of pollution vary widely, including the idea that certain kinds of human beings defile by their very presence. In apartheid South Africa and the Jim Crow–era U.S. South, race mixing in restrooms was probably the site of most intense resistance to sharing. Swimming pools were another flashpoint, perhaps because of the same phobia of contact with bodily waste, even perspiration or spit. Or was it because of whites' felt vulnerability of being undressed and at risk of ridicule in their display of nakedness and dependence?

Whatever the particulars, the dynamic of psyche and society becomes complex as social stigma converts to repulsion, which then reinforces the practices of exclusion. As cultural studies scholar Ruth Barcan remarks,

> When I hear of people afraid to touch a tap, I think less of real germs than of the fear of the Other. . . . Surely fear of "the prewarmed seat" is less a rationally grounded fear of infection than a fear of the touch of the stranger, the Other who is so like us as to share our bodily shape and our bodily needs, but unknown to us, and therefore potentially contaminating.[16]

U.S. cities have been actively closing down their public restrooms for the past several generations. In New York, the subway system alone once had 1,676 toilets.[17] Only about ten facilities still function.[18] Scarcity imposes special difficulties for members of some occupational groups, like those who make their living on the streets as vendors, for example. At the extreme, they face arrest for relieving themselves through inappropriate means. New York has five city departments that can take action against those who pee or shit outside: Sanitation, Parks and Recreation, the Metropolitan Transit Authority (MTA), the Police, and the Department of Environmental Protection. Fines up to $1,000 for public urination and defecation can be levied. Police also have discretion to charge offenders with disturbing the peace or with lewd or indecent behavior, especially if children happen to be nearby.

In New York, where parking is hard to find, especially in Manhattan, which is where 85 percent of all rides originate and end, taxi drivers have a tough time. They hold it in rather than risk losing a fare, and this could mean going an extra hour if a paying passenger orders a trip to the suburbs.[19] As remedy, some men pee in bottles they keep in their cabs. These options are less available to women. This may be part of the reason only 1 percent of New York cab drivers in 2005 were female,[20] a low number compared to some other U.S. cities like San Francisco and Chicago. (Lack of proper facilities may also keep down the number of women among the city's 3,000 plus street vendors). Although New York authorities have taken up various taxi system reforms (fare increases, acceptance of credit cards), improving the cab driver's way of life is not among them. A recent ambitious effort by the New York "Design Trust for Public Space," in league with the city's taxi commission ("Taxi 07 Campaign"), resulted in innovative new cabs and places for passengers to queue. But the campaign report did not bring up the creation of additional taxi "relief stands," as they are called. These are places where drivers can leave their cars for up to an hour without being fined. Some of the few that exist have been closed because neighbors apparently complain that drivers' "loitering" constitutes a threat to children.[21] Those that remain, alas, have no trashcans, no seating, no overhead protection from the sun or rain, and no place to pee.

Sidewalk street vendors also have specific requirements for places to go and some way to secure their goods while they are off from their posts. Otherwise the police can legally confiscate everything, at least in New York.[22] Vendors do make informal arrangements, but those arrangements are not facilitated by city policies that take their needs into consideration. Street-based prostitutes, dependent on proper sanitation as well as facilities to maintain attractiveness, are not welcome in most commercial places and city authorities harass them continuously. If they must make their way to places for relief that are too remote or untraveled, police or thugs can pick them off.

GENDER

Women and girls lose most when public facilities are thin on the ground. Particularly in poor urban regions of the world, such facilities can be available only in a few places and at certain times of day. In India (and other places), it is permitted for men to go outside to urinate or even move their bowels; they engage in "conspicuous defecation."[23] Women without facilities, however, must relieve themselves only after dark or in a secluded location. Where facilities are present, they can be severely crowded and not necessarily safe even when gender segregated.

Without a reliable place to go, people—but again, particularly women and girls—must alter their lives in strong ways, with bad results in terms of bowel and urinary tract diseases. Some may go the whole day without elimination rather than face the danger, embarrassment, or dirt of the available communal facility should it exist.[24] They report "having a system" in which they restrict their intake to affect what they eliminate and when. The anxieties of basic bodily care thus shape ability to gain an education or practice a livelihood. In refugee settlements, placing water points or latrines at the edge of the camp exposes girls and women to attack.[25] Wherever they are located and whether they are intended for men or women, latrines in India are cleaned by untouchables; only those from the lowest castes (and usually women) do the job. It carries stigma as well as subjecting the worker to harsh environmental conditions.

While de jure racial toilet separation has now been eliminated in the United States, gender segregation is omnipresent—"a kind of segregative punctuation that serves to reaffirm and reestablish differences between the sexes despite almost continuous contact between them," as Spencer Cahill noted.[26] Unlike those pertaining to race, laws requiring gender segregation arose with the rationale not of excluding members of the "lesser" group, but of protecting them. If not kept at home for their own good, women should be provided facilities specifically for their own use. So spaces were set aside for women—these included special train cars, hotel parlors, and ladies' reading rooms in public libraries and ladies' windows at the post office. In response to women's growing role in factory production—and aligned with the mid-nineteenth-century sanitation movements—laws required restroom facilities to be not only present for factory women to use but also gender segregated. Reformers were sometimes even disturbed that approaches to women's rooms were visible to men; the urge was to remove women's toilet facilities from men's purview as completely as possible—even conceal the fact that women used them at all.[27]

Of course, gender segregation was invented long before the nineteenth century and the practice has ranged across virtually all spheres of occupational and social life. But more than anywhere else, restrooms continue to inscribe and reinforce gender difference. Restroom regimes treat separation as a matter of simple fact, and limit some of the easier means for redress of security problems. As benign as the rationale may be, separation increases women's anxieties and predicaments, at least in some regards, as I will point out. And it plays havoc with the anxieties of security experienced by those who do not fit well into one gender or the other.

The obvious logistical solution to women's lack of access is for women and men to share the same facilities. As a simple matter of queuing theory, open access increases efficiency by equalizing the load across all types of users. Without such sharing, even when the number of women's rooms is equal to that of men's (which it often is not), women experience special scarcity. Women's bodies generate needs not shared by men, such as menstruation. They are more often care givers—nursing infants, for example, and more generally having to tend to the needs of children (of both genders) as well as to those of the old and infirm. Pregnancy generates additional urination. Aging women must go more often than aging men. In part due to inability to relieve themselves as the need arises, women's rate of urinary tract infections surpass that of men—half of all U.S. women will have a urinary tract infection in their lifetimes.[28]

It takes longer—and more space—for women to do some of the same things, like peeing, as men do. Getting ready—going into a stall, closing the door, pulling down underpants, arranging skirts and blouses—takes time. The greater amount of space required by toilets than by urinals means that even when an equal amount of square footage is allocated to men's and women's rooms, individual women will still be at a disadvantage compared to individual men. Hence the long lines at the women's room even in places where the restrooms are of equal size.

Because women rely on toilets for urinating, a case can be made that the women's room should receive more maintenance attention than the men's. For one thing, long skirts and other paraphernalia may land on the floor where they might be soiled. More attentive maintenance might also lessen compulsion to hover. Hovering over the seat is a common practice to avoid physical contact. This then increases the likelihood of urine being deposited on the seats by those with bad aim, thus encouraging still more hovering. It is a vicious cycle and a collective action problem. Those lacking the musculature to hover must deal with the waste deposited by prior users and clean it away themselves (with what?) or just sink into the mire. As part of the silence on the topic of toilet use, people are restrained from giving tips to one another, lending physical support, or learning how to develop the muscles that would do them the most good (unlike having visible abs, mastery of toilet squatting is not on the list of "goals" to be met by trainers at the gym).

When they do get into a restroom, women have more complex arranging work to do. They wear longer hair and fix it in more complex ways. Not having hair, cosmetics, and clothing properly arranged can humiliate. An architect of public buildings told me that he tries to install mirrors in women's rooms in places other than above the sink, because hair stops up drains in the women's room—evidence of disparate amounts of primping, depending on gender. Women wear more jewelry and other decorative accessories (shawls, buckles, barrettes). And, while the reasons may be debated as they often are in feminist circles, pulling off the right result is hard work. I have many accounts from women that reveal, from so many standpoints, the nature of this effort and its high salience.[29] Women socialize over the sinks in ways that men do not, perhaps because of a lower degree of homophobia. They may consult with one another on their grooming or maybe to conspire on ways to deal with men who are (appropriately, in their view) excluded from the scene. These observations lead to one ready solution to the challenges experienced by women in restrooms, which would be to acknowledge women's physical as well as cultural traits by giving them more space not only for elimination but also for grooming and socializing than that provided for men.

This brings us to a principle more generally relevant for dividing resources so that disadvantaged people share in life opportunities on an equitable basis and do not pay an extra anxiety tax by virtue of their status. To help equalize the security level of women vis-à-vis men, at least in regard to easing difficulties of elimination and other toilet-related needs, unequal resources must be distributed to the two groups. Indeed, this is a rationale and consequence for affirmative action of any sort: *one must deliver unequal resources to groups in order to provide equal opportunity to the individuals within each*.[30] In restroom practice, this often pans out to a 2:1 ratio favoring the women's facility, sometimes 3:1. The proper ratio can't be universal, because gender-linked cultural practices of dress and sociability do differ among subgroups, within nations, and certainly across the world. Women with long hair, to take one mundane example, need more counter time than women with short hair. Not to mention the fact that user sex ratios differ across venues. We need a calculus based on both habit and respect to come up with the right ratios. We need to acknowledge not only gender difference but also cultural variations in gender practices. Or, to take the more radical road of dealing with toilet insecurity, we need a system of gender sharing, such as the implementation of unisex facilities, which makes ratios moot.

Or should women be encouraged to change how they do things in order to enhance their collective security and not impose additional costs of privilege and financial sacrifice on others? Why can't women adhere more closely to men's practices? "Why can't a woman be more like a man?" asks the classic song from *My Fair Lady*. If we press women to change their ways, like spending less time primping, wouldn't that help? More radically, women could save themselves by using a female urinal. Various devices exist that a woman places over her vulva to direct the bladder's contents into a container that can then be emptied into a sink, toilet, or urinal.[31] There is also a female urinal that, placed lower on the wall than a man's, enables women to urinate in a semi-standing position while using the hand to help direct the flow. Under names like "She-wee," "I-Pee," and "Shee-Pee," variations have existed for generations. Finally, women could pee in a crouched position, and that means wearing skirts or sarongs without conventional underpants—an ensemble common in Africa and other parts of the globe. Perhaps from a male perspective, these may seem appropriate requests to make of women. All these options would require women to change their practices, but, it could be argued, for a greater good. Variations in people could be altered by changing how they do things, making them more alike.

The custom of hard separation into two—and only two—gender camps ignores the existence of transgender and biologically intersexed people. They are nonstandard people. Misrecognition is in itself an injury to their sense of belonging. But it also forces them to risk humiliation for being seen using the "wrong" facility, or indeed it subjects them to name-calling and even violence. Disparaging them for their misuse, gives opportunity for the straight and narrow people to celebrate their own evident normality.[32] In struggling to ward off such assaults, individuals transitioning to female (or just butch women) report tactics like keeping showy necklaces at the ready to display in the Ladies Room. A butch woman transitioning to male reports that when she uses the women's room, which evidently still suits her biology better, she sticks her chest out to accentuate her breasts—ironic, in her words, because they otherwise "don't exist for me, except when I use the washroom."[33]

Again, we could solve this and a number of other problems by ending separation full stop, which would lead to a true restroom revolution and a bold alteration in gender relations. Such has been the argument put forward by some gender rights groups—including those representing persons whose identities do not follow the binary. But then what does this solution take away from others? What about men who already suffer from paruresis (shy bladder), which they fear will be exacerbated by the presence of the so-called opposite sex in the vicinity? What of the women who use the women's room as a respite from male supervision, a place where "the girls" can let their hair down and exercise solidarity?

Some women fear that men on the premises would expose them to crime and violence. Apparently no reliable data exist—silence again—to indicate the specific location of criminal acts within restrooms (including the use of stalls by shoplifters who go in to rearrange their booty).[34] But we do know, or at least I do, that some crime in the restroom is committed by other women and not by men. My friend Annette watched with disbelief as she sat on a toilet at the midtown Manhattan Bloomingdale's as a hand came over from the adjacent stall and lifted her purse off the hook where it had been hanging. The perfect crime. By the time my friend could pull herself together, the offender was out of range, sprinting through cosmetics. In terms of the much more feared crimes of violence against women, the lack of data persists. But it seems clear enough that the sign on the ladies room door may provide the illusion of security more than the substance of it. Women and girls are accosted and murdered by men in women's rooms. "The potential expected presence of both sexes in an integrated restroom," legal scholar Mary Ann Case surmises, "could also on occasion act as a deterrent, by decreasing the likelihood a perpetrator will be alone with his intended victim and increasing the chances of a bystander able and willing to offer aid."[35] Again, an anxiety-bred measure to enhance security does, at least plausibly, undermine it. As security devices, the door signs may be theater props more than mechanisms of security. Indeed they may act to signal to violent men that their prey is likely alone.

Toilet gender segregation, and its disadvantages for women, thrives in a context of silence where anxieties can take their own direction, deprived of the kind of inspection and correction that open discourse could make possible. And again, like other things done in the name of security, this includes the presumption of standardization: that men and women are sufficiently alike to need the same amounts of space. And that men will, by virtue of gender identity, obey door signs even when they are up to no good.

Disability

People with disabilities have their own special toilet security concerns just as they have challenges on other fronts. The "disabled" is not a small category. All humans go through childhood, a life stage of special needs not only in terms of supervision and care but also in simple matters like being able to scramble up to the toilet seat, reach for the soap, or scamper across a sanitary floor. And they need latches that do not lock them in. Old people encounter a different battery of challenges. Twenty-five million Americans are incontinent (the great majority of whom are women):[36] they may choose to stay home and miss work, school, care giving, or care receiving. Such appurtenances as colostomy bags and pouches are not complete substitutes for restroom access and indeed need to be serviced along the way. Specific restroom location matters. If toilets can be reached only by stairway, people in wheelchairs or on crutches can't get to them. In Britain during previous eras, this is where they were often located—in places underground—either to assuage moral anxiety or just to free up rentable space. Stairways pose similar problems for people with prams or rolling suitcases.

Some people become temporarily disabled from a ski accident, car crash, or disease. Whatever the cause and for however long a period, a certain question arises: Will there be grab bars for hoisting above the seat? Those who are blind want to know if the paper towels will be in the usual spots that can be located precisely because of standardization in restroom layout (an important plus in this case). People using wheelchairs need doors light enough to give way without causing backward rolling when pulled open—not the "high-quality" heavy doors that occur, ironically, in some deluxe circumstances.[37] Where does a man put his cane when peeing at the urinal? Who picks it up if it falls? Given that men are reticent about talking, and much more resistant to touching in the men's room, how will disabled men gain assistance—especially because no helpful women are around? Anyone who is somehow off standard is under particular difficulty; and, given how undependable restroom provision actually is, this means that mobility is problematic.

Able-bodied men have troubles of their own. Perhaps the most intense of restroom features, urinals, line men up with their penises exposed and nothing to do with their eyes—not a situation most men anticipate with relish. And so unfolds the drama: men must not observe the penis of the man standing next to them, but they must never appear to be *trying* not to look at the penis next to them.[38] No wonder some men are made so anxious they cannot pee at all in such an environment and must retreat to the stall.

MORAL SENSIBILITIES

There are always people (and organizations) busying themselves with possible transgressions performed by others. Howard Becker calls these individuals "moral entrepreneurs,"[39] and most of us are led into at least a bit of a moral entrepreneurship. A starting point of modern judgmentalism is the concern about sanitation—the worry that vermin, bacteria, fungi, and viruses abound by the billions in and around our own being. Many have trouble accepting this plenitude and want to control it, even totally. Some people retain a ridiculous sanitary ideal of everything being dead except one's self and the creatures we need or admire. Hence there is anxiety about precisely how close others, especially strangers, get and how their body parts touch what our body parts touch.

Fears are fed by the small-scale disorders of the restroom because they signal, like a broken window on a building's façade, that things are not right in these zones—where we are already so suspicious of biotic impurities. People find paper towels and toilet paper scattered about, liquid puddles of unknown nature, or see substances treacled across surfaces—all from other suspect persons. Knobs may be sticky. Even soap itself, otherwise connoting cleanliness, becomes noxious when in the form of deposits (scum, odd solid bits left behind). An adhering strand of hair, on a soap bar or resting on a drain screen, further disgusts. Prior users may have broken a mirror (inadvertently or deliberately) or a door handle. Any sign of sanitation failure implies disrespectful humans about, maybe even out of control individuals. As increasing numbers of users come and go, accidents occur (the toilet may even overflow). Anxiety grows.

There are other troubling elements, some explicit, such as the instruction for "food handlers" about needing to wash. Instructions also tell people never to flush "objects" down the toilet drain, meaning tampons and sanitary napkins. But for those who do not know, like children and some men, mystery abounds as to just what those forbidden objects might be. Other signs instruct us to put the seat down after use or wipe the sink as a courtesy to the next patron (airplane toilets carry this message). These signs, confined as they are to the restroom realm, are further evidence of the taboo against bringing the topics up—not mentionable, for example, at a business or academic department meeting.

Restrooms are often focal points of moral panics. Drug injection recurs as a prevalent collective fear as does sex. So we have instances where stall doors are removed from men's rooms to ward off homosexual behavior—thus depriving all men access to civil privacy. This was commonly done at U.S. bus stations and, quite notoriously, at the major science classroom building on the Harvard campus.[40] In the United Kingdom, to discourage intravenous drug use, special fluorescent blue lighting has been installed in some public toilets, creating a hideous pallor to the setting. This light makes it harder to see veins. But users struggle to inject anyway, some moving to a different nearby location or adapting by injecting in their groin or neck—which is less difficult under the antidrug fluorescents, since veins in such bodily locations are easier to feel with the finger and thus require little light.[41]

For the moral entrepreneurs, there is both a need to see into spaces when they want to monitor activity and a desire to be insulated from others' gaze. We want it both ways, and this is a real dilemma at the toilets. It becomes reflected, especially in the U.S. case, in a highly ambivalent restroom physical apparatus. Stalls are made of hollow metal panels, weak and unsubstantial, with large openings above as well as below. See-through seams are left open; panels do not quite join. I assume this configuration came about to forestall bad things from going on, like sex and drugs. Perhaps the motivation was (also?) to enhance safety by making it easier to rescue a sick individual or trapped child by fishing them out the open bottom. Europeans are struck by the difference with their own stalls, which typically go floor to ceiling or almost so. They also have solid latches and fewer peek-a-boo possibilities. Stall construction is an American thing reflecting, somehow, American priorities. Almost regardless of building budget or function, restrooms retain mean and weird designs that emanate from U.S. sensibilities and political order.

Given the tense hardware compromise between privacy and surveillance, each individual is left to negotiate his or her own settlement. From conversations with friends and associates, I learn that some stall users look out, but not in; others look in but not over or under, and so on. The very flimsiness of the construction induces behaviors to compensate and "fill in" for what is physically lacking by, at least in some cases, refraining from looking at all (like the men staring ahead while they pee). In the more wide open spaces of sinks and urinals (where construction is also more solid), people do carefully monitor glances, gestures, and speech acts, enacting separations through sociality rather than hardware. In the face of all such challenges and potential indignities, the alternative again is to wait until one gets home. Or as my informants tell me, they do number one but not number two. They may restrict their use of public toilets only to particular conditions, as when they are caring for children or if they themselves become ill. They may go at work, but only to a different floor where their feet do not give them and their sounds away.

For some gay men, at least in a prior era in the United States, and still in many places of the world, the men's room becomes one of the few places to hook up. However degrading this arrangement, itself a source of self-stigmatization, they take to the toilet as a last, but practical, resort brought by repression in more open public venues. For some gay men public toilets, including their depravations, evidently provide erotic charge. As the sociologist Laud Humphries detailed in his classic study of men having restroom sex, minutia of signals, placements, lookouts, and excitements turn on the precise configuration of urinals, stalls, windows, and soundings.[42] Men do not simply have sex "in" rest rooms; the facility, its surveillance regime, and the erotic acts may indeed be intrinsically related to one another. Like 1950s honeymoon beds that stand in for long-postponed consummation, the fixtures shape the particulars of actions, social arrangements, and participants' sentiments toward the scene. Separateness and the added frisson of police danger build the currents that spill out when the floodgates open. While much signaling is done at the urinals, inter-stall communication occurs through ritualistic foot gestures—an erotic choreography made possible by those bottom openings of the stall panels. What emerges from these construction elements is an eroticism that defeats the very intentions of anti-sex design.

Whether it is part of the thrill or its inadvertent accompaniment, patrols against toilet sexuality unleash their own forms of toilet nightmare. Arrest and exposure have destroyed lives and careers—with suicide at least an occasional outcome.[43] Surveillance takes many forms, including one 1912 instance reported by historian George Chauncey, where agents of the Pennsylvania Railroad cut a hole in the men's room ceiling to observe what went on below.[44] The university where I began my career, the University of California at Santa Barbara, lost its otherwise distinguished provost (at that point the highest official of the campus, equivalent to chancellor or president) to a vice squad entrapment while on a trip to New York City. He fled to a life in South America, and the campus, post-scandal, worked through a leadership void that held back its development. The pinch was organizationally and not just personally consequential. Similarly, and with a more mixed reaction at least from me, the right-wing Idaho Senator Larry Craig was set up, in 2007, by a plain clothes detective who performed the under-partition foot signals in the Minneapolis airport men's room. Police trained in the art (do they sit all day, putting up with the usual scents and sounds produced by acceptable users?) evidently know the habits of their prey. The arrest ended Craig's political career.

At the airport, there is little choice but to continue to have public toilets and ones that respect existing privacy expectations of American men, however minimal they now are. So rather than closing them down or removing stall doors, entrapment is a way to accommodate basic needs while still policing immoral deeds. Again, the repugnant game involves waiting for the rare event—the appearance of a black swan of sorts—thus requiring long stays, high costs, and the risk of severe hurts to the so-called "deviant," Republican or Democrat alike.

What to Do?

On all these fronts, there are better options, and I offer some of them up in the spirit of my design consultancy.

- *Build more toilets, especially in poor parts of the world but in the rich places, too.*

Make them appropriate functionally, culturally, and aesthetically. Support organizations that directly and outspokenly confront scarcity and social indecencies. Sulabh International, based in New Delhi, makes sanitation the keystone of its reform agenda. It promotes the notion that inadequate sanitation is at the heart, both as cause and effect, of unequal access to both material resources and human security. The organization portrays the "toilet as a tool of social transformation."[45] It is an intrinsic part of Sulabh's larger agenda of education, gender equality, and the elimination of caste. It operates a system of schools and sponsors new toilet technologies that are cheap, culturally appropriate, and ecologically sound. It operates the Toilet Museum in New Delhi. Sulabh convened a World Toilet Summit 2007, also in New Delhi, and it sends its "toilet missionaries" to Africa and Asia. Its allies include the World Toilet Organization (WTO), based in Singapore, which, with Singapore Polytechnic and funded in part by the Schwab Foundation, supports a modest World Toilet College offering courses in restroom design and technology.

• *Service existing users.*

Follow how individuals actually behave toward the artifacts in their environment and then try to service their evident needs (a standard approach in the professional design world). There may well be moral and political boundaries that make some needs impossible to take on and stigmas that prevent them from receiving high priority compared to other public needs. But rather than striving to eliminate intravenous drug use through police, danger, or inconvenience—to remain with the drugs example—create a way to get better results for drug users. Treating drug use as a public health issue, including lowering fear for those who may already be suffering from psychological stress and social exclusion, involves providing users with a sanitary way to self-administer. We could take advantage of toilets as sites of injection by making them points of needle exchange. There already exist simple vending machines that crush deposited needles in the process of discharging sterile new ones; they are being used in some countries.[46] More consideration for drug-users would also benefit diabetics self-administering insulin, who also need good stall lighting and a small shelf for tidy manipulations.

• *Do design.*

Approach the contemporary restroom as a fruitful opportunity to re-work physical and cultural elements toward a better architectural and

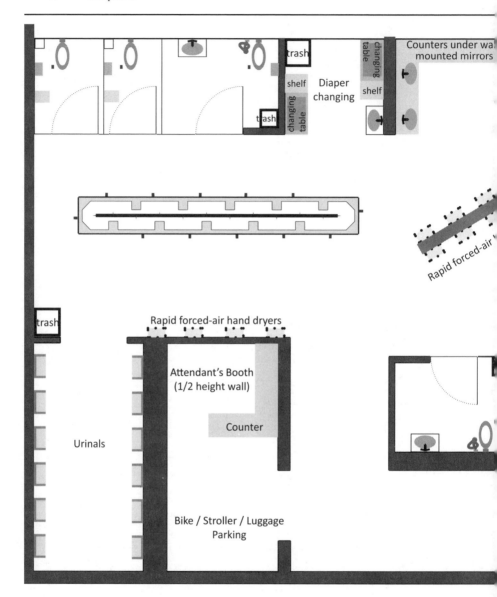

trash

changing table

Counters under wall
mounted mirrors

shelf

Diaper
changing

changing table

shelf

trash

changing table

Rapid forced-air

trash

Rapid forced-air hand dryers

Attendant's Booth
(1/2 height wall)

Counter

Urinals

Bike / Stroller / Luggage
Parking

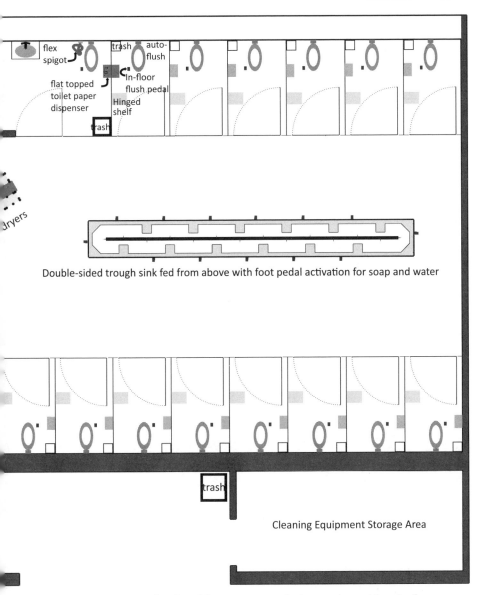

Figure 2. Norén-Molotch public restroom redesign, unisex with urinal zone. Reproduced from *Toilet: Public Restrooms and the Politics of Sharing*, edited by Harvey Molotch and Laura Norén (New York University Press, 2010).

social space. Attend creatively to detail. Architectural firms typically hand off design of a building's restrooms to the lowest-ranking member of the team, just as the stall partitions are chosen from catalogues of the low-end supply houses. There is seldom substantive discussion of how they will be internally configured; I have observed this on many university architectural committees in which I have participated. Similarly, in examining the writings of the great architects, including the avant-garde figures of the modernist and postmodernist era, we find little guidance on how to think about what goes on, much less how it could be accommodated. With all their talk about being "honest" with materials as well as with the actual functions of their buildings, modernist architectural visionaries stopped short when it came to the toilet—a lone exception is Denise Scott Brown, characteristically frank, bold, and feminist.[47]

Amateurs though we are, sociologist Laura Norén and I sketched out our own scenario for a better public facility (see figure 2).[48] The most ambitious move would be to go unisex—not just have women and men *alternating* in their use of a single restroom as on airplanes and in some restaurants, but *sharing* a common space at the same time. Besides improving efficiency, such gender mixing also fixes the women's room long-line problem and allows people with nonconforming gender identity to just go in. It also probably increases safety, but to learn if this is true we would need some gender-mixed facilities, at least as experiments, to get the right information.

In our mixed-use dream, we retain urinals for their ecological and spatial efficiency. We know that at least for a time, many women (and some men) will have trouble with that. So we locate the urinals in an area that makes them and their users less conspicuous. The largest bank of toilets occupies spaces that are at a distance from the urinal zone. Stalls are fully enclosed. All are outfitted with conventional toilet paper dispensers, but at least one is set up with a flexible spigot to accommodate those preferring the use of water for the cleanup. An area nearest the entrance and potentially under the purview of an attendant is set up for nursing mothers.

There are other anxiety-lessening amenities. Each stall, as now not uncommon in Japan, would have its own sound system, activated by a touch of a button: music, waterfall, or the white noise of, say, a bustling

Figure 3. Ceramic urinal, "pink orchid," from San Francisco artist Clark Sorensen. Image courtesy of Clark Sorensen, San Francisco.

airport. Or such sounds could be pumped into the restroom overall. Noise could be abated through use of sound-absorbing surfaces and other acoustic devices—instead of the fetish for hard and reflective surfaces now prevalent. Proper ventilation would mask or at least make unidentifiable odors of a particular person. Perhaps there should be one-way glass looking onto the common area so that people could be assured of their security as they exit—or just to be able to learn if they were keeping others waiting. This would be especially useful for airplane loos, where demand so often, but unevenly, presses on passengers who could use some extra time.

Figure 4. Roca space-saving "W+W" toilet-sink. Image courtesy of Roca Corporación Empresarial, S. A..

In terms of physical décor, a reformed restroom would be *normal.* Posters, advertisements, and notices found in other parts of the establishment would continue on in the restrooms. Bouquets of fresh flowers, a major feature of the restroom that helped transform New York's Bryant Park from abandoned wasteland to thriving public space, would display that maintenance is routine and caring. Urinals can be fanciful; they might be in the shape of orchids—as in the delicate design of San Francisco artist Clark Sorensen (figure 3).[49] All these ideas are examples of how design can be used to address problems, including security of various sorts, once things come into the open.

• *Go for the toilet-sink.*

Although not depicted in our scheme, which defers to the convention of sinks and toilets as separate appliances, a superior option would be to have sink and toilet combined in a single unit, each installed in its own stall. This gains back space and water efficiency that would be lost to urinal elimination, should that be a necessary compromise. This type of apparatus is (again) widespread in Japan. Elegant versions are available in the U.S. and European markets like the one depicted in figure 4 . When one flushes, the water coming out of the faucet at the top of the toilet gets used for hand washing. This water then drains into the toilet tank (now that is has become "gray" water), where it is available for the next flush. We get instant recycling, right on the spot and in real time. It also results in clean hands before one touches the knobs and levers to exit. It is pure genius, from which we are needlessly kept apart through demon fears and silences.

- *Feature waste.*

Perhaps most profoundly, public restrooms can be *featured* for their ecological and social importance. Precisely because they are places where people congregate and produce a lot of waste, they would make great sites to demonstrate how to make urine and shit more positive as parts of buildings and life. Restrooms could include visible on-site recycling and properly exhibit what goes on in the transformation process—through, for example, transparent tubing and window-walls of feces treatment (like at the car-wash). Each aspect might be a conversation piece, giving people, even male restroom users, something to talk about. Restroom design might then model ecological innovation more generally. Being at the outer edge of what thought possible for material reuse and didactic exhibition, such display ingenuity might inspire still more ambitious ecological schemes across the board. This is the radical toilet.

CHAPTER 3

Below the Subway: Taking Care Day In and Day Out

with Noah McClain

The New York subways are obvious sites of security concern; many measures get taken as a result. Such concern is not folly and nor is the disposition to try and address it. Attacks on the trains in London, Tokyo, Moscow, and Madrid have unleashed, each in their own time, death and destruction. New York has 468 subway stations, each with multiple entries. Depending on time of day, some crowd together hundreds, if not thousands of people in compact spaces. It surely dawns on most who are ever there that these are rich targets.

One way into understanding how security actually works in the subway is to talk with the people who are there a whole lot—the subway workers. They are employees of the Metropolitan Transit Authority (MTA) and most spend many years at the job. Noah McClain and I studied just what workers see and what they do as part of the routines of their jobs. We aimed our interviews to learn, in particular, how they responded to a range of troubles, from minor ones to those at the level of disaster. There is a connection, we came to think, between what goes on during routine work and what happens—or will likely happen—when genuine emergency strikes. Disaster studies, oddly enough, seldom attend to the way in which people work through more ordinary troubles. But doing so, it seemed to McClain and myself, was a good way to understand what individuals might do should a bigger threat develop. Given what we learned in our research, we concluded that workers' encounters with ordinary troubles shape response to difficulties of whatever sort and scale.

Our interviews, conducted mostly by McClain although occasionally with me trailing along, involved a total of eighty workers—station agents (the people inside the glass-enclosed booths), station cleaners, train conductors, and train operators (formerly known as "motormen"). We also spent much time in the subways observing, taking photographs, and doing other kinds of field research. In some cases, those we interviewed, usually in their homes or some neutral place like a coffee shop, invited us to their work location, where they could point out to us exactly how they operated their equipment, called for aid from police or fire, or managed to innovate on their own. From these various maneuvers we were able to see how their "eyes and ears" —what they see and hear—link up with concrete actions. To learn from those with a more overall responsibility for the system, we had extensive and numerous interview conversations with union—Transport Workers Union (Local 100)—and MTA officials, including present and past heads of security.[1]

Reacting to the terror attacks, officials in charge of the system experienced the obvious need to "do something." Like the security planners in Boston observed by Kerry Fosher (see chapter 1), they responded to Department of Homeland (DHS) color alerts—a system that several of our informants indicated began within the MTA itself, or at least within New York jurisdictions. As alert levels rose, more plainclothes police were put on platforms and in train cars. There was also a beefing up of uniformed Transit Police placed on duty. Whatever the source of heightened concern, armed troops are sometimes put on patrol in heavily used spaces, like Penn Station and stations serving Times Square. Police also conduct random inspections; they have the right to check bags and belongings of passengers, a program begun in 2005 following the London Underground bombings. Out of concern for civil liberties and to lessen likelihood of profiling, anyone singled out for inspection has the right to decline by exiting the train station. But those who resist may, of course, face disconcerting follow-up once they get above ground. A Brooklyn hospital manager of Kashmiri descent, whose case was taken up by American Civil Liberties Union, complained that he had been stopped twenty-one times in the subways— most New Yorkers have never been stopped at all.[2] So another cost of doing something is indeed profiling, and the costs and resentments to which that leads.

A not-incidental additional cost occurs in the ridicule these measures stir up among workers who take note of the more absurd aspects of the programs. One is the concentration of troops and equipment in the densest stations, like the one at Times Square, which no doubt rank high in official risk assessment analyses. But the heavy security squads at central Manhattan stations make sense, some workers reason, only under the presumption that bomb makers would drive with their bombs into the densest part of the city and park, and then descend to the subway station, where their suspicious behavior would be detected and lead to their arrest. These measures don't just provide mirth among workers, they also shape how workers interpret other policies announced as security related.

Part of the MTA "do something" involves deployment of new technologies that would replace or at least supplement human guards and inspectors. The federal government, augmented by state and local financial support, makes security dollars available for advanced technologies and equipment (but not, for example, routine training and maintenance). At a city council hearing I attended with McClain in early 2005, council members took turns lambasting MTA officials for failure to spend the money "to make our city safe." Almost $600 million in federal and state security funds had been left untouched for years after 9/11. Partly in response to these confrontations, the agency made its first funds commitment to Lockheed Martin in August 2005 for $212 million, a contractual commitment that eventually hit $453 million—with still more millions to follow in future contracts—for the subway's surveillance system.

These were not to be ordinary surveillance cameras. They would detect a human separating from a suitcase or package, something that *then* would trip off an alarm that *then* could trigger emergency response. At minimum, the system would generate "intelligent video" that would integrate moving images from across the system to certain centralized locations. It was clear to us, based on our interviews with MTA security officials, that the agency had not been "foot-dragging" in avoiding commitment, but instead were discouraged by genuine concerns that, even within its own terms, the pattern-recognition aspect would not work (there had been no demonstration of the promised technical capacity). Indeed, New York subway stations are particularly inhospitable to even ordinary surveillance photography, given the unevenness of lighting, plethora of nooks and crannies, and vulnerability to vandalism. But authorities were under great pressure to spend, and the new cameras provided a means to do it. Some MTA officials were particularly skeptical, both of contractors' motives as well as capacities. As the head of transit security told us at about this time (in June 2005), "Everybody wants to sell you what they say is the best security technology in the world. And then you find out they're trying to sell you closed-circuit TV cameras. We don't want a *picture* of the event."

The contracts went forward with the sad outcome of, in the words of a state comptroller's office press release, the program falling into "disarray."[3] Lockheed sued to withdraw from the project after the city complained of performance failures. The MTA countersued Lockheed arguing "that Lockheed had provided faulty technology that did not pass basic operational tests."[4] As a transit official testified to the City Council about the legal and financial morass, "The technology does *not* work in our subway system." She continued, "We piloted the technology in a subway tunnel–like environment. It's dark, there are too many columns, there are too many people and there were too many false alarms."[5] It had been, it seems at least in retrospect, a sci-fi pipe dream, a Reaganesque Star Wars for the subway.

But what if the surveillance equipment had worked? Worked at what? We still would have faced the same problem: we don't know what kind of terrorist is going to strike what kind of target and use what kind of method. A suicide bomber, as we know, never separates from his or her bomb. We still would have been stuck with a stupid "working" thing tripping off all sorts of false alarms as folks forgot their backpacks or teenagers tossed belongings to one another. Or a New York fly got on a lens. Without the right kind of attack under just the right anticipated conditions, the system would have done little but screw up the routines of workers' and passengers' lives.

Other subway initiatives are designed to further the vigilance of passengers themselves as surveillance instruments. Most famously, people are instructed, "If You See Something Say Something." Under contract with the MTA, the ad agency Korey Kay & Partners designed signs and posters, starting in 2003, that the agency placed throughout the transit system—in subway cars, on buses, in stations, and on the agency website. It comes in different languages (¡*Si Ves Algo, di Algo!*) and its use has spread to authorities around the world.[6] There are also TV spots. "Since the phrase was introduced by the MTA in 2003," the MTA website indicates, "dozens of municipalities in this country and around the world have asked permission to use it in their own anti-terrorism campaigns." The slogan has been officially licensed by the MTA to the DHS for a national campaign. The loudspeaker systems within subway cars and at station platforms recite the same admonition. Given the poor quality of the public address apparatus, the messages add still another garbled set of noises to the din of screeching trains, yelling kids, and buskers asking for money, selling candy, and performing musical numbers. Striking a higher-tech note, New Jersey Transit invited passengers to use their cell phones to text authorities ("text against terror") as the media reported it.[7]

Another front of the MTA drive to enlist public support was a campaign to assure people that their calls did indeed matter, and that they are not alone in making them. So, as part of a three-million-dollar program, posters on buses and subways, as well as ads on TV, proclaimed, "Last year, 1,944 New Yorkers saw something and said something." The ads include a hotline number to call: 1-888-NYC-SAFE. According to a *New York Times* article by William Neuman on the subject, neither police nor transit officials could say where the number 1,944 came from.[8] Indeed, in our own interviews with transit officials (conducted both before and after the *Times* story), including the heads of public information and security, McClain and I similarly could come up with no method or sources that could confirm this number. Our informants did not claim confidentiality, they just did not know. Putting up the number, the precise number, enables the MTA to show that it is indeed competently dealing with the problem, "doing something" in fact, and that many New Yorkers, through their active participation, believe it as well.

In all, according to the *New York Times*, the hotline received 8,999 calls in 2006, including calls that were transferred from 911 and the city's official nonemergency help line (311). The next year, the total shot up to 13,473, explained perhaps, according to the police department spokesman, by the ad campaign touting the readiness of New

Yorkers to participate. No calls, however, involved terror or terrorist threats against the subway or any other target, although there were false reports and phony allegations. Some people used the hotline to turn in people against whom they evidently held a grudge. A total of eighteen arrests over the two-year period (2006–2007) could be traced to the calls, but for offenses like making up a phony ID or possessing an unregistered handgun. Several calls led to deportations. Eleven reported on individuals said to look like Muslims, who were taking photos of train tracks or "counting people." Muslims use hand-held counters to tally their prayers as they make them, the way Catholics use rosary beads to keep track of the number of Hail Marys they say.

A total of 816 of the calls in 2006 led to follow-up investigation by the police intelligence division or its joint terrorism task force with the FBI. Of the calls about suspicious packages, most were about backpacks, briefcases, or other items accidentally left behind by their owners (who were grateful, one suspects, for their return through security). None had bombs. Neither newspaper reports (we have searched all data bases) nor our workers' accounts provide any cases where "Saying Something" revealed a bona fide attempt to inflict terror in the subways.

In response to the *Times* reporter's query, the police spokesman explained, in reference to the "See Something" campaign, "It's just one small part of the initiative the Police Department has to capture any information that might prevent another 9/11 or another catastrophic attack on the city. One call one day may be the one that stops an attempt to destroy the Brooklyn Bridge." The Director of MTA Security commented that officials in Madrid said that several passengers interviewed after the bombings remembered seeing the unattended knapsacks that turned out to contain the bombs, but for whatever reason decided not to alert anyone. The head of the MTA (Katherine Lapp at the time) indicated that this is something that needed to be avoided at all costs, even if it meant dealing with a deluge of false alarms.[9]

There have indeed been plots against New York since 9/11, most recently a failed effort to detonate a car bomb at Times Square in May 2010. The device did not explode; smoke detected by those on the streets alerted authorities, who closed down Times Square and gathered clues from the intact vehicle. It was an amateurish Rube Goldberg assemblage of home-made ingredients, according to police officials—by a miscreant who had "more desire than ability."[10] Faisal Shahzad, a U.S. citizen born in Pakistan, was readily caught and pleaded guilty.

The most serious plot against the subways, per se, was a 2009 scheme by an Afghan American, Najibullah Zazi, to set off simultaneous bombs (with two accomplices) at the Grand Central and Pennsylvania Railroad subway stations. The plan, or at least an early version of it, was evidently first detected by British intelligence, which intercepted communications between Zazi and his purported al-Qaeda handlers in Pakistan.[11] U.S. authorities trailed his activities as he bought bomb-making materials in Colorado, where he was working as an airport shuttle bus driver (the airport–downtown Denver route), and then as he made his way to New York to commit his crime. Before he could act, but with plenty of evidence accumulated against him, he pleaded guilty. His accomplices were also charged and face severe sentences. As per pattern, detection came not from the "See Something" campaign, from on-site inspections, or from any of the security operations set up by the subway system. It was external intelligence that found the threat.

The other big attempt to commit subway mayhem, a plot ended by arrests in 2004, was frustrated through a different scenario. It was a conspiracy to set off an explosion at the 34th Street–Herald Square station (the busy station that serves Macy's—the "world's largest store"). The plotters never reached the point of purchasing any materials for making a bomb, or going beyond amateurish drawings and speculations about what it would take to do destruction. The charge of conspiracy was also complicated by one of the plotters repeatedly saying, as captured by police recordings, that it was important to him that people not be hurt.

The NYPD's paid informant in the case had a central role, as made evident by the tapes played at the trial of one of the plotters. The informant was double the age of the two young men charged with the crime, James Elshafay (nineteen at the time) and the only somewhat older Shahawar Siraj. The young men regarded the police informant, Osama Eldawoody, as a father figure, and he called Elshafay "son."[12] The younger two seemed anxiously deferential toward his wishes, expertise, and what he convinced them were his impressive connections with Islamic scholars in the Middle East. Eldawoody had in fact been trained as a nuclear engineer, although he made his work in the United States by driving a taxi and performing other miscellaneous occupations. The three of them were all in frequent and lengthy conversations over many months. The interactions of the informant with Siraj are recapitulated in an impressive book on "snitching" by the journalist Ethan Brown, who presents the informant as clearly leading the young men toward schemes they do not seem capable of hatching (alas, Brown does not consistently provide sources for his paraphrases of the conversations).[13]

A defense lawyer for Elshafay argued in court there was little evidence that his client—young, uneducated and clinically schizophrenic— "had any ability whatsoever to carry out any kind of plan."[14] The informant received about $100,000 from the NYPD over a little more than a two-year period, with his weekly stipend rising as his reports became more forceful (he was to complain later of underpayment). The case resembles another highly sensational plot (not involving the subway, but also out of New York) where it turned out that some of the defendant's incriminating statements were made while both he and his NYPD informant were smoking pot. The alleged plotter, Jose Pimentel, later emerged as "unstable," having twice attempted to circumcise himself, among other unusual acts. And, again, we have an informant whose aid was crucial given the incapacity, evident from still other details of his biography, of the man charged.[15] In this instance, the issues of entrapment were sufficiently strong for the FBI to refuse to be part of the prosecution effort, considering the case unwinnable in court. Taking a very different stance, Mayor Michael Bloomberg, Police Chief Raymond Kelly, and Manhattan District Attorney Cyrus Vance all appeared together to eagerly announce the plot when it was first "revealed."

Finally, I turn to the example of one of the very few bombs ever to go off in the subway system and the only one to do so in the post-9/11 period. It was a pipe bomb explosion at the Times Square station just before the start of the Republican National Convention in 2004. It was reported by New York subway police officer Joseph Rodriguez, who himself was injured in the explosion. The event caused a lot of tension in the city in the immediate aftermath and led to an intensified police presence in the subway. Police brass and the media lauded Rodriguez for finding the bag and taking the hit when it went off. But the next day police changed their account and filed charges against Rodriguez for planting the bomb himself. Police found incriminating evidence on his person and in his personal computer, including instructions on bomb making. He had not called 911 when the bomb went off (he was not seriously hurt), a basic part of police protocol, and had other incriminating materials in his Manhattan apartment. Further, there was a history of psychological disturbance; Rodriguez was about to be retired from the force at age 27 on a psychological disability pension.[16] There was no hint of motive, other than what has been called a "hero complex," in which individuals yearn for acknowledgment for having saved the day.[17] Perhaps wars on terror create not only heroes, but also hero wannabes who create their own kind of disturbance.

Looking back at these various attempts at grand violence, patterns emerge. They have been amazingly few in number. None has been successful. All are amateurish, performed by people lacking the relevant skills, not always having even the healthy psychological disposition that anyone needs to be effective at any task (as in the Rodriguez pipe-bomb case). The security apparatus of the subway system did not foil their plan—although intelligence from communication interception was crucial in the Zazi case. The city was spared destruction from miscellaneous things going wrong, such as mishaps of machinery (as in the Shahzad car bomb), and from an apparent lack of seriousness or capability on the part of the plotters (as in the Elshafay "plot"). All such elements imply relevant lessons for thinking about the nature of threat and how possibly to deal with it.

ARSENAL IN PLACE

Against the background drama of bombing conspiracy, injury and death do take place in New York and in its subways. Despite the city's substantial decline in crime (murder rates are now one-third of what they were in the early 1990s), crime still occurs, and this is true of the subway as well as the streets. There is the occasional murder (only one in the subways in 2006), but quite a few robberies—819 in 2006. There are reasons to think this an undercount because of sharp and inexplicable shifts in numbers from various years and because of ambiguity in determining whether to attribute a crime as occurring at a particular subway station or at the corresponding aboveground location.[18]

Whatever the actual numbers, one feature of crime victimization is people's fear of it. Criminologists devote a great deal of research to understanding "fear of crime," partly because of the direct costs it exacts from citizens. There is also, however, a causal relationship between fear and victimization that criminologists focus on: if people fear crime they will be less likely to go out, and that, in turn, increases vulnerability for the increasingly few who do. Subway workers protect passengers from this kind of fear first by simply being there in uniforms, which likely reassures the public, especially with all the signs that advise customers to "alert" a train operator or station agent if they see something. But workers do other, more concrete, things, to make passengers feel they are safe, and—no small matter—that makes them safer in fact. Combined with actions by passengers and others on the scene, they enact day-to-day solutions that hold routine mayhem at bay. In essence, many people are already deeply involved in making things secure, albeit in ways not evident from looking at posters or newspaper reports on security. They involve garden-variety mechanisms in some nonobvious ways.

First among these mechanisms are the passengers' own tendencies to solve problems. Despite the so-called bystander effect, in which people supposedly do little to intervene to save others from assailants, individuals actually do help one another out—a whole lot (as is consistent with the bystander effect follow-up literature).[19] We encountered sixty-two different instances in our interviews, and a few more as reported in the press, in which passengers (not counting off-duty police or subway workers) intervened, usually spontaneously and not infrequently at some risk to themselves. Their actions included jumping down into the tracks to rescue people who had fallen in by accident or on purpose, as in an attempt to commit suicide. These rescues sometimes meant close calls for the passengers in the face of oncoming trains.

In other instances passengers subdued a violent wrongdoer. A twenty-six-year-old named Jonathan Cohen, after seeing a disturbed man (who later turned out to have been psychotic) push a woman to her death in front of an oncoming train, pursued the assailant up escalators and through corridors, eventually to hold him in what the police called a "bear hug" until they could arrive to take over.[20] In another case, a passenger was stabbed as he tried to break up a fight among people he did not know. Still another good samaritan waylaid a man after his attempt to molest a child, physically holding him until police eventually came. Following a passenger's apparent diabetic seizure, and after a conductor announced it to others who might not otherwise have seen that the passenger needed medical assistance, seven people (doctors and nurses) made their way to his car to help.

There are other examples where passengers stayed behind to staunch others' wounds, in one instance, alas, where a woman nevertheless bled to death. Evidence of spontaneous helping runs consistent with what researchers have documented over and over again.[21] Instead of succumbing to passivity and inaction, survivors quickly move to do what can be done. We sometimes see it in TV news footage, whether the responders be Israelis or Palestinians; Hindus, Sikhs, or Muslims; or tornado survivors in the American Midwest. Most often, however, it seems from a close inspection of media coverage that official responders are the ones depicted as the helpers. Even though this is most certainly not the prevalent pattern on the ground, media coverage does often depend on official responders arranging journalistic access. Or maybe it is the pattern because journalists favor the uniforms and rescue equipment that make for good theatrical narrative.[22]

Presumably there are times when people do not come to the rescue and when indeed some are content to let the "hero" take care of the problem; they are passive. But we could find few instances from the subway where somebody who was in a position to do something failed to initiate aid when there was imminent bodily threat to another (some of our workers do report, however, that police have walked off, leaving it to good samaritans, for example, to deal alone with fracases involving teenagers). An exception of workers coming to others' aid seems to be when violence occurs among people who are in some sense outlaws in common, as when two young men who were engaged in the illegal fare-beating system known as "selling swipes" (see later in this chapter) got into a knife fight over access to customers. Under such circumstance, people will call for the police, but do seem—sometimes appropriately—unwilling to physically step in. There was a case where private contractors working in the station did not physically stop a crazed assailant attacking an innocent man with two sabre saws (one in each hand) that he grabbed from a worksite.[23] It also seems, as more of a matter of routine, that passengers do not intervene in minor rule breaking, as when people hold open train doors or, as one woman conductor complained during our interview with her, when men exhibit themselves.

Subway workers indeed *presume* customers will help out, at least by calling police or, at times, taking a more active role. One example became clear to us through McClain's participation in MTA's fire safety and evacuation training, with real-time simulations of train and tunnel darkness. As explained by the MTA veteran who was directing the training, only with the assistance of passengers could there be effective movement of people out of cars when stopped in poorly lit or smoky conditions. People would be needed to assist at every turn to prompt customers to move right or left or to go up steps or across thresholds—for example out of trains and on to catwalks. McClain estimated that a minimum of four helpers would be needed for a simple evacuation. Without the assumption that passengers lend a hand, the whole training protocol would make no sense. Our interviews similarly revealed assumptions among workers that passengers help out when needed—like doctors and nurses who come to the aid of the injured, or those who spontaneously arise to deal with a miscreant.

While customer help is strictly voluntary, subway workers are charged in various ways to maintain order, including guarding against passenger injury. Injury can derive from direct assault or, for example, from a fire (perhaps inadvertently started by a pile of free newspapers catching a spark). Passengers can become ensnared in equipment. Or there can be flooding, which, although not necessarily a danger to life and limb, does threaten the smooth operation of system equipment and trains. In warding off any such threats, workers know and, to a substantial degree, do attend to the formal organizational rules, while at the same time enlisting ad hoc work-arounds as situationally warranted—a central theme of McClain's own research conclusions.[24]

One of a subway worker's intense worries is passenger suicide. Being part of a suicide or some other fatality becomes a trauma. Workers know about coworkers' experiences with such incidents and other types of danger through news reports but more vividly through shared word of mouth. The union, through its own safety initiatives, also provides information regarding such incidents, and how to avoid them—and how to recuperate once they occur. Subway workers find themselves dealing with what they sometimes refer to as "knuckleheads," "crazy people," or, also in their argot, "EDPs" (emotionally disturbed persons). Many worker interviewees report having themselves been victimized. In the most extreme case, a woman worker was subject to one attempted and one actual rape.

Workers' routines, including observance of official regulations, expose them to danger as a matter of course. Very specific work protocol requires conductors to put their heads at risk. They must stick their heads out of their cab windows in ways that do not allow them to see an assailant intent on hitting them on the head, perhaps with an object. Located in a middle car (the train has eight or ten cars), conductors open train doors by depressing two buttons simultaneously, each opening half of the train's doors on to the platform. But they close them in two separate operations. Conductors look first to the right (head out the window) to make sure it is safe in that direction. All doors to the right are then closed with the push of a single button—head remaining out the window and looking right. Then they repeat the same maneuvers but to the left, pressing a different button. Their heads must remain out the window during both maneuvers, sometimes repeatedly at a single stop, often for long moments and looking in only one direction at a time, focused on the car doors. As the train exits the station, their heads remain out the window until it has moved a prescribed seventy-five feet forward.[25] Taking advantage of these conditions, according to our informants, miscreants have punched conductors' heads, slashed them with blades, thrown glass bottles at them, hit them with various objects, and spit at them or doused them with other liquids.[26] But in the mean-

Figure 5. Signs and notices block views at station agent booth. Photo by Noah McClain.

time, conductors' assiduous looking (and risk taking) means that few if any customers are caught in the doors and hence dragged through the tunnels. This maneuver also ensures that children are not separated from a care giver—a high priority for conductors, as they brought up repeatedly in our interviews.

Station agents are almost always alone in their booths and, depending on location and hour of the day, also alone in the station (a minority of stations also have commercial news kiosks, which are open for at least some of the hours of train operations). Station agents answer travelers' questions, an activity that itself is sometimes helpful for learning about problems in the system (how come the right exit is blocked?) as well as providing answers that enhance passenger safety. The glass-enclosed walls behind which they sit make it possible for them to visually survey their surroundings. They have access to an intercom button to call for outside help. Their views of space surrounding the booths are often blocked by signs that the MTA puts up over the glass, some of it ironically warning passengers to be on alert for unattended packages, that their stuff might be searched, and, of course, that if they see something they should say something (figure 5).

One worry that station agents have is that miscreants could spill or spray a flammable liquid or gas through the opening at the base of their booth's window, followed by a match to set the booth afire. A number of station agents were killed or maimed in the 1980s through the mid-1990s in such attacks, accompanied by robbery attempts. Ironically, prior efforts to increase booth security contributed to the problem. To deal with station agents' vulnerability to shootings, authorities made the booths bullet-resistant. But specifics of the design had the effect of decreasing ventilation, which made explosion (rather than fire) more likely. More recent add-on remedies, particularly a fire-retardant system, have had an apparently corrective effect.[27] But since 1995, there have been seven additional attacks reported in the press, which indeed support the stories that workers have told us and which they continue to discuss with one another. In four of the seven accounts, attackers used an unidentified liquid; in the other instances, one used anti-freeze, one gasoline, and one lighter fluid. Besides dangerous items hurled through the opening, a man inserted his erect penis to shock a female agent—another account that made the rounds. If they sense trouble in time, workers can quickly shut the aperture to their window (ouch!).

Some of the station agents' safety routines are not for self-defense but for defense of others. As school lets out each day, hundreds of pre-adolescents or teens may descend into a station. They jump on and about one another as they approach the turnstiles, risking human crush. Some station agents have told us that at these times, they disengage the turnstiles allowing anyone to go through with a simple push. The agents fear that someone attempting to go through the turnstile will discover they have no card, that their card will malfunction, or that they will just fumble and take too long. Rather than risk a pileup, station agents disengage the system—something not permitted for workers to do under MTA rules, but done anyway.

Similarly, station agents are not to leave their enclosures to service the needs of customers, but if a child is in dire trouble, for example, they simply do it. If there is a difficult person at a station, the station agent can give him or her a free admit through the turnstile to enter a train, albeit then perhaps to become a problem at a different station. Workers on the trains also have options, not in the rulebooks, to deal with safety concerns. One strategy is to lock wrongdoers out of trains or, depending on circumstance, lock them in. Conductors have the capacity to key lock car doors individually, both the doors that lead off to platforms as well as doors between the cars themselves. A worker reported to us that on one of his runs he realized kids in a car were shattering bottles against windows, ripping seats from the train floor, and trying to throw them through the glass. Among other hazards, their actions could have resulted in objects on tracks with potential for derailment or sparking a fire. He also saw they had knives. The conductor—who happened still to be in his apprenticeship—took the impromptu strategy of turning the last car, where the disruptive kids happened to be, into a holding cell. He closed all train doors. He then made his way back to the penultimate car and got the remaining innocent people out of the car still containing the troublemakers. As he explained in our interview,

> So I went to the ninth car. I motioned to the people [who could see me through the glass window], "come this way come to me," but I didn't want to give it away because they [the miscreants] would have probably attacked me. Locked what they call a storm door, which is at the end of the car.

This trapped the offenders where they could be held while police were called.

When the police did come, they were on the wrong side of the platform. Some crossed over the tracks (contrary to policy because of the danger of electrocution and exposure to moving trains), while others took the stairs up, crossed over on the street above, and then came down again (several flights each way). By securely penning the offenders, the conductor saved the day regardless of the wait-time for the police. While the capacity to key lock individual cars stems from the need to protect them while in storage or in yards while awaiting repair, the feature comes in handy when workers need to make an ad hoc security application.

Figure 6. "Shoe slipper" used by conductors to disconnect a train from its power source. Photo by Noah McClain.

Similarly the public address system on a train can be oriented toward safety, albeit in an unauthorized way. A cleaner working inside a train reported,

> I'll go to the intercom system where the conductor gives his announcements, and I'll go, "All right, people, be aware. There's a pickpocket on the train." And I'll make an announcement over the, uh, you know, the PA system.
>
> Now if my supervisor caught wind of me doin' that I'd be in trouble . . . [asked why by the interviewer] because I'm not supposed to be in the conductor's cab makin' announcements cause I'm not a conductor.

Another instrument at hand that train workers can put to unauthorized safety use is the hardwood "shoe slipper" or "shoe paddle" as it is also sometimes called, which is yellow in color (figure 6). According to official procedures, train workers may use it to disconnect the train from its power source, by inserting the shoe slipper between the shoe and the third rail. They may need to do so when, for example, someone is under a train and could be electrocuted by train components in live contact with the third rail.

Here is a conductor interviewee showing us the shoe slipper's common use as a security instrument:

> We're not supposed to carry that for any other reason but to do that function [disengage the train]. But, when I go out there in the middle of the night, I don't go out there without something [to protect myself].

One conductor describes how he was able to divert a ranting drunk away from passengers. He employed the shoe device to prop open the door to his compartment (which otherwise closes on its own) to divert the angry man's attention away from passengers and toward himself:

> It was a homeless person. He was getting up in peoples' faces while they were sitting down. He was screaming at them, cursing at them. Daring them to get up and fight him. He was really really out there. And I was telling him, "Sit down and shut up already. Stop bothering these people." And he'd come and scream at me, and I said, "Sit down. You want to sit here?" I propped my door open with a shoe paddle.[28] I said, "Go ahead. You can scream at me all you want 'til the cops get here and take you off!"

While rules do not permit MTA employees even to touch a passenger, workers use the shoe slipper to wake up sleeping passengers sprawled across the seat or to nudge them along from one location to another. Other instruments as well have served as defensive weapons, according to reports—for example, a detachable train break handle. In a very uncommon report, a worker used his brake handle to hit a violent person.

Train operators also have horns they sound to herald their coming to anyone who may be in the way of the train around the next bend, including impatient passengers on platforms leaning forward to see if a train is coming. The horns are very loud, and hence operators sound them only as short bursts and only prior to entering passenger platform areas. They can go to full volume, which is literally deafening,[29] to warn of danger, as in cases where workers or others are on the tracks.

In many instances, such as an assault or robbery on board, train operators are instructed to "blow for police en route." Blowing the horn in a particular pattern (long-short-long-short) sends a signal to police who might be within earshot, even several stations away. But horn blasting can also deal directly with perpetrators. A train operator once used his horn when he noticed a mugging attempt as he came into a station. He blew his horn loud and long as he came on the scene and kept it blaring. As he explains,

> So the woman was getting mugged on the platform. Avenue H I think it was. So I blew the horn. Try to get him to leave her alone. I was slowing down in case these guys think about pushing her in front of the train. . . . And I started chasing them with the train but I couldn't go any further cause I came to the end of the platform.

The operator had hoped the sound of his horn, indicating an approaching train with an employee on board who could see what was going on, would dissuade the mugger. Or that the continuous blast, by sheer aural force, would disrupt the activity. As it happens, it did neither; the perpetrator got the woman's purse and made a successful escape. But the operator's reaction shows how the horn, and indeed the moving train itself, can be operated in an extemporaneous way to address a problem.

Besides locking in perpetrators, workers can use the individual car key feature to protect passengers from a repulsive and bloody mess, and hence the fears and anxieties that such visible residue of violence might induce. During one of McClain's sessions observing train crews, a teenage male was assaulted in one of the rear cars of a train. After police and ambulance responded to the call for help, the car had blood on the seats and floor, and rush hour was fast approaching. Lacking equipment or personnel to safely clean the train car, the MTA worker "keyed off" all the doors in that car—ensuring its doors would not open at station stops. The train was thus able to remain in service without further alarming passengers.

Admonitions to report all problems to supervisors pervade the *Rules and Regulations* book (MTA, 2003) and all deviations from strict procedures require permission from supervisors. Workers do strictly adhere to some rules, like the instruction for conductors never to close train doors without simultaneously having their head out the window, as explained earlier. But in many other cases, the rules (as with the equipment) are treated in a more ad hoc manner.

Unlike many other kinds of workers, such as members of a construction crew or clerks in a government office, subway workers do not typically have the resource of calling on adjacent workers for tips and real-time help.[30] When they do communicate with supervisors—known colloquially as "Control"—it is via radio or phone. Such communication is an example of what has been called "interaction in isolation."[31] Subway workers are not allowed to call police and firefighters directly. Although not all such contacts between a station agent and Control is for a major emergency, the contacts are voluminous—on the order of over 150,000 calls each year.[32]

Summoning help always carries some risk of being misunderstood by the call-center operators or generating delays in action being taken. Examinations by social scientists (conversation analysts, as they are known in this case) of "calls for help" to 911 in the United States, clarify how, quite beyond the subway context, systematic difficulties can arise from phoned-in requests for aid.[33] In the 911 case, emergency dispatchers require specific information to fill in data fields before sending assistance, sometimes insisting that their questions be answered in a required order. This can lead to misunderstandings, delays, and disastrous consequences, including—in one instance yielded in the research by Don Zimmerman and his colleagues—death.[34] (A woman died as her frantic adult son was unable to follow the proper information sequence demanded at the other end of the line.) In responding to forest fire reports in Southern California, dispatchers cause response delays with questions aimed at determining who or what started the fire.[35] Emergency aid dispatchers, as in fire or crime reports, have two goals: gaining clues to who may be an arsonist or criminal and also attending to the need for aid. It can be a tricky balancing act trying to decide how much time and effort should go toward one goal versus the other, given the urgent need for fast action.

In the subway, workers must satisfy the information needs of Control (for example, "Are the people fighting on your train male or female?").

They may be prevented from following what for them, at the moment, might seem a more common-sense narrative that would mobilize police or fire immediately. By the time help is on the way (and sometimes promised help just never arrives, according to our informants), the damage may be done, a culprit gone from the scene, or the problem already solved by workers and/or passengers. Control may not agree with workers' evaluation in any event, or the type of response may not correspond to what the worker thought necessary (for example, fire fighters arrive when it was police who were needed). For all sorts of reasons, then, workers may "take care of it" on the spot, as best they can. The arrival of help can also disrupt train service, and the request for this help, if not considered the proper response to a bona fide problem, can reflect poorly on the employee.

Especially when situations are highly ambiguous (they are always ambiguous to some degree), it comes in handy for those at the top of organizational hierarchies to decentralize responsibility for emergency aid "as far down the organizational line as possible."[36] If things go wrong, those below can take the blame. As Robert Jackall explains, "When blame is allocated, it is those who are . . . politically vulnerable or expendable, who become 'patsies', who get 'set up' or 'hung up to dry' and become blamable."[37] As much as possible, blame is set up to go downward.[38]

Perhaps the most instructive instance of a subway worker under high stakes and organizational uncertainty comes from the World Trade Center site itself on the date of 9/11. One of those McClain interviewed was the operator of a train headed right into the World Trade Center–Cortlandt Street subway station as the building was about to collapse (the only such train reported to be doing so at that time and place). The train driver defied his orders to *not* stop. As he said during the interview,

> They said continue in service, but bypass Cortlandt Street–World Trade
> Center. So I made the station stop at Whitehall and right around then is
> when they said, "All trains, northbound southbound, bypass Cortlandt
> Street." What happens is Command Center has to go by what they're
> hearing. They're in the office somewhere in Brooklyn: Jay Street. They

can't see what's actually happening, so they just run their playbook. They were running it as a "smoke condition." And as a rule of smoke conditions we bypass the station. You don't want to put customers onto a platform with smoke. You don't want to take smoke into the train.

But the train driver saw a waiting crowd, about four persons deep. The station was indeed in a smoke situation. As he entered the station, the train driver locked eyes with a woman anxiously waiting to board. He recalled,

And I had never seen that kind of fear in my life. I couldn't see her facial expression. All I could see were her eyes, and it was fear.

This cue of "her eyes" apparently convinced him to stop the train and take on the new passengers. As he told McClain,

Cause, um, I was disobeying orders. My order was to bypass the station. I made a judgment call. I made a judgment call based on experience, basically.

The train driver was intensely concerned about the immediate circumstance, but also how he was going to report the fact that he stopped the train against standing procedures as well as the specific instruction on this occasion:

Well, in my mind I'm thinking, "I know I'm going to have to hear about this one." So I was trying to figure out how I was going to write the . . . we call it a G2, and it's in the report. I was trying to [figure] out how to word it. Where, um, I minimize myself and my conductor getting into trouble.

As it turned out, the train operator made the right call; he surely saved many lives.

But he was right to have concern. Workers are wary of calling attention to themselves in general. It may force them to stay beyond a shift to make written reports or meet with agency officials. This may disrupt personal schedules, like complicating child-care or causing a worker to miss a ride home or commuter train. In these after-shift sessions, supervisors might scrutinize workers' accounts (or workers fear this will happen), as they look for rule violations, including actions not even related to the reported incident. Perhaps the workers were standing in the wrong place at the time of the occurrence or they were wearing an unauthorized type of clothing or insignia.

By far the most prevalent reason for workers to resist rules, especially security dicta, is the risk of stopping the whole system. Not everything can be reported and corners must be massively cut in this regard. Given the range of things that go on in the subways, there is huge potential for false positives. Someone may tell an MTA employee that a suspicious bag has been left on a station platform. A worker tells us she "just kicks" bags to see what might be in them. Calling it in to Control risks a station closure, just like a conductor calling in a box left on a seat means that the train goes out of service. Major delays then occur and a worker who does not use common sense is, in Harold Garfinkel's apt term, a "judgmental dope."[39] That could mean discipline, including being "targeted," as the workers say, for some other potential infraction.

Some instructions aimed against terrorist acts are seen as not capable of being of any use in an actual emergency. For example, the MTA issues masks, known as "escape hoods" to protect against chemical or biological attack to conductors, train operators, and track workers. The masks hang from belts at hip level in a plastic pouch. Station agents have a single mask in their booths. The MTA issues no masks at all to cleaners (who are on the lowest-paid rung of the job scale). Some workers think the masks add security to their work yet note they are meant for only fifteen minutes' protection, maybe enough time to get themselves out of tunnels but not to aid others in doing so. Evacuations, they say, require great patience and the power of speech (which is muffled by the mask). The actual evacuation that McClain encountered in fieldwork in September 2004 (as opposed to the simulated one in the training reported earlier) occurred at midday on a lightly populated subway. A conductor and train operator collaborated to move all passengers into the rear car, which was very near a station platform. Passengers stepped from the train directly onto a two-foot-wide catwalk and proceeded fifteen feet to the platform. This calm and uncomplicated evacuation (as no one had to walk through tunnels or climb emergency ladders) took about thirty minutes. In the experience of other evacuations, between 2003 and 2006, it took an average of one hundred minutes from incident to "open sky."[40]

The transit union has publicly complained that the emergency training offered to workers is merely perfunctory—the MTA distributes pamphlets to workers and offers a brief course that is especially inadequate in terms of showing how to assist the public. Workers are basically told, as one of our interviewees complained, to "cut and run"—something we know they don't in fact do, judging from the examples already described. But given the paucity of equipment and other practical exigencies, cut and run may at times be the only realistic course. And beyond a mask shortage, or the proliferation of masks that hinder communication, there are deep problems of infrastructure, like inadequate lighting and signage, indecipherable audio messages, and emergency platforms that are only marginally accessible—they are often too narrow for a significant group of people to make their way out.

The details of turnstiles, otherwise so routine, become critical during evacuations. Early New York subway turnstiles provided relatively little obstruction for those needing to exit in a hurry, as evidenced in a 1943 photo (figure 7). But that meant they also did little to obstruct people from entering without paying their fare. Whether young or old, frail or obese, people could climb over or crawl under and get a free ride. Out of concern to "protect the fare," the modern turnstile emerged with sloped entry panels, bars placed just above head level, and angled flanges on the turnstile itself (figure 8). Although claimed by its creators to have been "designed with reference to the human body," it was based, as made clear in the patent application for the equipment, on the bodies of U.S. military servicemen. Even within that constricted population, only the bodies of the middle 90 percent of the sample were taken into account. The design method traveled from the military to the subway turnstile without adjustment for sizes and physical capacity of the civilian population. Some people have crutches, guide dogs, babies, strollers, large packages, or luggage. Bulky coats, worn in a New York winter, add further girth.[41]

The most ambitious turnstiles for warding off fare beaters are the so-called high-entry (HEET) models, which are harder to cheat, at

Figure 7. Subway turnstile, 1943. Image courtesy of New York Transit Museum.

least by using the usual techniques. Observing with McClain and me, sociologist Christine Nippert-Eng, while spending a few days with us as a consulting field researcher, named it "the garlic press" (see figure 9). It prevents people from jumping over or crawling under (although not from coupling up and squeezing through on a two-for-one entry). Whatever has been gained or lost in paid fares, there is a potential security cost. Entry or exit takes more time. Especially when a crowd is trying to exit, people can routinely be seen in line waiting their turn, many dozens of them sometimes. When the MTA originally installed the modern garlic press, they were in noncompliance with the state fire code, which requires greater capacity for exit. Any evacuation will take longer than in the past when the very vulnerabilities of the machinery for fare beating provided a kind of emergency safety valve.

Figure 8. Contemporary turnstile with sloped side panels and other features to ward off fare beating. Photo by Noah McClain.

In one vivid example of security backfire, police were delayed in responding to a platform shooting because they lacked MetroCards. They had to borrow fare cards from others to enter.[42] A man bled to death in the interim. Getting medical equipment in is made more difficult as is getting an ailing person out (imagine a gurney trying to pass through the turnstiles). In partial compensation, the MTA announced it would provide police (and fire officials) with MetroCards, and I've seen them use them.

Responding to the evident problem of the HEET turnstiles, the MTA installed additional emergency exits at platforms (see figure 10), untested in terms of evacuation numbers but certainly an improvement (although in some exit corridors the HEET models remain the only way out). The emergency exit doors have now been thoroughly tested in terms of unauthorized use. People hold open the exit doors (one kid pays to go in and holds the door open for his friends). Or

Figure 9. HEET turnstile, a.k.a. "garlic press." Photo by Noah McClain.

people happening on the scene take advantage of someone making his or her way out and grab the door to go in. Either way, non-payers gain free entry, making the whole system more permeable. As people push open the emergency doors, an alarm sounds for about thirty seconds. These alarms, contrary to early specifications, are connected to nothing. During busy times in busy stations, the opening of these doors creates a continuous piercing noise, adding an unwelcome sound to an already noisy environment—but also rendering incomprehensible, or potentially drowning out all together, any instructions made over loudspeakers or by emergency personnel.

System redesign may not end cheating or add to security, but it does alter the ways to cheat and the kind of people who do it. It turns out that a spent MetroCard can be bent in such way that fools the machine. People with the right skills stand at the turnstiles and sell swipes, usually well below the price of a normal ticket (one dollar instead of two).

Figure 10. Emergency exit. Photo by Noah McClain.

They can also guarantee themselves plenty of business by jamming up nearby MetroCard vending machines with chewing gum in the money and credit card slots, making their swipe business the only alternative for some customers. Subway cheaters have been pivotal in the city's anticrime quality of life campaigns; arresting them is thought an important part of the "broken windows" strategy to head off big crimes by stopping small ones. Perhaps because of the nature of the culprits (poor and black or Hispanic young men), authorities have increased penalties of fare evasion. By explicitly alleging that they were hurting efforts to fight terror,[43] the state legislature increased the penalty from simple violation to a misdemeanor to a crime with penalties of up to three months in jail for those selling swipes. In 2005 prosecutors began interpreting the crime as felony forgery, with a potential of seven years imprisonment. In the first six-month period, sixty-one individuals had such charges leveled against them.[44]

In any event, the cheating problem remains unsolved despite the legal and mechanical interventions. At one recent point in time, the authority estimated as many as 10 percent of passengers to be free riders. For the year 2008, the MTA had estimated lost revenue of $7 million; a recalibration led to a reestimate of losses at $27 million.[45] Unlike when phony tokens deposited in fare boxes could be counted up and proper estimates made of that mode of cheating, newer technologies eliminate such precision. Card-bending leaves no trail. As McClain elegantly summarizes, "Through these progressive iterations against fare evasion, the MTA in effect chased the problem out of accountability."[46] And this also means, as does happen with increasingly complex technical apparatuses, the organizers are hoisted on the petard of their own technical sophistication.

What to Do?

Our master guiding remediation principle for this chapter on the subways is the need to acknowledge everyday work practices and their instrumentation as guiding emergency response, in the past and for the future. The key ingredient is people's ordinary sense making that, in Karl Weick's term, must not be pressed into "collapse."[47] That means there needs to be integration of security precautions with the actual jobs that workers do and the manifold tasks they undertake. And, yes, this may mean accepting some fare beating and other inconvenient outcomes. Some of the specifics follow on.

- *Attend to workers' practices.*

Authorities should know and respect workers' repertoires for dealing with ordinary problems, including those based on their experiences with outside agents. If workers think their supervisors have bad information, they will not treat instructions given to them as bona fide. If they think their supervisors do not take into account job exigencies at hand, they will discount their directives. If they think bosses' initiatives are silly, they will deride rather than follow them. Remedies for dealing with such disjuncture are either to change the routines of the work situation (easing, for example, the vulnerabilities to human and mechanical challenges) or to make sure instructions take those contexts into account. Understanding the mundane is the best route for addressing the spectacular.

This orientation aligns well with that of the master security analyst and distinguished psychologist Elliot Aronson. From his studies of how people respond to campaigns to use condoms or conserve water, he concludes that they will ignore advice they do not consider trustworthy.[48] Besides their own routine experience with how the system operates, our subway workers know that the "See Something" campaign is preposterous and the signs that tell how many New Yorkers "Said Something" are no less ridiculous. Unless advice, following again Aronson, is concrete, doable, and credible, it will yield nothing—something judged to have been the case with the DHS color code warnings and the much-derided advice to have a "safe room" sealed off with duct tape.[49] An alternative to all of it is to abandon these earmarked and official security measures and concentrate on the daring alternative of just making things better—creating conditions that have the effect, quite counter-intuitively, of indeed adding to security. I list some of them for the subway system.

• *Improve ventilation.*

If there is a chemical attack or just a pile of newspapers set on fire, better ventilation will save people from smoke inhalation or visibility problems. In terms of workers' long-term health, less steel dust from wheels on tracks will reach their lungs. And, until an attack happens, everyone will breathe easier; perhaps also, if the MTA plays the infrastructure right, stations will be less stultifying in summer and cold in winter.

• *Fix communication.*

In an emergency, people need to be in touch, two (or more) ways if possible. During the World Trade Center disaster, almost all systems collapsed: radio, television, and even cell phones. The notoriously primitive loudspeaker systems of the New York subways (a routine joke among passengers), as well as the so-called emergency communications system for workers, leave much room for improvement. Indeed, the workers have only the most primitive means of communicating with one another and with their supervisors. Think of the poor subway conductor approaching Ground Zero, trying to get accurate information.

Passengers need to know if they are being advised to go to a particular exit, to remain in train cars or to vacate, to walk to the right or the left in the tunnel, away from the third rail. Like those in the factory pulling at the locked doors, they will, without being able to understand what is being said, perish. But again, good sound brings a bonus for the everyday. People will be less tense because they know which stop is theirs and which train has been rerouted to what track. New York's subways, at this writing, still do not have cell phone service in most places, in part out of authorities' fear that cell phones could be used to trigger a bomb. With cell phones, of course, individuals could also warn one another as well as authorities of real-time danger. Another way to improve communication would be to decrease noise levels. The antiquated cars and tracks screech and squeal; that creates a communication problem as well as aural discomfort. Modernizing them would be another everyday amenity that would also enhance safety.

• *Improve signage.*

Even on a good day, passengers have trouble figuring out which way to the street and, where there are multiple exits, to a particular street. If passengers are to learn that a particular exit is closed, they need clear markings so they can know, without hesitation, the best alternate route. And they need it, in a polyglot city, in a way that does not require knowledge of English. "Way finding," and there is something of a science of it, is another aspect of emergency infrastructure, and if it is good, it is good 24/7. It's a simple as this: people are safer when they know where they are. And the learning occurs in the routines of everyday use as individuals notice out of the corner of their eye the markings for exits and routings they ordinarily have no reason to use.

• *Make better stairways, corridors, ledges, and platforms.*

Because of their origin as separate competing private companies and also years of deferred maintenance, the subways are mazes of make-do add-ons. Anything that clarifies and simplifies helps with safety—and again makes things more pleasant day in and day out. Stairways should not be limited by their "behind the scenes" functionality like toilet stalls left in architectural silence. They should be made visible from floor areas to enhance safety as well as to let in light to enhance pleasantness. Vertical columns now press bodies close to the platform edge, complicate evacuation, and obscure vision. They need realignment or elimination.

Also making matters worse for quick exits, escalators break down and are blocked off routinely—not just put into disuse, but left with empty voids where landings need to be. So in a power failure they can not even be physically climbed. Lack of an escalator does not just create inconvenience and pain for the aged, injured, and those with luggage, it yields hazard by pressing passengers into a narrow stairway. Routine maintenance and fast repair thus not only make life better, but also make things more secure. In some instances, escalators are blocked off for years because the developers who pledged to maintain them as a condition for their high-rise building permits fail to do so. Unlike friends and neighbors, these developers are less likely to spontaneously jump in to help; they need to be forced into compliance.

• *Lose the HEET.*

Designed to protect against those who would cheat, turnstiles evolved to become increasingly difficult for all users, and the HEET models must go. They reflect a continuous narrowing of the range of human beings who can pass with comfort and safety. They embody the opposite of "universal design" —the idea that in serving the needs of everyone, including the disabled, a good device enhances benefits for all. One of the most famous lines of universal design products are Oxo Good Grips kitchen tools, first developed to aid people with limited hand capacity but then found to be better for everyone. And they now dominate in their industry.

An even more universal alternative is to get rid of all turnstiles completely. An honor system, as practiced in various parts of the world, sometimes involves random checks with penalties for nonpayment. In other cases, I have been told Norway is one such place; people there consider transportation enough of a government responsibility that authorities are not too exercised about some cheating. In the United States, much of central Portland, Oregon, is a free ride zone as are ski resort areas. It is life enhancing to just walk in and walk out, spared the ordeal of finding the card, making sure it has enough money on it, and assuming the swiping pose (while balancing packages, babies, and suitcases). Some business models have a built-in degree of theft ("shrinkage"), sparing employees from scrutinizing every customer. Not just luxury stores but also low-end chains and web-based merchants allow returns "no questions asked." Some museums have only "voluntary" contributions, but a great majority of patrons do choose to pay the "suggested" fee with the result that admission income is no less than 75 percent of what would result if everyone paid full price.[50] Meanwhile the museum can let up on fare policing, while expanding its audience and serving those with financial difficulty, which is useful for private fund-raising as well as public relations. At Apple stores, as with Singer sewing machine centers generations ago, people get free advice regardless of whether or not they buy. But buy they do; Apple's midtown NYC branch had the highest per-square-foot gross of any retail space on Fifth Avenue.[51] Starbucks lets pedestrians come in off the street to use the toilet and provides sofas and electricity for laptop users. Many if not most private employers let workers use paper, copy machines, and other goods and equipment for "unauthorized" private purposes. It is all part of the slack.

For subway workers, doing away with the turnstile would also mean a nicer day. They would have less exposure to customers' anger about cards that don't work, machines that malfunction, and rides that were paid for but not taken. Staff could devote more of their time to other aspects of the job, including watching out for real trouble. Homeless people, who ride the rails all day, could more easily exit and reenter the stations, which in turn would allow them to come up and relieve themselves in a more appropriate place rather than urinating or defecating in the subway system.

• *Light better.*

Enhanced lighting and durability, particularly at exits, would pay off in a moment of crisis, as well as improving conditions at most all other times as well. Will there be disorienting glare or will lighting be crisp? What objects are lit, not just on the platforms but also in the system's innards that people may have to negotiate? And what is the system redundancy, not just to handle catastrophe but routine troubles of power failure? Improve on all fronts.

• *Clean it up.*

Ordinary construction crews know that an unkempt workplace causes accidents. In the subway, dirt and grime obscure signage and may cause people to slip and fall. Helter-skelter environments facilitate chaos in times of emergency. After exhaustive investigation, officials judged track debris the culprit for the 2001 Baltimore freight-train-tunnel derailment and fire that lasted five days and virtually shut down central Baltimore. In the chemical conflagration 2,554 gallons of hydrochloric acid were released from one of the tank cars, with additional toxic chemicals spilled from others.[52] The solution for Baltimore, as for subways in general, is to implement regular inspections and a higher standard of order and cleanliness.

Greater cleanliness brings a much-used public facility into conformity with how people routinely live in their private spaces. Societies differ in the standards of comfort and pleasantness between the public and private. In the United States the discrepancy seems extreme, with the standard for public facilities, especially the subway environment, falling far below the level of cleanliness that residents achieve in maintaining their own living space. This means that people notice the low standard of the public facility and might well support a higher one, and pick up some nonobvious security benefit in the bargain.

• *Keep humans.*

Finally, what about the MTA employees? We learned that real security is provided by context-sensitive inventiveness by people not charged with doing security—without benefit of special budgets and without armaments or much coercive authority over others. In the language of security organizational analysts, they have "high mission valence"[53]—they are committed to keeping people safe. And they do countless things for others along the way, including giving advice to tourists, uniting families with lost children, and compensating for decrepit and faulty artifacts. They are security bulwarks. Humans alone scan, know, and remedy. Somewhere and somehow their presence and goodwill seem key.

Whether in respecting the role of the workers or upgrading the passenger experience, the best way to enact security is by doing things that do not look like security at all. Improving subways to make them more efficient and pleasant can make them more resilient and safe. Such improvements are not *alternatives* to investing in security, but the most important aspects of it. Officials can lessen danger by implementing measures that are inconspicuous, passive vis-à-vis both customers and workers. It is akin to what has been called "crime prevention through environmental design,"[54] but more generous in spirit, delivering benefits that can stand even if there are no attacks, which is the overwhelming likelihood for any given context. Improvement in everyday infrastructure bodes well for resilience, and at relatively low cost. A gentler subway provides for people and enables them toward solutions of their own safety and survival.

CHAPTER 4

Wrong-Way Flights: Pushing Humans Away

Airports have turned out badly. It takes about the same amount of time to travel through air today as it did dozens of years ago, but a lot longer time to get off the ground. Security procedures change not just the timing, but exact huge costs in money, mood, and resentments with consequences far and wide.

When I was young, my family was not the only one that, however bad the food, would go to the airport to have a meal. Just being *around* air travel was a treat. The idea of travel has long been an excitement. We find it in prose, poetry, and song—particularly since safe and fast mechanisms, especially planes, have appealed to a wide audience. Air travel feeds on the basic human desire to "get out"—up, up, and away. The Italian song, "Volare" ("to fly") won two Grammies and was the Billboard top single of 1958. "Come fly with me," echoed Frank Sinatra in his huge hit album of that name in the same year. Some of the frisson may have been fed by a sense of some danger; flying was indeed less safe in those days. To help assuage and assure while at the same time performing little miracles of hot meals even on short flights, air carriers larded on cocktails, shrimp appetizers, and attractive young stewardesses. And people could visit the gates to see one another off and meet those coming in, sometimes with large (and animated) groups of well-wishers and greeters.

Before 1973, when a number of hijackings prompted the U.S. government to take restrictive action, people entered airports as casually as they now go into department stores. Indeed, air travel's festival nature invited joining the "jet set." Security was so informal that people could actually give their tickets away or exchange them with one another (as long as genders more or less aligned with the names on the tickets). This could provide quick and easy solutions to life problems that might arise—for example, "I can't go to the wedding, so you go." A "fly-away" Michigan fraternity party, held at the Detroit airport, featured one couple being presented with tickets (phony names were on them) to a surprise destination—that very night. Everyone came packed for the possibility. On board, things could also be festively informal and boisterous. A large group I was part of (conventioneers on an appliance company junket) was able to convince the flight crew to allow one among us (Sam Moss, from the Zenith television wholesale distributor, who was very funny) to get on the intercom and regale passengers with his singing and off-color jokes. Those were the days, my friend.

For people much lower on the social totem pole than appliance dealers and closer to our own time, airport openness served another function. Airports sheltered the homeless. According to the research of sociologist Kim Hopper, hundreds of people once lived in airports. It was a plausible solution to a host of practical problems.[1] Airports have heat in the winter and air-conditioning in the summer. They have running water and bathroom facilities that are mostly empty for long periods of time. And there is also a good supply of free food, cast off by restaurants or left behind by hurried passengers. Also, sleeping at the gates is common enough to allow homeless people to have a rest without being too obtrusive. But now without a boarding pass, homeless people cannot get very far. They were living in the interstices, and interstices are inimical to security regimes.

TENSIONS OF TRAVEL

So modern security helped turn something a little wondrous into trials and tedium. Travel carries some built-in emotional baggage, regardless of security regimen. There may be concern about the journey to the airport, making connections, arrival times, and seat assignment, plus all the other details concerning hotel, car rentals, and meeting preps. An aspect running through it all is the anxiety of being dislodged from a home base, including being separated from the tools and goods through which we ordinarily manage routines and intimacies.

The act of packing is an effort to secure the transition. Deliberation goes into choosing the right clothes, prescriptions, and more idiosyncratic paraphernalia that needs to fit within luggage—a small fraction of one's normal holding capacity. Many air passengers pack with care, folding to avoid creases, protecting gifts against crushing, or shielding important documents from liquids or derangement. Attention goes to figuring out what will be needed at the destination. It may take a lot of money to compensate for what has been forgotten, with precious time lost to borrow or shop for replacement; sometimes replacement will be impossible altogether. Tension is especially high for the carry-on luggage, which usually holds the most precious cargo and undergoes the most intensive security invasion. Careful trade-offs must be made to deal with restrictions of luggage girth and issues of weight. All this pre-worry contributes to human vulnerability in the meeting up of self and the security apparatus.

The Standard Personage

The idiosyncrasies of packing up contrast starkly with the thrust of public authority. Any public infrastructure, especially if it involves separate jurisdictions and intersection with commercial operators, requires common standards both of artifact and procedure. Everyone must drive either on the right or on the left. Sometimes it doesn't even matter which is which, only that there is conformity. So the advent of railways required a consistent railway gauge within a continent. Air travel requires minimum runway dimensions to which plane manufacturers conform.[2] Infrastructure also implies individual conformity; air travelers must check in at appropriate spots, attend to details regarding the proper "concourse," "departure gate," luggage retrieval area, and all the rest. An onboard suitcase must fit dimensions of the overhead bin. Passengers need to have a common sense of how to stay out of the isles when the food is coming through. These standardizations permit individuals varying arrays of choice within them—which route to drive, for example, where to fly, chicken or pasta.

As James Scott points out in his major treatise, the state "sees" the world to gain control over it, and that means generating conformity and a certain degree of obeisance.[3] Besides eventually weighing in on which side of the road to drive on, the emerging state forced individuals into actions less evidently for the pure purpose of coordination. It required individuals to have two names (in medieval Europe, they typically had only one) and then some form of identity numbers, as social security numbers in the United States. These innovations made it possible to differentiate one person from another and hence to levy taxes and conscript soldiers from local populations.

At the security gate, state thinking similarly needs a standardized person. The pressure is to break down each human, her or his behaviors, and accompanying artifacts, and to convert each into an actionable item.[4] In practice, it is a shifting system of demarcation—for example, does ethnicity count (and which ethnicity?) and just what items can be placed in a carryon (nail clippers, yes or no? baby formula, how many fluid ounces?). Passengers and employees need to keep up.

The great difficulty, of course, is human variation in physical form as well as in biographical contingencies, as we saw with subway turnstiles that fallaciously assume a standard person. While many behaviors and modes of life are recurrent and patterned, idiosyncratic things happen in biographies as lived. There can be peculiar objects, perhaps a jokey gift for a friend or a school child's science project—or an art construction with wires and tubes sticking out. Unlikely and implausible events occur among people chasing after romance or among those who just live in ways to which the inspectors are not accustomed. In a 2010 incident, Birmingham, Alabama, airport authorities became suspicious of a Yemeni man who checked a suitcase with a cell phone taped to a bottle of Pepto-Bismol and other cell phones and watches also taped together on his route to Amsterdam. American officials caused him to be detained "on the basis of suspicions of preparations for terrorist attacks."[5] While his were not the type of objects Americans might bring from abroad, a Yemeni cousin in Detroit explained, "This is our culture"—to carry things (often of a practical nature) back to Yemen as gifts for others. A big enough number of people, as a matter of simple probability, makes *anything* likely.[6]

RULES OF THE MACHINE

Confrontation begins with the airport roadway approach and warnings not to remain stationary in front of terminals, a restriction that can create special trouble, for example, when someone is waiting in a car with a suitcase to give to a departing friend who inadvertantly left it at home and now must come out of the airport to get it. On to check-in. Airline personnel examine identification papers and ask a few security questions. These must be answered correctly. Here are the usual questions, but with some hypothetical answers that must *not* be given—all taken from a single anonymous blog:[7]

> Has anyone asked you to carry anything aboard this aircraft? (Yes, my mother and my girlfriend.)
> Has anyone asked you to pack something for them? (I packed a shirt for my wife, because she ran out of room in her suitcase.)
> Did you pack the bags yourself? (No, Alfred the butler did, but I don't think he's a threat.)

Answering correctly does not mean you provide factual truth. It means you respond so as to get on the plane and allow airline employees to move forward with their job. There are, no doubt, individuals who may truly fear that speaking an untruth, in this day and age, might result in detainment. So they may fail at common sense and hold up the line by answering literally. Still others, perhaps with weak English skills, may also not "get" the right nuance and also provide right, er, wrong, answers. For everyone, it is a negotiation to take seriously so as to tell the right lies. Adding into the tension is the involvement of the computer, whether through a human being intermediary or at a check-in "express" machine. If the system is down, if one's name is on "the list," or if there is just some glitch, trouble can happen.[8]

On to the security gates and, in the United States, the Transportation Security Administration (TSA) employees who staff them. One must again show ID, this time simultaneous with display of boarding pass. Many times I see people put their documents in their mouths (that others will handle) because they can't figure out what else to do.

I watched a teenager toss an empty water bottle over to a bin, miss it, and then run with her laptop over to the area where it landed, pick it up, and place it properly in the can. The TSA agent yells out to let it go, but to no avail. More noise and confusion. One can see such small dramas unfold at practically every security gate. As passengers struggle, fiddle, and fumble, officials remind them what is the right stuff to take off one's body, where to put it, and to move along. People repeat the instructions to one another and do some debating about what they have heard and what it means (can both laptops go in the same bin for the TSA scanner?). Is the requirement to stand still and await a signal to move forward or does one inch onward, maybe with one's child or spouse? Now given the variety of scanning devices that TSA has established at some gate areas, one must also figure out which portal to approach and how to place arms and feet within its particular configuration. At the most "advanced" machines, the "Rapiscan" in the version I have come across (see discussion in the section "Scan Escalation: Hands on Bodies"), you hold your wallet over your head as a scanning bar moves over your body, and then as you come out, you hand your wallet to a TSA guard, who takes it from your fingers and runs a wand over it. At least this is what happened to me on my encounter with the appliance; I was truly bewildered when told to hold my wallet over my head. What kind of stick-up is *this*? I refrained from asking.

Ergonomic difficulties intersect with ambiguity to intensify dilemmas and concern. Each individual hoists up baggage, pushes it along, and pulls it down at the end. Shoes are an issue. Even the able-bodied can have trouble if there are laces, high-tops, or, as with workmen and backpackers, heavy boots. Our stuff disappears with access only to TSA workers while we await the uncertain moment of reappearance and return. It might be thought of as a "total institution" moment. Erving Goffman famously distinguished total institutions, like prisons, the army, and mental asylums, from other settings. In total institutions, even people's micro moves are under the administrative control. But in fact we all move through settings that vary in their *degree of totalness*, and for many of us, airport security is the most "total" of environments we know in our adult lives.[9] A certain arbitrariness occurs: belts off, yes or no, shoes in a bin or on the conveyor (or in Europe they remain on feet), jackets off or not, sweaters okay unless they are like jackets, which is just when?

Taking off shoes makes bodies touch foreign surfaces in unaccustomed ways, bringing to mind the ass on the restroom toilet seat. But here the danger is clear and present. Bare feet on airport floors spread fungus more frequently than toilet seat residue spreads disease. At the main Moscow airport every traveler is given thin plastic slippers that they wear through security. But these do not solve the problem of random objects like paper clips, pens, pencils, wire bits, and tacks that fall to the floor where they can puncture the skin. My friend James Jasper—a fellow New York academic—was pierced by a flag lapel pin dropped by a patriot who had gone before.

Moving through security resembles a prison routine not only in the submissiveness required but also in the standardization of the equipment as well as the sharp limits placed on what can be done with it. The trays for overcoats and laptops must be used only for the purpose of temporarily holding such goods. One is not, for example, to put one's baby in one of them to gain a few moments of composure, or to give a fun ride to a toddler while waiting to go through. One is not to turn a tray upside down to give a boost from the floor. Nor can you take one with you after security to gather lunch items at the food court.

Despite constituting a market in the billions of dollars, the artifacts at the gate are essentially off-the-shelf products that are now pressed into ad hoc airport service. Hence the bins are adapted commercial restaurant gear used for busing dishes. In the early years, this is exactly what they were, some of them stamped "Rubbermaid®" on the underside. Bowls for coins and keys derive from picnic wear or dog food bowls. Until quite recently, at least at smaller airports, the tables and platforms where you place your suitcases were the fold-up variety like those used in school recreation halls. At some airports, the tables are kitchen gear from the restaurant industry. At a time when the design of a routine can opener receives deft attention from focus groups, aesthetic connoisseurs, and ergonomic experts, artifacts at airport security remain dumb to the issues of design competence. The mechanistic and control-oriented setup inhibits effective pleasantness; it represents a militant absence of design forethought.

True, some of this varies by national and even local setting; inspections seem more intense and authoritarian in the United States than in most other places. Some airports, as represented on blogs and airport ratings systems, generate consistent complaints of rudeness (Frankfurt), others of friendliness and efficiency (Stockholm), both in regard to security and other matters. At the airport in Sydney, Australia, apparently it is still permissible for family and friends to meet and greet at arrival gates and to see others off (although all must go through security). In my experience, workers at New York airports aggressively yell out commands in a way not found in more genteel parts of the world, like Vancouver and Santa Barbara airports, which have been frequent spots on my own travel itinerary.

The rituals become familiar at least until a new edict comes down the chain of command. Everyone knows box-cutters will generate a full stop. There are also random selections of individuals for closer inspection; I've heard guards shout out the words "I've got a random" to a colleague. For the passenger, the gate performance aims to avoid being singled out, for whatever reason—not unlike the subway worker who just wants to get home. Most know the airport drill of what to put where. These are *strange* things to be doing and thinking about however much we have become accustomed to them.

Passengers are alert. They keep pace with the needs of those behind and closely observe the progress of those in front. Based on his close observation of people's behavior at airport security, Ole Pütz documents their vigilance as they follow procedures.[10] When a guard instructs an approaching passenger to remove his belt (because of visible metal in it), those behind this passenger also remove their belts even when there is no need to do so (because they contain no metal). Similarly, a woman removed her eyeglasses when she saw the guard ask the person in front of her to remove his sunglasses ("shades" must be off, but spectacles can stay on). The guard had to tell her to keep her glasses on, forestalling a sequence of eyeglass removals as chains of conforming passengers mimic those in front of them. At security, a coal-face of the state, people relax their need to know and to have cogent theories of the world; they strive instead to conform.

Not being at the ready holds up the progress of other passengers as well as perturbing the guards. Our regard for their needs merges with organizational goals to keep us on task. We assent to having our things disappear out of reach and view and with some risk of being commingled with the stuff of others. For myself, and I am likely not alone, the big worry is my laptop. Besides the dark thoughts of its being mixed up with another passenger's, it could somehow be damaged in the flurry of the process, including being dropped by me on retrieval. My colleague Douglas Guthrie told me he watched, with sinking heart, as a security agent—thinking the tray containing his laptop was empty—slung the tray toward an open stack, causing the laptop to sail through the air before landing on the floor. It was okay.

There is a lot of self-consciousness regarding what one indeed has in one's possession that might be, by some reckoning, illicit: Recreational drugs or the trace of some old pot? Pornography? A dildo? Materials that are politically incorrect—or maybe racist or fascist, or religiously blasphemous? A prosthetic device? An "Islamist" tract? Many have something to hide, even when not committing an act of terror. During all this quasi-fracas, one hopes to look "normal," especially during pat downs—eyes trained to the middle-distance and not on The Man.[11] As at the urinals, it is important not to look at certain things or appear to be trying not to look at certain things. Showing anxiety *is* on official lists of suspicious behavior.

An imperfection like forgetting about some metal content may lead the guards, post-portal, to run an instrument over the body or take one aside for a special frisk. They may not easily find the cause of the alarm going off, which then generates a close pat down. Whether randomly or in compliance with some unspoken criterion, agents can and do open, rearrange, and take things out of one's carry-ons. In one instance, a colleague watched an agent lift his toothbrush out of his personal effects kit, holding it by the brush end. The inspector was wearing plastic gloves, but these gloves had touched many other things. My colleague now had the quandary of how to buy a replacement toothbrush at his hotel when arriving late at night—or did it not really matter, those strange fingers on an implement to go into his mouth?

Amidst all this worrisome assemblage, we have a distinct lack of helpfulness. In the effort to pare down procedures and equipment to no-nonsense security, officials disable other elements of human capacity and interaction that might be useful. Passengers do help each other, but help does not come from those in charge. Even when staff is not rushed, passengers are on their own. Guards treat each traveler as a potential offender, a carrier of a shampoo bottle that, if beyond the three-ounce limit, may be lethal. In other occupational realms, people doing a given job are multifunctional. While serving food, cleaning teeth, or selling stock, they offer up words of encouragement or even helpful hints on unrelated issues like good gyms, nice recipes, the best place to buy gas. People in such trades may even touch a patron perhaps with an encouraging pat on the shoulder or offer up something helpful to assuage a cranky child. A restaurant worker or clothes sales person may help with unwieldy bags, equipment, and packages a patron is trying to manage. The airport security regime, however, blunts this impulse to facilitate and share, an impulse that I think TSA workers themselves also possess but not in a way that can easily come through.

People also fool around quite a lot in real life, even with strangers. At security, one must be cautious with humor. Making a gun, knife, or bomb joke, however much on the mind, is a special no-no. In a 2009 incident, a thirty-year-old-on the way to his wedding on a United flight from St. Louis to Washington, D.C., was asked by the flight attendant if he needed anything. He said, "No, I'm fine. I've got my shoe bomb—I'm good." He was removed from the plane and booked on felony charges. His fiancée explained to media, "He is smart, but he still does stupid things."[12] In another incident, authorities arrested an Air France pilot who joked at JFK that he had a bomb in his shoes—with a resulting twelve-hour delay of the New York-Paris flight. A transportation security administration spokesman told *The New York Times*, "We have zero tolerance for those kinds of comments."[13] But there is always intrinsic ambiguity of what does or does not signal offensive intent.

Take the case of a twenty-seven-year-old man convicted in the United Kingdom after tweeting a friend that he would blow the airport "sky-high" unless it reopened after a snowstorm. He had been on his way to link up with a woman he had met online and was frustrated by his flight's cancellation while waiting in the gate area. Seeing the post a few days later, the airport manager reported it to police, who picked up the offending person at his workplace, questioned him for eight hours, and took his computers and phones. The court convicted him of causing a "menace" under the British Communications Act, fining him a thousand pounds. As the convicted criminal himself explained, "People who meet and work with me make all these comments all the time—'I'm going to kill you if you don't get me a coffee in a minute.'" He also added, "To me, it is clear that it was hyperbole."[14] But now because of his criminal record, his employer fired him. A second employer found out about the record, which he had failed to reveal in his job application, and also fired him. In the phrase of sociologist Aaron Cicourel, it is a case of "death by dossier."[15] It is a latent effect of any security system that expands the number of potential offenses that then, thanks to modern technology, follow the individual even into realms where security has no relevance.

A dumb and fear-based system feeds individuals into an authority apparatus and makes them official deviants. Normal ways of speaking *always* require use of context to be properly understood. Even the word "kill," maybe especially that word, needs proper interpretation. A graduate-student friend of the twenty-seven-year-old was quoted at the time as expressing alarm: "It could be anyone of us. Every single person I know has said or done something on the Internet that could be classified as criminal if someone took it like that." The whole affair was to become a minor cause célèbre among tweeters, who are especially aware of how expressivity works among those sending out short blurts. They followed up with further tweets of menace: "I am going to blow up the entire universe with my giant blob." "I think I'll blow up Parliament . . . Oh, wait, that was a JOKE."[16] Besides being natural among all cultures, joking is at least potentially a source of information if it is allowed to be. It can reveal, in a subtle way, intentions otherwise being masked and also, just as important, meanings that are utterly benign.

Rules against fun have also come to the Department of Motor Vehicles here in the United States. The DMV was never a place for much mirth, but now some states have explicit rules against smiling, at least when posing for pictures. By 2009 four U.S. states ruled that photos used for drivers' license applications could not show smiles. Apparently computer recognition software needs similar expressions across photos in order to recognize identities, and, unlike what we like to see in family photo albums, the smile was not chosen for the standard. Effective citizen identification requires a standard *looking* citizen—just as restroom toilets and other automated equipment need people who perform consistently (automatic flushers are thrown off by kids' bodies or someone repeatedly rising out of the sit position). At the DMV facial mirth threatens order. For security personnel, accepting a display of good humor risks accepting passenger moves that are outside the serious business of proceeding in the prescribed order from point A to point B. Standard security operating procedure assumes single and unvarying focus for all, a meta-message of authority not to be trifled with.

SCAN ESCALATION: HANDS ON BODIES

The Rapiscan machine, developed by TSA contractors and being deployed nationwide, enables every passenger's body to be seen on screen as it moves through the security portal. These images reveal all exterior elements of the body, including outlines of breasts and penises (figure 11).[17] The screener watching the body image is in a separate space without the possibility, we are told, of seeing the actual person moving through the machine. Authorities say they do not retain the images and passengers making the request can substitute a full-body pat down, in private if they wish. But once having entered the security area, it is against the law not to go through with at least one of the options. A person is not free (as was the case with those subject to subway inspections) to leave the airport. That would allow would-be terrorists to get away.

Some individuals do not welcome these "virtual strip searches" regardless of officials' assurance that they and their employees have no

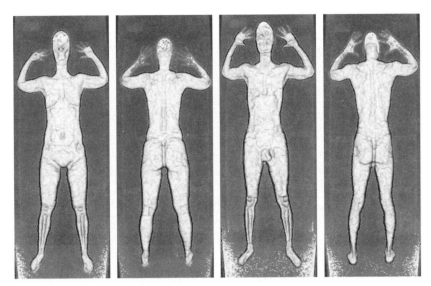

Figure 11. Body images as seen in full-body scan. Images courtesy of the Transportation Security Administration.

intrinsic interest in the sights on view. I do not know what Transportation Security Officers (TSOs) or their supervisors actually inspect and keep on record. I am not privy to any informal banter about passengers' biological features. No one knows how screeners in any security system, for obvious reasons of their inaccessibility to researchers, observe and share information among one another. But we have one good study, from Clive Norris and Gary Armstrong, who were able to spend almost six hundred hours observing men stationed in surveillance rooms watching, in real time, the goings-on at three separate commercial sites in the United Kingdom.[18] One of the things we learn from the Norris-Armstrong study is that out of boredom, if nothing else, surveillance workers focus on things that titillate, particularly on women they find attractive or situations involving erotic events. They call one another in and replay these special excitements.

Concern among worried passengers that such things go on is thus not misplaced; we are confronted, as we were with the toilet stall, by the contrary goals of providing human privacy while also achieving aggregate control. There needs to be a way for authorities to see things that the individuals involved may regard as private. Once again we head for an awkward solution — in this case of having a designated seeing-eye person, kind of like the proverbial doctor who sees but benignly doesn't really notice.

On privacy grounds, a San Diego man named John Tyner resisted both the machine and the pat down. He recorded some of his interactions with two TSA inspectors at the San Diego airport by leaving on his cell phone audio-video feature as he went through the ritual. Here is a transcript, based on the CBS broadcast of the footage:[19]

> MALE TSA WORKER: Also we're gonna to be doing a groin check. That means I am going to place my hand on your hip, my other hand on your inner thigh, slowly go up and slide down.
>
> TYNER: OK. (perfunctory)
>
> MALE TSA WORKER: And if you would like a private screening we can make that available for you also.
>
> TYNER: But if you touch my junk I'm going to have you arrested. I don't understand how a sexual assault can be made a condition of my flying.
>
> FEMALE TSA WORKER: This is not considered a sexual assault.
>
> TYNER: It would be if you weren't the government.

The TSA disallowed him from boarding his flight; he left the premises and faced possible criminal charges for failure to go through the system (I could find no evidence he was prosecuted).

Others, of course, besides this one individual, resist what they consider to be an excessive government intrusion. Conservative political figures as well as liberal commentators complain or at least ridicule the goings-on. Public surveys on the topic, however, are inconsistent. A 2010 CBS poll found 81 percent expressing approval of the stronger set of measures.[20] An ABC/Washington Post poll had 64 percent in favor. But the same poll had half saying that "enhanced" pat downs, in particular, go too far.[21] Opposition runs higher among more regular flyers.[22]

Some individuals resist on civil liberties grounds. Others fear the cumulative effect of small amounts of radiation from metal detectors or x-ray equipment, a concern echoed by some scientific experts.[23] And still others think that these full body searches are ineffective in any event. If chemical contraband (or even hardware like razor blades) is worn flat and close to the sides of the body they will not, according to academic researchers writing in the *Journal of Transportation Security*, be detected by the new machinery.[24] Placing materials like explosive plastics in body cavities puts them beyond physical as well as electronic scanning detection. It may also prove possible, especially with future miniaturization, to implant an explosive within the large intestine (one report in Saudi Arabia of a bombing set up in this way has apparently been debunked).[25]

Whatever the technical failings and human complications, I have seen and overheard numbers of people at the security gate avidly proclaim their acceptance. They proudly and enthusiastically volunteer for each successive indignity, eager to do "my part." It almost seems that the more humiliation they are put through the better; they "understand" how "important" security really is. They see like their state.

DISTRIBUTION EFFECTS

As per pattern of differential impacts depending on social and economic circumstance, some types of people have more airport security problems than others as authority enters life.

Disability

Keeping in mind the capacious nature of this category (see chapter 2)—which includes the very young, the aged, the sick, the injured, the crippled, and those caring for them—people with disabilities face special difficulties at the gates. Long lines impose costs, although some may claim and qualify for the right to jump the queue. People with metal in their bodies typically must face a pat down, which needs to be accomplished either with special finesse to avoid offending a person sometimes already in a vulnerable state. In one intense instance, a guard oblivious to a passenger's warning caused a urostomy bag to overflow with urine on that traveler's body and clothing.[26]

Gender

Again as with public restrooms, which are historically biased against women in public space, security favors men. Moving a baby, with or without stroller, is a whole big deal, and toddlers must be separated from their parent, each of whom has to go through the apparatus separately. Indeed, toddlers are not acknowledged *anywhere* in a U.S. airport, quite in contrast, I am reminded, of my modest neighborhood bank in Sweden, which had a gigantic Lego installation for children to manipulate while adults attended to business. Back to the feet: women's nylons are more fragile than socks, if the female passenger is wearing foot coverings at all. Women have more stuff and more stuff that matters to them—besides cosmetics, there can be sanitary napkins, birth-control materials, lotions and potions, diapers, and toys for dealing with the young. There is jewelry, some of which may have high financial or sentimental value. Women are more sensitive than men, the surveys reveal, to a stranger going through their stuff. Purses are special "islands of privacy" in Nippert-Eng's phrase, and are to be guarded against invasion.[27] And, I am told by at least one woman friend, loose-fitting dresses attract hand searches. As with the floor-to-ceiling stall, they make it harder to know what is fully going on by just looking.

Women have more to lose in being subject to orders of what to take off and where to put it. Their bras may have wire for uplift. In one extreme case, a woman with a nipple ring was harassed and made to remove it with pliers when guards would not accept a visual inspection.[28] Some religious sects have strict notions of female modesty, including which body parts need to be kept covered. Women have lodged numerous complaints of sexual harassment and groping by guards.[29] Despite the obvious evidence that women are far less likely to be involved in terrorist or any violent activity than men (whether Christian or Muslim) they do not seem to be getting a gender break. A woman at security must raise her arms above her head, as must a man, just as women must deal with closed restrooms even though it is the men whose sexual practice has been the cause of the concern (see chapter 2). "The law, in its majestic equality," to adapt the aphorism of Anatole France, pertains to women and men alike without favor.[30] In fact, women who refuse to go through x-ray portals may face extra delays, particularly at smaller airports, where there are fewer female guards around to do pat downs.

And, again as at the restrooms, airport security presumes heterosexuality among both guards and passengers. On the assumption that it neuters erotic exploitation, a member of the (nominally) "same" sex is supposed to do the pat down. This can be wrong in regard to either the guard or the passenger's sensibilities. It may indeed offend the homosexual or homophobic passenger, male or female, who is subject to a patting down by a member of the same sex.

Class and Hierarchy

At larger airports, those flying business or first class (or otherwise with special elite privilege) go through their own separate security line. It is shorter. Security thus enhances class distinction rather than mitigating it as an opportunity for equally shared sacrifice. If they qualify for membership in an airline lounge (for example, Red Carpet Club at United, Maharaja at Air India, Dynasty at China Air), passengers can leave unattended luggage around and are spared announcements of security warnings. On the plane, when sitting in business or first class, passengers are less likely to be hassled by attendants about items left on the floor (and not under the seat in front of them) during take off and landing.

People who own or hire private aircraft do not have to pass through any type of security to get on their plane, possible bomber though it may be. The TSA does not even station personnel at many terminals serving private craft—"general aviation," as it is called. This means that even those who charter a 757 or 777, capable indeed of mayhem if commandeered in the sky, are free to come and go at will. The TSA administrator, John Pistole, when asked about the absence of screening, indicated that there is less danger from this sector of the flying public than those who use the airlines. And, he added in an interview with the *Atlantic Monthly*'s Jeffrey Goldberg, "Clearly the general-aviation community has a lot of equities and interest in our rules"[31]—an apparent reference to why private aircraft customers are not monitored in the same way as is the general flying public. During the U.S. Civil War, it was perfectly legal to pay a stand-in to serve in one's place in the army, something done by Grover Cleveland, among other prominent Americans. People like him continue to avoid sharing the pains of citizenship by buying their way out.

At times, outside threat is manipulated to help sustain control over civilians who get too uppity. Airlines have long had trouble with coach passengers using business-class toilets. For some years they instructed over the intercom that all passengers (rich and poor alike) must use the bathrooms in their designated class cabin. After 9/11, they added the words, "as a matter of security." But people do, as indicated in the prior chapter on toilets, sometimes have pressing needs that conflict with class (or security) prerogatives. In one case, a resulting transgression led to a passenger's two-day jailing. On a 2009 Delta flight (Honduras to Atlanta), a man in coach, according to his account, found a serving cart blocking an urgent trip to the loo. So he went into business class (disclosure: I have done this myself, albeit on rare occasion). The flight attendant put out her arm to block his way and he pushed past. He says he grabbed her arm to hold his balance; she says it was a violent act. Charged with a felony, he spent two days in jail before a U.S. District Court judge could hear his case.[32] A trip to the toilet became, literally, a federal case. Of course, if this man had been traveling in business class in the first place he would have not got himself into trouble, highlighting the fact that membership in a disfavored group increases vulnerability to authorities.

One way to see how privilege works at security is to look at what happens when procedures such as pre-board screening portend penalizing those who are supposed to get better treatment. Frequent business travelers, for example, can have similar profiles to would-be terrorists and thus be a basis for suspicion and delay. Flying with a last-minute reservation, using a one-way ticket, or not checking luggage can signal a terrorist or just a rich person who hops from one office or home to another where they keep wardrobes and personal effects. They don't need luggage and may not be making round-trips.

Addressing such dilemmas is leading to new programs that enroll individuals as "trusted traveler," "secure flight," or "registered traveler," akin to the EZ-pass used on the highways (some of these programs are now in early deployment at some U.S. airports). Those covered go through separate lines and are spared at least parts of the usual rigmarole. They pay a fee, with $100 per annum being mentioned as the probable rate.[33] A RAND study geared toward creating a version of the system advanced a checklist for eligibility, providing further clues of what profiling looks like as a systematic, as opposed to spontaneous on-the-spot, enactment.[34] Here are the criteria for being low-risk:

Passing a "national agency check"
Absence of criminal record (as indicated by fingerprint check)
A verified, stable employment history
A record of demonstrating firm community roots
A record of financial security with no unexplained deviations from typical
  patterns
A travel history consistent with occupational history
An employer's statement of confidence

Beyond the imposition of the fee, a list like this de-privileges those lower in the social and occupational scale. They are more likely to have criminal records, unstable employment histories, and no evidence of "community roots" as might be shown by organization memberships and leadership roles. It is also a list that disfavors those who, as a matter of lifestyle preference, are less consistent in their patterns and choices—bohemians, hippies, and free spirits. And being put in the database as *noneligible* is itself stigmatizing, probably in a quasi-permanent way. The victims would tend to be persons who lack the resources, or the stomach, to battle their classification. If all the bona fide "good people" get on the OK list, being left off will be penalizing, even for those who merely failed to apply. And, to reiterate, private-aircraft flyers need to pass no criteria, except that of wealth, to escape the apparatus altogether.

In terms of costs and benefits for the security workforce, overwhelmingly a working-class population, the security gates do provide them with jobs. But they are the ones who have to put up with the disgruntled people who may have contempt for those who inspect them. Many of the workers do not in fact enjoy intruding on others' bodies and find it a mutual humiliation. And they may not enjoy putting others under stress. In one event witnessed by a close friend, an elderly woman, when told to raise her arms above her head in the Rapiscan, began sobbing that she was "really innocent." Two TSA workers immediately offered gentle reassurance and helped her become calm; they too, according to my trusted witness, seemed disturbed.

At the aggregate level, TSA (and Department of Homeland Security [DHS] more generally) uses security concerns as a way to inhibit unionization; union-busting was part of the plot in creating the DHS in the first place. Federal workers once protected by unions lost the privilege when their units were merged into DHS. Under the Obama administration, the ban on organizing was lifted, but workers are prohibited from bargaining over wages, benefits, screening procedures, or discipline. In the words of a TSA spokeswoman, "We will not negotiate on security." The massive exclusions do not satisfy critics from the right, with the president of the Heritage Foundation complaining that the TSA's "first mission has to be to protect Americans, to protect the homeland and the people . . . letting them unionize removes TSA employees' focus in that area—into 'Am I going to get short-changed on my coffee break'. . . . That's all a distraction from what they should be focusing on."[35]

Ethnicity and Race

The big gorilla in security discrimination is the "Arab," regardless of what authorities might say. We know that in routine life, where the imperative is less strong, people use physical attributes to mark humans from one another. In racial terms, it is a hazard to drive while being black, and the official data on "stop and frisk" make overwhelmingly clear the presence of police focus on young black men.[36] Surely it is reasonable to accept testimony from those of Middle East "look" and surname that they experience special troubles as Arabs trying to fly. In what I take to be a symptom of a much larger and omnipresent problem, a young man was allowed to board a Jet Blue flight only if he covered over his tee-shirt that displayed the words "We Will Not Be Silent" in English and Arabic.[37] Problems arise no matter what the costume or how ambiguous the message. He did cover up, was allowed to board, and gained a settlement of $240,000 from the airline in subsequent litigation.

It's quite likely that profiling, whether based on ethnicity or some set of other attributes, makes things less safe—an argument made by the estimable and ever vigilant security expert Bruce Schneier.[38] If the profile is made into an official list, bad guys can use it to build their scheme. If flying first class is on the list, the bomber can go coach. If traveling with a small dog spares the passenger a full-body scan, the terrorist can get a Chihuahua as a security companion. If a bigger dog can hold a bomb, wire up Rover and put the dog through check-in. Profiles bias scrutiny toward those lacking the wit to fit in, not the sophisticated plotter. It can perhaps capture the blundering amateur—which has been the preponderant type apprehended thus far, but always nabbed without the help of profile. Moreover, abandoning profiles, besides not undermining real security, has the advantage of democratic decency.

Less egregious than profiling, some routines also create particular penalties for specific ethnic groups, however unintended. Japanese people abhor direct physical contact between a part of their bodies and a surface that receives outdoor foot traffic—they do not, for example, sit on steps. Shoe removal forces those from tropical zones of the world to remove sandals and flip-flops and expose bare feet in a way that stocking-footed people are spared. The yelling and confusion may especially trouble people who are less accustomed to it in their public lives. So there may be special bother for those from the more genteel cultures of Polynesia and Scandinavia—and pardon my ignorance—wherever else people enjoy subtle silence and demure sociality. Those who do not speak English misunderstand commands and thus take on additional risks of nervous fumbling and losses of objects and documents.

IMPOTENCE

One reason for the great concentration of security at airports in the first place is not that that it is effective, but that it can, quite simply, be arranged.[39] Against the inherent ambiguity of securitization, having controls at entry gates presents itself as something doable. Planes are nice discrete people holders that have narrow points of ingress; passengers can be bunched up for clearance at specific choke points. Logistical possibilities of this sort influence just where security operates *within* the airport, even when it in fact creates crowds that otherwise would not exist. The extra questions at check-in slow down movement and cause people to cluster up. The security gate furthers the gathering up, making for dense crowds — still not yet scrutinized for weaponry — often in a snaking queue. This is a security-generated target often consisting of a larger number of people than would be on any airplane.

It is a common observation in the security business that in hardening a particular facility against perpetrators, you may deflect attack to a more opportune location. For a private individual or firm, it may make sense to take advantage of this fact by shifting threats to another setting — a competing bank or restaurant. With public facilities, such deflection makes no sense — it doesn't matter much to people and their loved ones if they die before or after screening. In my discussions with former high officials at TSA, they express frustration with this problem, which has evaded solution.

As far as I know, the vast airport apparatus has not stopped a single incident of mayhem; foiling of plots comes from other forces, such as advance intelligence or actions on board. Each restriction is a remedy for a technique used in a prior attack. As the list of contraband items grows, add-ons intensify complexity, and increase the time it takes to process an individual through. The growing pressure to notice details of more items and behaviors, according to one report of the RAND Corporation, taxes the capacity of TSA inspectors to spot even obvious items of threat.[40]

Further, boredom among the guards can breed an "atrophy of vigilance," in the phrase of sociologist William Freudenburg.[41] Laboratory researchers refer to the phenomenon as "instrument decay," in the same way that equipment wears out, becoming less effective over time (and thus affecting experimental results). Some analogous shift can happen with the equipment that is human, and indeed, as one indicator, labor turnover has continued at a high rate even after federalization of the security system.[42]

The classic studies of assembly lines show how people manipulate the pace of work by either ganging up tasks—running ahead or "catching up" with items moving past them.[43] Josiah Heyman has observed how border patrol workers sometimes make a game of catching people and their illicit materials by competing with one another— who can catch more bad guys today? In part, these games are in response to job tedium, while also fitting in with larger organizational goals, as they interpret them.[44] Our subway workers also developed game-like strategies, including ways to move boisterous kids out of their stations to keep lines moving ("popping" the doors on them). Airport screeners we learn, from a Reason Foundation strategy paper, "select additional passengers for manual inspection, to maintain a desired workload level."[45] They too adjust official rules to deal with work context.

In some cases, airport guards just do not do their job at all. A traveler through Abu Dhabi (some time ago) reports security guards deserting their station to go for a smoke, with passengers just walking through. At Accra airport, and likely other parts of the world, guards look for a little money to facilitate passage. Their attention is not on the contents of the scanning machines. At Newark Airport in 2010, a TSA officer guarding the concourse exit against intruders left his post only briefly, but that was long enough for an intruder to enter the departures area without clearance—resulting in a six-hour shut-down of the terminal.[46] Anecdotes of such incidents can be found on various websites that carry passenger comments about airports and also on the Bruce Schneier security blog.[47]

So it happens that, even in efficient societies like the United States, there are not infrequent failures to detect contraband. A particular problem is detecting bomb parts; because bombs disassemble into individual elements, each of which will appear innocent to a screener. But screeners also miss grossly inappropriate artifacts. A report leaked to the press on TSA's own undercover operations, again at Newark Airport (conducted in October 2006), found that screeners failed twenty of twenty-two security tests, missing numerous guns and simulated bombs (these tests are not about liquids or scissors). There had been previous and repeated failures of 100 percent at some U.S. airports, according to an ABC News report.[48] Because it is against TSA policy to reveal the results of covert operations, it is not easy to find accounts of the agency's own internal undercover research and the degree to which it tests for more subtle elements passing through the gates (like parts of weapons, as opposed to finished artifacts). Occasionally a passenger tells after the fact of being able to carry through illicit material, including a gun in the case of one businessman who had inadvertently left the weapon in his hand baggage.[49]

The two most dramatic efforts to blow up U.S. aircraft post-9/11 both involved failures to detect. In the first, the now notorious "shoe bomber," Richard C. Reid, placed a plastic explosive in his hollowed out soles with enough C4 PETN to blow a hole through the fuselage of the plane he was on. On his first attempt to depart Paris for a flight to Miami on December 21, 2001, authorities would not allow him to board because of his appearance and other suspicious indicators, like having no checked luggage. But after further interviews by French National Police, he was rebooked for the following day's Paris-Miami flight. This time he got on the plane, but when aloft he failed to ignite his shoes despite numerous attempts. Apparently, it has been reasoned, moisture had penetrated his shoes, either from body sweat or being out in the rain during the day before his postponed departure. Reid, British born to an English white woman and a Jamaican immigrant, had converted to Islam as an adult. He had spent time at an Afghanistan training site and had extensive history with al-Qaeda operatives during his two years living in Pakistan. Not only had the French authorities (and U.S. airline operatives) missed these indicators, so had the vaunted Israeli security apparatus; Reid had flown to Israel in July of 2001 and had passed through the El Al screenings as well. At his eventual U.S. trial, he admitted (proclaimed, really) membership in al-Qaeda.[50] The result for Reid was lifetime imprisonment. For the rest of us, it meant taking off our shoes at airports.

Objecting to the "shoes off" policy, a blogger asked what he took to be the preposterous question: "If Richard Reid had stuffed C4 into the crotch of his baggy pants would we all be dropping our drawers every time we tried to board a plane today?"[51] He was to get his answer some years later after the "Underwear Bomber," Umar Farouk Abdulmutallab, tried to set off an incendiary on a Northwest flight from Amsterdam to Detroit, Christmas 2009. He had strapped the same plastic compound (PETN) into his underwear, in a six-inch-long soft container. The PETN incendiary does not show up in the scanning machines—the PETN in Richard Reid's shoes would have also gone right through(!). But the fact that underwear could carry such non-detectable contraband generated a search for response. Rather than demanding total nudity of passengers, as sarcastically suggested by another blogger, authorities turned to the presumably more acceptable whole-body-imaging scan, as performed by the Rapiscan appliance. In my own experience, security gates do not have enough such scanners for everyone, and so, on whatever basis, TSA guards point some to the full-body machine while most others move through the usual channels.

For my own various reasons, including the desire for data, I have five times now refused to go through the full-body scanner. In the most recent instance, the TSA worker just excused me and let me go through the normal scanner (excused completely, like those who decline a search in the subways by going to a different station entry). The other times I was not excused, but the guards were courteous and carefully instructive in language identical to or very closely resembling the greeting given to Tyner (the San Diego refusenik quoted earlier). Unlike Tyner, I did allow the full-body searches. They were below par in thoroughness. The screeners never touched my genitals or anus. Maybe human civility, at least at times, trumps devotion to security. Or perhaps a type of profiling was in play, one that allowed me (advanced age? white skin? academic demeanor? Premier member status?) to receive gentler treatment. The screeners do not, as consistent with earlier evidence of their own struggle with decency, like having to do the "enhanced pat down" (as it is called). This appears to be the case according to TSOs who responded to a blog's ("Flying with Fish") solicitation on the experience. Here is one screener's report:

> It is not comfortable to come to work knowing full well that my hands will be feeling another man's private parts, their butt, their inner thigh. Even worse is having to try and feel inside the flab rolls of obese passengers and we seem to get a lot of obese passengers![52]

Other reports align with this one indicating that workers resist being invasive, however much this lessens capacity to detect chemicals, powders, or poisons. On the other hand, several friends—one man and one woman—told me their (gender-appropriate) inspector went all the way, down, around, and across). I obviously have too small a number of cases to draw aggregate conclusions.

Clever people can play with the boundaries of what is or is not contraband. They can fashion parts of luggage (sharp metal used in frames, pull handles) into weaponry; they can also take apart pieces of the plane itself, particularly those accessed in the privacy of the toilet on board. One lesson can be drawn from prisons: inmates show vast talent to convert ordinary objects into weapons. They can turn a toothbrush, comb, or part of exercise equipment into a shiv. They use pieces of fencing, wall fragments, or exposed wiring to make into weapons, typically to be used against one another rather than the guards. And this is in an environment that is under total control—where there are virtually no civil liberties and where inmates are under constant surveillance. In the administration of Gaza, prisonlike in its ways, Israel banned concrete, steel, and other building materials from entering in (even though these were needed to build schools, houses, and infrastructure) because they could also be incorporated into weapons and bunkers. And so they could.

In the complex and also more open site of the airport, many types of disruptive possibilities arise. In a complexly ingenious scheme, a Dutch investigative journalist used the duty-free shop to breach security. A lot of duty-free goods are liquid: liquor and perfume. And so journalist Alberto Stegeman bought a bottle of clear rum at a pre-security Schiphol Airport Duty Free—the same airport the so-called Underwear Bomber had only months earlier boarded his flight for the United States with explosives. After making his purchase, Stegemen then went to the men's room, dumped out the rum, and refilled the bottle with tap water (simulating an explosive liquid). He then went back to the shop and returned the bottle to the shelf he had taken it from, and re-bought the same bottle. The sales clerk put it in a sealed duty-free bag for him to take on the flight, which he did.[53] Because this reporter had achieved notoriety for prior successful security breaches (and had published reports of same) he was subjected to extra checks by extra guards. Even so, he got his liquids through. The point is not that this particular exercise is going to be common, or even feasible; it is to indicate the potential for finding intricate ways to get around the system.

The capacity of outsiders to outwit a target has been demonstrated in another way by two MIT students using computer-based mathematical simulations. Under their scenario, bad guys could just keep sending proxies on flights, seriatim, under different circumstance of airline, flight type, luggage arrangement, payment method, and artifact. They would learn who gets through and with what. This gives a counter-profile of what a good guy and good stuff look like. The MIT students concluded that the best option is to perform random searches; randomness provides no intelligence advantage to the potential attacker in the way that focused searches do.[54]

Those who run the TSA know much of this. In my interviews with several former officials, I learned they are aware of what happens in prisons and the remarkable plasticity of physical elements in the world. They also know the capacity of smugglers to continuously innovate and hide contraband in places it would be impossible to examine on a routine basis. But the list of forbidden items and some TSA procedures do not arise from autonomous expertise of sophisticated people such as my informants. Instead, as I learned, there are other parties involved. One of them happens to be private companies who have a stake in expanding the market for high-tech equipment that they develop, such as those full-body scan machines. General Electric tried, without success, to market a dedicated instrument to scan shoes. As we saw with subway surveillance, purveyors exaggerate how effective their appliances can be. There is an ongoing bias in favor of technological instruments as magic bullets.

This brings up "the Hill," which is another force shaping what is or is not the right procedure and what should be on the contraband list. Because security is everybody's business, members of Congress take satisfaction in expressing their support to "have" it. While a bit reticent to opine on the details of high-technology solutions, they have less hesitance about certain things like what types of people and what sorts of artifacts should or should not be "on the list." When TSA announced it would allow scissors on board (up to four inches from fulcrum), some members of Congress denounced the loosening of standards.[55]

For their part, my TSA informants stressed the goal is to keep out items "that can bring a plane down." With the advent of a secure cockpit, they think small tools—even the proverbial box cutters—are not worth the worry. This viewpoint, however, has its own sharp edge: it places a lower priority on preventing a perpetrator from killing a flight attendant, for example. As the head of TSA explained in congressional testimony, "Sorting through thousands of bags a day at two or three minutes apiece to sort out small scissors and tools does not help security. It hurts it."[56] In response, according to the *New York Times* report, Senator Ted Stevens of Alaska said he found that logic "difficult to follow." He proposed instead reducing allowable baggage from two items to one to save time for the screeners. Scissors were taken off the contraband list despite the politicians' wishes, but other contested items remained on it (and in my experience, small scissors are still selectively disallowed). The ban on liquids also remains despite experts' doubts of its relevance. Liquids give the TSA the problem of proper disposal, since the captured bottles of water, shampoo, sun lotion, and all the rest cannot, by definition, be classified as benign. Their disposal is neither simple nor inexpensive, I was told—although I was not given the details of their processing.

It is not possible to frisk babies or examine inside their diapers; however possible it is to put a bomb on a baby, parents (and the public) would not tolerate it. Colostomy bags and other such medical devices are also off limits as are orthopedic shoes. Gels and ointments related to prosthetic devices are okay, as are medications that are so "identified." Animals are never put through x-ray machines and are subject to visual inspection only. Guns, while not allowed in hand luggage, are permitted in checked bags, along with unlimited quantities of ammunition (TSA has no limits, but individual airlines may). These items must be declared at check-in, be properly packed, and placed in locked luggage; the relatively permissive U.S. position, versus tighter procedures in other countries, obviously follow from U.S. gun politics. The list of forbidden items and related implementation represents compromise and, perhaps for this reason, is unevenly enforced. As at the subways, with their specific campaigns of "See Something" and arrays of controls and cameras, the setups do not arise from some disembodied expertise but rather from an amalgam of pushes and pulls.

INSIDER THREAT

Beyond the threat of trouble from outsiders is the threat of trouble from insiders—the growing number of people hired as part of the security apparatus itself. In what must be the most rapid startup of any organization in history, short of mobilization for World War II, the TSA began with the hiring, in a single twelve-month period, of fifty thousand people. Combined with those playing other roles in police, military, and service functions (including air freight), this amounts to hundreds of thousands of individuals on the inside of the air transport system. Potential grows for those up to no good to gain positions of responsibility, and it is amazing how rare any acts of betrayal have been. After all, even those once innocent of any conniving can eventually go bad. People cannot be assumed constant in their ways of looking at the world—either continuously loyal or continuously disloyal (an issue taken up in a later chapter of this book). Like the Rodriguez bad apple in the subway case (the cop who set off the pipe bomb), the more apples you have, the more likely one will be bad.

Those participating within the system can systematically weaken it not through desire to do harm but through more mundane organizational motives like trying to make the outfit look good—something all bureaucracies tend toward. So it happened that the TSA connived for two years, 2003–2005, with its screening contractor at San Francisco Airport (Covenant Aviation Security) to tip off workers, in real time, as undercover inspectors approached with their fake bombs and other contraband. According to the DHS Inspector General's office,[57] TSA was feeding screeners with precise descriptions of the undercover personnel, reporting along the way on their movements in the airport (TSA rehired the contractor anyway with a $314 million four-year contract).[58]

Organizations, we also know, often exaggerate the threats they are under, and those involved in making the threats may also be exaggerating them—thereby disrupting the security apparatus in the process. One of the most sensational plots was the reported attempt by four men originally from Guyana and Trinidad to blow up Kennedy Airport, its pipelines, and its fuel tanks, and cause massive destruction to the city as well. One of the suspects boasted to a federal informant that "he had a vision that would make the World Trade Center attack seem small." Arresting authorities followed suit, citing the potential for an explosion that would eclipse 9/11. But it came to be revealed that the existing pipeline technologies would have prevented the series of envisioned cascading explosions. Furthermore, it turned out that a government informant was also an enabler. It was he, for example, who purchased the camera used in surveillance missions. He also had to show the supposed mastermind, a sixty-seven-year-old immigrant and former cargo handler at the airport (said to be a "homegrown extremist"), how to work the technology.[59]

Ordinary to the Rescue

There are various reasons, as we keep learning, for security systems to misfire. As a critical element, the myopia of command and control blunts the process of how real humans learn about situations and one another. People utilize all their senses, simultaneously applied, pretty much with "no time out." People see not just forward and back, but sideways as well. They take in details and particulars from all sorts of cues: verbal, touch, visual, olfactory, including facial expressions, laughs, kinetic movements, and side conversations. They grasp elements not in an additive way, but as gestalt, as simultaneous comprehending how things "add up," either instantaneously or in sharp iterative instants. So-called security workers could be doing this but are deprived, in systematic ways, from easily being able to do so. The sociological field of ethnomethodology has the word "indexicality" to explain how we manage to understand what goes on in our world by relating everything to everything else in our purview. By eliminating whole ranges of information that come with "small talk" and jokes from routine interactions on "irrelevant topics,"[60] the security regime blocks information that might otherwise come out in passing. In the subways, as we learned, workers have trouble specifying how they know when there is trouble in the making. They "just knew," they repeated to us again and again. There's a "sixth sense," they sometimes say. So it is, always and ever, the human instinct toward the wide scan that is done with tacit competence.

It thus might not come as a surprise that the handful of would-be perpetrators (and occasional actual ones) were caught mostly through the alertness of ordinary people as opposed to those charged with doing security itself. It was passengers and flight crew who foiled shoe-bomber Richard Reid. A passenger notified a flight attendant of the smell of smoke. The attendant, seeing Reid trying to light a match, warned him off. When the attendant subsequently returned and found him making another attempt, a physical altercation ensued with other passengers and another flight attendant joining in. They bound Reid up using lengths of plastic seatbelt extensions and headphone cords.[61] Two doctors on board injected him with a tranquilizer from the plane's emergency medical kit.[62]

It was similarly passenger and flight attendant action that foiled the Underwear Bomber headed to Detroit in 2009. He had been screened before embarking on his trip aboard a KLM flight and then again when changing planes in Amsterdam to the U.S. carrier. After nineteen hours aboard two flights across three continents, he finally made his effort to ignite his syringe of incendiary powder.[63] Passengers detected smoke, this time with fire. They sprang into action (a certain Dutch video producer was hailed as a particular hero) and forcefully restrained the perpetrator. Flight attendants doused the flames with fire extinguishers. All the sophisticated airport devices, including the ban on liquids, sharp objects, and contraband metal, had failed to detect the bad guy or bad stuff. There had been no panic on board.

BOTTOM LINES

Militarism seems to trump even the market, creating a stark contrast with the behaviors of airline flight and gate crews who greet at check-in and then become lights at the end of the security tunnel. A Cornell University study estimated, for 2002, that extra airline costs due to security issues were over $4 billion.[64] The head of the International Air Transport Association put the 2004 price tag at $5 billion.[65] After 9/11, there was a 6 percent drop in air travel by Americans shifting to car, rail, or bus (a 9 percent shift at the country's fifty busiest airports) with the implementation of just one new imposition —screening for checked luggage (this was over the 2001–2002 period). Because the requirement was phased in at different airports over time, the Cornell researchers were able to discount other plausibly relevant factors, like changes in the overall economy and fear of terrorism.[66]

According to an Orbitz survey, 11 percent of travelers report cancelling flights or flying less because of security procedures. Women, in particular, objected to the "intrusion from security" (31 percent) compared to men (only 4 percent), and this was before implementation of full-body scans and intensive pat downs.[67] To whatever degree security chased people away from flying and into car use—so much more dangerous—it killed some of them. Again according to the Cornell analysts (in a second paper), 2,300 lives were lost in the two years following the attack, with disproportionate losses in the Northeast corridor, where switching to car travel was most feasible.[68] As *New York Times* columnist Nate Silver pointed out, it would take "four fully loaded Boeing 737s crashing each year for air travel to kill that many people."[69] The Cornell researchers remarked in their own summary, "Terrorist attacks can have unintended consequences that rival the attacks themselves in their serverity."[70] They deduce that it is a matter of "balance" between imposing inconvience at security while at the same time showing enough precautions so as to assure people they are safe. In my view, the balance wrongly tipped in the direction of imposing trouble on people rather than protecting them from it.

Security created other potential conflicts with the airline business besides the problem of lost customers. Following on heightened anxiety from the Detroit Underwear Bomber, TSA issued a directive asking passengers to check as much of their luggage as possible and travel with a minimum of carry-on luggage. This would, in the rationale provided, speed passengers through the additional security measures. It also probably adds some time to the check-in process and certainly adds time on to luggage retrieval. This would increase crowd accumulations at both security-vulnerable sites. More checked luggage also means that more flights would be held up to remove luggage of those who do not show up for boarding—something that must be done as still another security measure. In any event, the check-in remedy conflicted with airlines' efforts to decrease checked luggage to enhance profits.

Again treating the Underwear Bomber as a security lesson, TSA acted on the fact he had waited until the last hour of his last flight before trying to explode his device. So TSA issued a new rule against having anything on one's lap in the last hour of travel, laptops included. I happened to be flying late on that fateful Christmas day. Since my flight from Vancouver to Los Angeles was only two and a half hours, we passengers spent a large portion of it under zero-object conditions. I later saw the following posted on the official Air Canada website: "New rules imposed by the U.S. Transportation Security Administration also limit on-board activities by customers and crew in U.S. airspace that may adversely impact on-board service. Among other things, during the final hour of flight customers must remain seated, will not be allowed to access carry-on baggage, or have personal belongings or other items on their laps."[71] This surely does not help the airline industry.

Potential foreign travelers must complete an electronic form before their trip, answering questions regarding their history of drug use, mental illness, and arrest. Coupled with requirements for fingerprints and sometimes-complicated visa requirements, the U.S. travel industry again loses money. The U.S. Travel Association has registered objections, especially in regard to China, Brazil, and India, which are rich sources of visitors but countries where citizens face especially stringent difficulties in travel to the United States.[72]

In a rare instance of open revolt, the head of British Airways, Martin Broughton, complained in 2010 of the required "kowtowing" of the airline industry of the world to U.S. demands—as in forcing passengers to unsheathe laptops and take off shoes.[73] The head of Airports Council International in Europe, the official organization of European airports, said it was "clear that most of the recent developments in aviation security have been driven by the US." He urged that there be an end, among other practices, to "useless duplications."[74] Echoing a theme voiced by multiple airline officials, an executive at U.K.-based EasyJet complained of the "crude, blanket security checks which inconvenience all passengers" compared to "more intelligent processes," which he argued were indeed available.[75]

U.S. domination over security regimens stems from the country's predominance in setting standards for world commerce by making its own policies ipso facto global policies. Much of the standardization grew out of the post–World War II era when governments established a network of bilateral and multilateral conventions. Coordination now officially occurs through an agency of the United Nations through which fifteen training centers around the world implement consistent security protocols.[76] Those who fly internationally are accustomed to hearing and watching the nearly identical recitation from flight attendants. Like so much else of the modern jet plane (which heavily derived from World War II bombers and cargo planes), these are American protocols. U.S. aeronautic centrality has been continuously coordinated through the Department of Defense and the Federal Aviation Agency. Specifications for aircraft peripherals, such as gangways, luggage-handling equipment, and even—especially in the contemporary no-knife moment—onboard catering, also follow U.S. standards. Plane manufacturers and airlines that do not conform are not allowed at U.S. airports—a very high cost for any company to face. Hence so much of the stuff looks the same around the world and with the same messages appear in different languages in waiting areas and on board. Regardless of cultural difference, the U.S. security model tends to prevail.

Theater of Domination?

Because so much at airport security (and other security settings as well) seems to make so little sense, it is tempting to use the term "security theater"[77] for the whole apparatus and to see it as deliberately engineered to engender supplication and deference to the powerful. Making people anxious is the whole point, some say. In an environment where there can be "no compromise with the war on terror," those motivated by significant and serious commitment—including concerned travelers—must join in the performance. Anything else risks a display of softness and reluctance to do our part.

However plausible it is to see the world that way, my own view relies less on organized and capable conspiracy. Believing in such connivance places too much trust on forethought and masterminding in a system that, as we have seen from the research of Kerry Fosher on the origins of 9/11 response teams, is just too helter-skelter. It stretches credulity to think these outcomes were envisioned by anyone. Instead of careful orchestration, I see the myopia of an obstinate command and control version of the world—quite dangerous, to be sure, in its own way but still indeterminate to some degree in its origin and effect. The devil is as much in the detail of omissions as in the commissions. There is no professional design, no considerate and artful setup at security, because thinking that way would involve addressing other aspects of life and ways of knowing and being. Agencies would have to develop an internal design staff or search for the right outside consultancy, and then stand up to officials at the DHS, Congress, and the White House to get the money for thoughtfulness and laterality The kind of people involved with airport security and the kinds of environments they work within do not auger for such actions and the alternative arrangements to which they might lead.

WHAT TO DO?

Any initiative for change must take on the fact that airports, as with other security venues, are indeed places of threat ambiguity. The authorities do not know what to do and neither do most of their critics. We don't know where trouble might be coming from, in what way, from whom, or precisely where. The solutions I offer—as with those for previous sites I've examined—are in keeping with the idea that something must be done, if for no other reason than that publics and politicians demand action, activity, and implements. The starting point is to ease up on command and move toward facilitation, empathy, and amusement.

Here is the breakdown:

• *Help.*

Helping is not just nice, it informs. Anyone who has helped children put on a jacket knows it is a learning experience for the helper. You learn if kids have a hurt arm, if they took a cookie, or if their body heat seems above normal. Touching people and their stuff in a helpful way, not just frisking them, is data rich. You also gain clues when people refuse help but who really need it: maybe they are hiding something, including an injury that might need attention.

Making inquiries, even what may seem like "insincere" ones, yields data. Flight attendants have told me that when they stand in the plane's doorway welcoming passengers and asking them how they are doing, they are also looking out for trouble—who has too much stuff? Or won't be able to reach the overhead bin? Who is drunk? Doesn't understand English? Making inquiries allows the attendant to generate remedies before the fact, something often belittled as rote and insincere or, in the sociological canon, emotional "labor" that is not sufficiently compensated. Either way (or not in any of these ways), affect is part of the multitasking intrinsic in life situations, occupational or otherwise. Being nice, being interested, and helping others is not, of course, ipso facto a complete source of intelligence—but it is one indeed. To help a person "get ready," you learn a lot about what is going on—an intelligence feature of kindness. The fact that it might also do some good for fellow human beings is no small advantage.

• *Design it, damn it.*

The objects and utensils at the gate could themselves be far more helpful. The bowl where you put your pocket change could use a funnel; coins would return more easily into the hand. If the gray bins (usually they are gray in the United States) were translucent, it would be easier to see if they had anything in them. Not only would this help with security, but also such changes would make it easier for passengers to track their own stuff as it moved through the system—helping speed the line, perhaps, while enhancing comfort levels. It would also make it less likely for a tray with a laptop in it to be mistaken for an empty one and the stuff inside put at risk (see above).

And why not, to stay at a primitive level of gadget remediation, have a simple bar across the bottoms of the platforms where we place our bags and stuff. That's where we could prop up feet to untie shoelaces at one end and then tie them back up at the other. And, to get slightly more ambitious, passengers should be able to place bags at floor level, with a motorized incline taking them up to the screening device. That would help not just the infirm but also many others. In Hong Kong, if you put small items in a container for the metal detector, you are given a number so that you can collect that basket when you've gone through the checkpoint.

Of course, we would expect far more from a real design reconfiguration than a well-placed spout, a footrest, or a claim check. Designers and operations researchers, knowing all the tricks of the trade, could reconfigure the entire process and each of its elements. This is something routinely carried out in both private and public enterprises all over the world and in regard to much less crucial activities. Consistent with my subway recommendations, the aspiration would also be to add assistance and pleasure through appropriate staffing and training.

Finally, in 2009, TSA and the design firm IDEO researched prototypes that would improve both physical design and worker capacities, based on a number of these suppositions. However, other than a trial setup at Baltimore-Washington International, I could find no evidence of implementation (although I now see some bins that are semitransparent). Why was it not done sooner and why did it not "stick"? I learned from my TSA informants that anything like design just did not occur to those running DHS or TSA. They had been only vaguely aware that such professions and consultancies existed. As the IDEO project unfolded, the very word "design" and some of IDEO's terminology— like "customer engagement"—put off some officials and politicians as suspect and "fluffy." Sympathetic TSA officials had to fight off suspicions from others in the agency, at DHS, and "on the Hill."

• *Calm the line.*

Calm is the opposite of commotion, and it is what security needs more of. Calm delivers a life benefit to passengers, but it also makes trouble more evident—whether it's trouble from contraband or trouble in the form of an ailing person. Ironically, perhaps, accumulating anxious passengers at checkpoints make it harder to pick out those who are on edge because they have something to hide versus those just trying to do the right thing. As part of its exercise with TSA, IDEO presented two images that dramatize the point: a shark in calm seas versus a shark in rough seas (figure 12). Of all the strategies used to communicate the point of calm, none was more effective in trying to enlist sympathies of the more militaristic (and shows the importance of graphic artistry in communicating substantive issues). IDEO also had suggestions for color, music, and even scent as well as informative visuals that would aid passengers in knowing what was ahead, how to "divest" their stuff at "composing lily pads," and be given a "rejuvenating send-off" (now we are really pushing some military buttons).[78]

Some airports have public art programs that go some way toward bringing in part of normal urban life. In the United States, San Francisco's airport has vitrines of wonderful objects lining the corridors and along the moving walkways—similar to the mechanism that moved multitudes past Michelangelo's on-loan *Pietà* at the 1964 World's Fair in Queens. Lessons could also be learned from Disney amusement parks, which process vast millions through use of entertainment figures—Goofy, Mickey, or Snow White—who distract people waiting in line. It is a version of providing a "nudge," in which people are not forced to obey but rather encouraged to make desirable choices from the standpoint of convenience, calm, and good order.[79] In some retail settings, such as Whole Foods grocery markets, I have seen samples offered out to those in line, a rather ingenious system for mitigating the wait, with employees offering cheerful guidance. Engineering niceness into the process is part of sound configuration. "Courtesy is contagious," and this could mean the lines would move quicker and more efficiently as customers do less grousing and fidgeting.

Figure 12. Shark in rough sea versus shark in calm sea. Images courtesy of the Transportation Security Administration.

The Guggenheim Museum in New York, in conjunction with one of its exhibitions, deployed a distinctive version of double-duty kindness and control. It aimed to enhance visitor experience while also protecting the art. The museum, in effect, created a new type of staff—people who rove the galleries, starting up conversations among visitors about the art, trying to demystify the work. Their presence also protects the works, keeping people from touching or otherwise disturbing the exhibited material. So a part of the art appreciation becomes information about the art's vulnerability to touch (for example)—

something especially appropriate for installations that are ambiguous as to the proper role of the museum visitor. Some works are meant to be handled, walked on, banged, or even eaten, others not so.[80] And the "guard" gently assists with information and prodding. It is an occupation resembling the party "enablers," attractive hired people who reach out to guests and dance with them to lubricate the dance floor so everyone can have a good time. An element of such sociability can be put into the security mix. The Guggenheim personnel were young and museum-quality enthusiastic, but the social type put on duty can be varied depending on setting and visitor profile, and made airport-appropriate. Maybe have some shtick for the New York-Miami run: "You don't laugh? You got a bomb up your ass, mister?"

Free verse eases tensions while yielding information of whatever sort. Israeli officials, forces of respect throughout the world's security industry, do not ask a mechanical series of questions like "Did you pack your bags yourself?" and instead ask, in effect, for answers that spell out a story. So travelers might be asked where they are going, why they travel there, who they will meet, why those people, why that place, what about after, and so on. The idea is that liars will have trouble maintaining a coherent narrative, and if they are providing rehearsed answers, they eventually will run out of script and show nervousness at being on shaky ground. Of course, some people are just shy, inarticulate, or indeed have an open-ended itinerary and live according to a more laid-back lifestyle. They may be swept into the suspicious category by following their own everyday normality. Better to embed inquisitiveness in a regime of help.

One way to address the liabilities of lines is just to have fewer of them. Reporting on its study of conditions at LAX, a RAND report found that a 20 percent increase in screening capacity would completely eliminate the line and wait time.[81] The same type of modest increase in capacity, the RAND report indicates, would eliminate wait lines at check-in. Reducing the wait time for luggage to one minute (admittedly a more difficult challenge) would, according to the operations research experts, reduce deaths from a bomb explosion in the immediate area by half.

• *OK with the funny.*

Allowing laughter may help, whether in the line or other stages of the apparatus. Southwest Airlines shows a way, building its identity by breaking role and actually encouraging mirth at least once in the plane. I have heard the following over the Southwest plane intercom:

> In event of emergency the lights will appear down the dirty blue carpet.
> If you don't like our service, use the exits marked over the wings.
> Do what we say and you won't get hurt.

More than once, passengers have applauded at the end of the flight attendant's "fasten seat belt" spiel. And here's one reported on a website devoted to the airline's humor:

> Your seat cushions can be used for flotation, and in the event of an emergency water landing, please paddle to shore and take them with our compliments.

The danger of fun at just the one airline is that it may get people in trouble. Passengers may joke around at other airport settings where their antics will unleash the powers that be. So we need general change across the flying world to make it safe for people who think they can be human when they travel. Otherwise, Southwest may be guilty of entrapment. Letting humor run its natural human course becomes still another source of intelligence: who is thinking what, needing what, threatening what—small troubles or big. It tips off.

• *End profiles.*

Profiling is an inevitable tool of consciousness. Sense making requires distinctions and that means using stereotype. Stereotypes are always rough and ready, blinklike, and only more or less adequate to purposes at hand. Features of dress, gait, skin color, body morphology, and demeanor figure in to judgments. We do not need *programs* of profiling; profiling can take care of itself. Official profiling has proven itself massively inaccurate and inefficient, says at least some of the security literature.[82] Whatever use it might have will play out—rightly or wrongly— among passengers as well as authorities..

Some have argued for "risk-based decision making"[83]—which means considering indeed the specifics at hand rather than following gross profiling categories by rote. But such schemes still typically embed profiling, albeit the word is skirted around or said to be just one element in a larger list of criteria. But again, offenders can learn the elements of any such system to blunt its effectiveness. Massively on the other side of the risk ledger from the potential gains is resentment and alienation, always a danger. Given the low pay-off and, yes, the injustice, we should end profiling to find the terrorist. The capacity to profile needs to be aimed at discovering those who need help and this, again ironically, may lead to knowledge of those who could be a threat, of whatever sort. Information, it is worth reiterating, is a good thing.

• *Make profile awards.*

A concrete antidote to profiling, official or otherwise, could involve compensating those who are made to suffer—a market-based remedy. This is a way to deal with false positives and also their injustice. If you are bothered a lot and especially if you are caused to miss a flight, you get something in return. Perhaps your prize should be a free flight or an upgrade. For lesser official mistakes (holding somebody for an extra frisk to detect metal that does not exist), the passenger gets some free air miles or snack box. This would build internal organizational incentives for minimizing wrongful interference. It could also change the social valence of "looking Arab" or whatever the stigma du jour happens to be. *They* would be the people in first class with cashews and easy access to toilets. Of course, this would add still more complexity to operations management, but I find it instructive that not even a hint of such institutional courtesy is mentioned in the security literature or public discussions. Why not give it a try, especially given the happy congruence of such profile rewards with other market-based policies of the neoliberal moment?

The point of many of these remedies is to break with the social sterility of security and to allow the outside world in: humor, aesthetics, sociality, and interpersonal caring and compassion—as well as frequent flyer miles. Like the public restroom that also bars so much of normal life on principle (with an overlapping albeit not identical list of prohibitions), enforced exclusion creates tension, per se, and—as it turns out ironically once again—decreases security in the process.

CHAPTER 5

Forting Up the Skyline: Rebuilding at Ground Zero

We are reminded by the remaining remnants of European city walls (now sometimes used as ring roads and the occasional urban park) of how security concerns strongly affect urban form. Physical barricades and tall fences are still used to keep the enemy at bay. But in the case of a country like the United States, with so much immigration as well as tourism—along with seeps, leaks, and escapes— building up the membrane becomes a true challenge. So we arrived at the solution of constructing security brick by brick, building by building, place by place within the territory, not just at its borders.

The central site of it all in the United States, both as cause and effect, is what is left of the World Trade Center; a site and now a reconstruction in Manhattan. It shows in a striking way what security architecture can be and reveals how competing goals and anxieties meld into physical form. Whatever their mixture in U.S. civic culture at the time of the attacks, fear and truculence became dominant. It twisted the nature of the building outcome, shaping its form, influencing its uses, and determining which voices and priorities would predominate. Well before the decisions about what would be rebuilt and how, security displays were affecting the texture of political and business life, including making City Hall itself into a forbidden realm surrounded by checkpoints, fences, and armed guards. All around post-9/11 downtown New York, there were (and remain) conventional elements of bastion, with bollards, Jersey barriers, and no-entry zones.

This was the temperament that was to shape the project on the sixteen acres once occupied by the twin towers. As things evolved, the program became one of big, tall, and strong and partaking of the national ideology being given strident voice by the U.S. president, the governor of the State of New York, and the mayor of the city. From early on, it was clear, this building or set of structures would be aggressive and in your face. "I can hear you, the rest of the world hears you, and the people who knocked these buildings down will hear all of us soon," Bush announced through his bullhorn to clearance and salvage workers at the site on September 14, 2001.[1] Although he probably had in mind the wars to come, buildings would also show what America was all about. As Mayor Giuliani proclaimed, "We're going to rebuild, and we're going to be stronger than we were before . . . I want the people of New York to be an example to the rest of the country, and the rest of the world, that terrorism can't stop us."[2] The "skyline will be made whole again," he assured.[3] "Stories are always important," says historian Kevin Rozario, "but at no time are they more important than in the midst of crisis and uncertainty."[4] We had our story.

The events of 9/11 were "smothered in an exuberant distinctly American embrace," to use the words of William Langewiesche, writing in the *Atlantic Monthly* at the time.[5] But the resolve to rebuild, common enough in the aftermath of disasters everywhere, packed in the drive to get even. Some punitive sentiment had been present in reactions to earlier U.S. urban destructions, of course. In 1871 Chicago and 1906 San Francisco, like New Orleans after them, there were exaggerated and indeed unfounded claims of looting and moral turpitude on the part of various groups: Asian hordes in the instance of San Francisco, the Irish of Conley's Patch in Chicago, women "of the baser sort," and the riff-raff of the slum areas in general.[6] Such sentiments no doubt helped ground anxieties already running amok and intensifying under stress of the occasions, including concerns about demon alcohol causing people to run rampant in the desperate aftermath. Temperance movements were in full swing. As Rozario says, "Narratives need disasters as much as disasters need narratives." The 9/11 attacks were useful for the narrative of untrustworthy foreigners of the early American twenty-first century, now with Arabs playing the dark role of the worrisome and uncontrollable Other.

Anger cannot be the only force behind U.S. city building; it must respond to the usual commercial interests in play, starting with the property owners and those with a larger interest in metropolitan development. Business owners conflict with many security measures; they need their area to be secure but not at the cost of deterring buyers (like the airlines at the airport, they want profit as well as safety). In Lower Manhattan, merchants in nearby Chinatown vociferously complained of lost revenues from street blockage and control points (the "frozen zone"). Their needs were not treated as paramount, but the long-term viability of downtown commerce was indeed a part of the calculus. And that meant looking for new ways to conjoin security with built form, hopefully—some had their fingers crossed—with urban growth and increased property value.

As part of responding to both symbolic needs as well as commercial ones, speed became especially important. Portrayed as responding to patriotic idealism, building crews went on a 24/7 schedule. Contracts were signed on the fly or not signed at all—an inversion of the slogging bureaucratic niceties sometimes observed even after disaster, as revealed, for example in the Katrina response (see the next chapter). With dispatch, the humiliating devastation had to be cleared and the visible scandal of weakness made less visible—with Wall Street commerce restored. One of the urgencies was the leaseholders' rights; Silverstein Properties has just taken over the lease from the Port Authority of New York and New Jersey before the attacks occurred and was obliged to pay $100 million per year in rent fees to the Port Authority. As part of negotiations and litigation, clearing the site both physically and legally was necessary to maintain the viability of the agreements.

Speed at the site meant minimizing any negative publicity about health danger to those doing the work or remaining in the residential and business structures left standing. Top officials assured there was no danger to the health of workers, and to only a limited degree, the residents of downtown Manhattan. One week after the catastrophe Christine Todd Whitman made an official statement that was characteristic of the U.S. Environmental Protection Agency (EPA), which she headed at the time:

> We are very encouraged that the results from our monitoring of air-quality and drinking-water conditions in both New York and near the Pentagon show that the public in these areas is not being exposed to excessive levels of asbestos or other harmful substances.

Her press release went on to say the following:

Given the scope of the tragedy from last week, I am glad to reassure the people of New York . . . that their air is safe to breathe and the water is safe to drink.[7]

The city's mayor echoed the sentiment. Mayor Rudi Giuliani told the people of New York, "The air quality is safe and acceptable."[8]

Such assurances about safety should, along with zoning permits, window-walls, and floor areas, also be considered as elements in the rebuilding of the downtown area. They do not necessarily make for an attractive feature. A 2010 study of five thousand first responders found that all had developed respiratory impairments, with one thousand of them placed on permanent respiratory disability.[9] Another analysis concluded that fire fighters serving at Ground Zero lost, on average, the equivalent of twelve years of lung function. Even state workers (as opposed to firefighters and police) with only "moderate exposure" showed persistent effects five years later.[10] Other evidence indicates those living within one mile of the Ground Zero site suffered higher rates of respiratory ailments than others in the city. Although the number of reported health issues related to the attack has declined over time, ailments remain disproportionately high among residents living near the site.[11] For children, heightened rates of asthma were detected within the five-mile zone of Ground Zero, with incidence in proportion to distance from the site.[12]

A senior EPA scientist, Cate Jenkins, accused the agency of having deliberately lied.[13] A 2003 follow-up by the Office of the EPA Inspector General provided support for the charge.[14] White House pressure had caused numerous changes to be made in EPA reports, consistently in the direction of minimizing danger. The White House intervened to downplay asbestos poisoning, as one major example, with the EPA assuring safety when results were, at best, ambiguous.[15] Studies of health effects continue on to this day, as do claims for costs of treatment. Apparently about 40 percent of those being monitored lacked health insurance at the time of the attacks.[16] It is evident that more will have died from the response to the disaster than were lost in it (not even counting, of course, the deaths of troops and foreigners in the military conflicts that followed).

Design Rises

Well before the dust began clearing, schemes began to unfold as to what, specifically, to build. Leaving the site open with a meadow for peaceful repose got a mention. The notion of a quiet sort of monument, one that might leave standing some of the shards of the prior structure, also surfaced. Several twisted steel arches from the lower floors had survived both the buildings' collapse and initial clearance efforts. They were indeed poetically evocative, in the manner of a sadly splendid ruin. Precedents for retaining bomb remains do exist, as in the Kaiser Wilhelm Memorial Church ("the hollow tooth") in Berlin's bustling center. The German authorities left the bombed-out remains to stand as a reminder of war-making horrors as well as of defeat. Indeed, much of German reconstruction, including the development of Bonn as the new capital, was done with understatement and humility to deliberately contrast with fascist bellicosity.[17] Similarly, at the Hiroshima Peace Memorial, a bombed-out dome remains in place. Both such memorials connote contrition and a renunciation of political violence. It is also true that the decisions to retain were both made while the respective countries were under U.S. occupation. But such a mode of memorialization would not do as precedent for post-9/11 commemoration.

In terms of the commercial real estate market, the most reasonable use of the property would have been for residential apartments, as advocated by the *New Yorker* architectural critic, Paul Goldberger.[18] The area's excellent subway access (the best service for any New York neighborhood) and its location at a stone's throw from waterfront parkland on three sides make it a highly desirable place to live. Finance had been, for about the previous twenty years, migrating in any event from the so-called Financial District to midtown. Back-office functions were moving to Brooklyn and New Jersey, a trend accelerated by the attacks. In effect—an awkward truth—the downtown devastation further rationalized land-use change as financial firms took the opportunity and gained the experience of being in places more suited to their activities—something predicted by the then-head of New York Chamber of Commerce, Kathryn Wylde.[19] In the wake of vacancies that began well before 9/11, developers were converting downtown office buildings into residential condominiums and rental apartments. The area, a.k.a. the "Financial District," received its residential real estate advert imprimatur "FiDi."

Partly to reverse the financial out-migration, there had been the goal, indeed, made explicit in post-9/11 redevelopment documents, to construct a "one-seat" mass transit line from downtown to JFK Airport—one-seat meaning no need to transfer from one train or bus to another as now required. This would finally give city users a way to their flights in a fast and comfortable way (thirty-six minutes from Lower Manhattan). But such a utilitarian type of public infrastructure did not sustain interest. It lacked the kind of glamour and excitement of a soaring tower and would, it must be acknowledged, have been expensive—about $4 billion. But that is within range of construction costs of, for example, a dramatic new subway and New Jersey commuter train terminal designed by Santiago Calatrava being built at the site. It is the cost for constructing the main tower at Ground Zero, also expected to come in at around $4 billion. A new airport rail line would have indeed made downtown an indispensable business center and provided a significant amenity for residents and tourists alike.

One big thing, spectacular in its way, would be to rebuild exactly what was there before—the twin towers in their dubious majesty. It is always a respected accomplishment to reproduce something that has already been around, using technologies, equipment, and materials as they have come to exist. Such has been a response to other types of disaster as well as to just the ravages of time. Re-create even buildings that have been totally destroyed. Thus, besides the hollow tooth, postwar German authorities rebuilt museums, churches, concert halls, and other landmarks to closely duplicate structures destroyed by allied bombing. The Austrian government reconstructed the Vienna Opera House, heavily destroyed in the war, as closely as possible in detail and grandeur (budgets permitting) to the original. Jerusalem is a virtually reconstructed center of the ancient. Donald Trump, interviewed about the proposed rebuilding at Ground Zero, suggested the replication option (as did Mayor Giuliani for a time), except Trump wanted it to be one story taller than the original—a sign of extra strength in his view.

But such would have been, by other lights, too prosaic a response. The architectural press had long condemned the Trade Center buildings. In part because the architect, Minoru Yamasaki, used fanciful gothic motifs at the base and building tops rather than going with the rectilinear style favored at the time; the modernists abhorred the structures. Rather than being the great sheets of glass, windows were slit-like, precluding the wide-open views that modernist buildings generally afford. Even after postmodernism came on the scene, critics never warmed to the structures—neither tradition-oriented fish nor modernistic fowl. As partial remedy, at least at retail and ground level, the leaseholder, Larry Silverstein, was about to begin a major remodel to fix some of the most egregious failings (some remodel efforts had been made a decade before). The huge plaza linking the two towers was a particularly desolate scene—a worst-case scenario of vast hard-surface expanse of the sort favored in 1960s urban renewal design. The combination of skyscrapers and big concrete expanse created howling winds in winter and exposed all to summer's broiling sun.

Besides design admiration, the buildings had, at least originally, lacked an even more critical asset: tenants. The towers were created not to fill a commercial need, but as an artifice of political desires and the era's enthusiasm for clearing out chaotic urban spaces and inserting structural behemoths. The Port Authority of New York and New Jersey—the agency that runs the ports and major airports of the New York metropolis—was in charge at the time. The Port Authority was somehow persuaded to get into the real estate business, and with this gargantuan project.

Only 40 percent of the floor area was rented to private business; all the rest went for government use, with federal, state, and city agencies signing up to pay the full rate. This amounted, in effect, to a massive public subsidy, with government agencies renting the kind of high-end office space ordinarily leased by prestigious private tenants. At the time of construction, there was the further cost of disruption to hundreds of local businesses, many of them making up the city's concentration of outlets for electronic products and components—"Radio Row" as it was called since the 1920s. Taken by eminent domain (each business was offered $3,000 regardless of its size), most did not survive. There was a vast excavation of dirt that ended up in the Hudson River as fill for what became the new residential high-rise zone of Battery Park City. This too, by contemporary standards, was ill conceived and would never pass muster at a present-day environmental impact hearing.

A great faceless bureaucracy, the Port Authority, was self-financed through highway, bridge, and airport tolls and revenues. The effort was goaded forward, actually conceived almost from the beginning by David Rockefeller, at the time head of Chase Manhattan Bank and also the creator of the Downtown-Lower Manhattan Association, a business group advocating for a World Trade Center project as part of an effort to develop the district. The bank itself had built its sixty-story headquarters in the immediate area. David Rockefeller's brother Nelson, as governor of the State of New York (1959–73) and then vice president of the United States, was also a strong force in making it happen. The Port Authority could issue low-interest bonds and pay them off with revenues from its bridge and tunnel enterprises—generating a steady-stream of income, insulated from the general fund needs of other state and local agencies.

The rationale for using such resources to build the towers, controversial at the time, was that they would serve "world trade" by housing shippers, brokers, and those representing them in accountancy, finance, and law. A fashion at the time (and other times as well) was to spatially "unite" functions nominally of the same sort into cultural and civic centers. Hence such colossal urban concentrations as the San Francisco and Cleveland Civic Centers, and performing arts assemblages like Lincoln Center in New York and the Los Angeles Performance Center. The World Trade Center would do this for "world trade." As dubious as the initiating idea of uniting world trade happened to be, it was not to be tested, because few such businesses located within the towers. In short order, its sponsors abandoned the highfalutin rationale for the buildings' existence. It ended up as an office complex of extraordinary height but with mundane uses. So to reprise, the World Trade Center was economically and functionally unwarranted, ecologically damaging, a design failure, and the result of un-democratic scheming. In physical form, it was a kind of screwy sedimentation of urban ideas, practical exigencies, and political ambitions.

None of this bodes well for restoration in the heritage sense; it is not exactly a worthy model to emulate. Instead something new would have to happen, at least equal in its monumentality to what had been before but also responding to some of the prior critique. Yes, it would have to be big and bold but likely as well to incorporate some of the lessons preached by the anti-modernist critics. It would be less of a superblock and pay some homage to the street grid and urban "texture." Nods had to be made to Jane Jacobs, the great critic of urban renewal and not just to Robert Moses, the New York government operative who did so much to foster it. It would be pedestrian friendly. And there would need to be recognition of architecture—glowing and gorgeous—as well as other elements of an art and culture environment. As part of making good economic sense, if for no other reason, it would have to attract the creative class and those who love them. And as a final uptake of the contemporary planning *geist*, there were ambitious programs for citizen participation, neighborhood input, and, in special ways, accommodation of victims' family members. Perhaps above all, honor would be paid to deceased first responders through respect for the wishes of their survivors, people who came to be considered "nearly unassailable."[20]

To manage the rebuild process, then-Governor Pataki created the Lower Manhattan Development Corporation (LMDC) made up of his appointees and those of the mayor of New York. An early LMDC initiative was the "Listening to the City" gathering at the Jacob K. Javits Convention Center in July 2002, which involved over five thousand people (there were actually two events, but with one much larger than the other). It was a massive and intricate arrangement of speakers and workshops that aimed, in part through Internet feedback, to create lists of goals and bases for consensus.[21] There was also extensive online follow-up with still more participants. The LMDC had commissioned, as a first attempt to get some official planning off the ground, designs from the New York firm Beyer Blinder Belle. Three others firms entered the mix: Peterson Littenberg, Alex Cooper, and Skidmore, Owings, and Merrill (SOM). The yield was a total of six distinct design proposals.

Alas, these schemes met with little enthusiasm from the public or political leaders, in part because they failed to show a dramatic addition to the skyline. They did contain, however, some planning-oriented elements, like grand promenades of green and new linkages of down-town to the waterfront. To little avail, the LMDC had emphasized that these were only site plans, but the distinction between site plans and architectural buildings was lost in the rebuild fervor and the need for a stirring gesture. It was, remarks architectural commentator Philip Nobel, "the death of reasoned planning at Ground Zero."[22] The plans went on display at Federal Hall in downtown Manhattan with an esti-mated seventeen thousand people visiting the exhibit.

Beyond the confines of the convention center and Federal Hall, thousands of suggestions poured in and from all over the world, many replete with drawings, mock-ups, and other forms of representation. Memory was still fresh of the Maya Lin triumph with her Vietnam War memorial proposal, sent in while she was still a college under-graduate. This must have especially inspired not only those submit-ting concepts for the new buildings, but also some of the additional five thousand people (a different five thousand than those involved in the Javits events) who sent in design ideas for the separate memorial also to be constructed at the site. In response to its special request for feedback from survivor family members, LMDC received a further 480 responses.

Rather than commission still another architectural practice of its choosing, the LMDC put out a general call to planning and architec-tural firms and received over four hundred submissions from around the globe. Six teams were chosen, representing thirty-four countries and a total of twenty-seven different design outfits. With a few interest-ing exceptions (Frank Gehry, for example, did not submit), they were a virtual who's who of great architects of the world. All these teams working on the same project and at the same time and in the same place, created what was no doubt the greatest charette on earth. The models, drawings, and video displays were publicly exhibited in the summer of 2002, this time with a reported one hundred thousand visi-tors. Countless additional meetings were held in various parts of the city, sponsored by community organizations, business groups, galleries, and universities.

Early on, the governor himself performed a fateful design stroke by assuring (and repeating) a promise he made to victims' families: "We will never build where the towers stood. Where the towers stood is hallowed ground."[23] That reduced the land available for construction and molded the shape of whatever might be coming. The hunger for symbolic replenishment as well as the "let's show them" urgency of the moment would have to play out from an abbreviated site for any type of replacement towers. The coming debate would be about which starchitect team would win approval to address this great challenge.

In the end, it came down to two different submissions, one from the Israeli-born, Berlin- and New York-based Daniel Libeskind, and the other from a group that called itself "THINK," which was made up of Shigeru Ban, Frederic Schwartz, Ken Smith, and Rafael Viñoly. Governor Pataki, reversing the recommendation from the LMDC-appointed design jury, chose the firm of Daniel Libeskind over THINK. Libeskind's designs typically have boldness, often with jagged shapes and thrusting edges, something much on offer in his Ground Zero submission. For the main signature structure of "Freedom Tower," which had been so named by Governor Pataki, Libeskind stipulated a height of 1776 feet. It would not be the tallest building in the world, which the prior towers were during some of their time on earth. Indeed, it would be smaller in total bulk than what was there before, although the shortfall was to be made up with lesser towers to eventually be built in proximity.

In terms of design, it was a whole lot more pointed, not only literally with the spire at its top (figure 13) but also with its many metaphoric gestures, such as the 1776-foot height and an elaborate scheme to mimic in architectural form the Statue of Liberty across the Hudson River. Libeskind said that his larger plan, itself called "Memory Foundations," created a "Wedge of Light" that would shine across the site's main plaza annually on the morning of 9/11 at the moment of the first tower being struck. It would be "a perpetual tribute to altruism and courage."[24] There was also to be a "Matrix of Heroes" formed by etchings in pavement to honor firefighters lost in the response. The wedge of light turned out simply not to be possible because existing buildings would cast shade most of the time during the memorializing moments; the matrix idea was to fall to other development considerations. But they were effective presentational devices for Libeskind.

Figure 13. Freedom Tower (on left) and other structures, as proposed by Daniel Libeskind, 2002. http://www.renewnyc.com/images_WMS/signature/ Libeskind-MODEL-view-3.jpg. Lower Manhattan Development Corporation and the Port Authority of New York and New Jersey.

It was the loss in scale that so disappointed Donald Trump, who voiced concerns of others as well. Said Trump of the Libeskind plan, "If we build this job the way it is, the terrorists win. If we rebuild the World Trade Center, but a story taller and stronger, then we win."[25] He preferred a grand public park (not a bad idea!) rather than let through what he termed such "egghead architecture." To gather support, he helped lead "the Twin Towers Alliance," which collected more than seven thousand signatures in favor of a stricter reconstruction.

However short of being a replica in physical form, Freedom Tower was a close restoration in other ways. In part to satisfy Silverstein, who still owned the lease and requested that the building be more commercially viable, the Port Authority director declared a name change to "One World Trade Center." He offered, as explanation, that this name would be "easiest for people to identify with."[26] Besides in name, it would also resemble its predecessor in not having much to do with world trade. Indeed, it was being built into a downtown office real estate market weak in any regard, but especially so for office space. As a general economic proposition, super tall buildings (over fifty stories or so) make only limited sense; too much of the core must be devoted to elevators and other elements of infrastructure.[27] The motivation to go taller must come from political, religious, or symbolic goals. The prominent New York architect James Stewart Polshek has said, "Skyscrapers are not socially productive, and rebuilding would be an act of super arrogance."[28]

Once again, government came to the rescue, signing up for a lion's share of the allotted space. Of the 2.6 million square feet of office area (amounting to sixty-nine floors), the federal Government Services Administration signed up for 645,000 square feet and the State Government Services took 412,000 square feet. This puts the ratio of rental bailout at about the same level as that of the prior project. If there were to be another terrorist attack, this time a more thinkable event than the first time around, hapless bureaucrats would take a lot of the hit. As for commercial tenants, Condé Nast was to sign up, in 2011, as anchor tenant for a healthy one million square feet of space (twenty-one floors). The trouble is, it is paying a rent level ($60 a square foot) that is less than half for the break-even point for this very expensive building

(Condé Nast will also benefit from a variety of other financial incentives, including exclusion from sales tax for furnishings and equipment that it purchases for its space).[29]

Besides forcing clearance at the site before health effects could be carefully assessed, *speed* of the reconstruction has also got into building costs. Initial estimates had put the Freedom Tower budget at 1.3 billion,[30] plus a billion or so more for the memorial and other features. By 2012, costs approached $15 billion, counting in the expense of newly constructed memorial pools, plazas, and other site amenities. There were also changes in the financial reporting methods. But security, in ways already described, added additional hundreds of millions to budgets. An official audit blamed some of the overrun on a "dysfunctional" Port Authority bureaucracy and, more pertinent here, the desire to have the memorial ready for the tenth anniversary of the attacks—which it was. That required shifting priorities at the site itself and incurring other budgetary burdens. In part at least, as with other World Trade Center shortfalls, increases in bridge and tunnel tolls (controlled by the Port Authority) will help make up the difference—an already instituted increase to $12 from $8 for a single-trip crossing of the Hudson River, for example.

There are still other twists. To reach its symbolically impressive height, the building relies on its especially tall spire—408 feet high (that's about thirty to forty stories of office building height), compared, for example, to the Empire State spire of half that height. At the building's bottom usable space does not actually begin until two hundred feet up; the space below is mostly empty. The first usable floor above ground will be identified as Floor 20 and the highest floor will be identified as 105, with 102 as an observation deck—a total of about eighty-five usable floors, at most. Without considering spire and other rooftop gear, Chicago's Willis Building (formerly Sears Tower) would remain the tallest building in the United States. It reaches 1450 feet in height (compared to 1368 for the new World Trade Center, and that includes the latter building's parapet structure—just under the spire). The Willis Building is thus the more honestly big and high, as was the design intention of its architects at SOM, the firm that designed it in the early 1970s.

As it turned out, SOM was to play the big role after all in the rebuilding of the World Trade Center. Despite all the charetty hullabaloo, Silverstein went back to the very same architect he had engaged for the remodel of the World Trade Center—SOM, represented by the respected David Childs, a forty-year veteran at the firm. Childs simplified the Libeskind design, omitting a lot of the jaggedness and abandoning some of the symbolic froufrou. It does retain a bit of the Libeskind edginess with a skin that changes dimensions as the building rises, transforming the square at the base into eight hugely tall isosceles triangles running the full height of the rest of the building. At about the middle elevation, the configuration results in a floor plate that is a perfect octagon (see figure 14). The size modesty, relative to the original structures, survived the Childs-Silverstein redo. The building's total footprint would be about equal to the footprint of a single one of the prior towers (200 x 200 feet).

At this writing, One World Trade Center is almost up, but it is not the structure even as envisioned by its most recent Silverstein-approved architect. For one thing, it has changed ownership: Silverstein got himself out of the picture by turning his lease back to the Port Authority in return for financing assistance on three adjacent skyscrapers. Besides the ownership switch, new design issues arose having to do with security. New York police officials complained that the building was too close to the street and thus vulnerable to truck bomb damage. Potential destruction rises exponentially with small increments of proximity. The Childs plan would allow an ordinary truck with incendiary devices to do tremendous damage from a curbside location. The solution was to move the building sixty feet from the nearest roadway, complicating routing of adjacent streets and other related uses of the site while also raising costs.

Most dramatic, both in commercial and aesthetic consequences, is the removal of the bottom twenty stories as usable floor space. It will be two hundred feet of windowlessness. The architects, making some lemonade of the ingredients, provide a soaring sixty-five-foot lobby height and put some of the building's mechanical equipment into the void. Also as part of the lemonade story, the designers came up with

Figure 14. World Trade Center, as designed by Skidmore, Owings & Merrill, Lower Manhattan Development Corporation. © Skidmore, Owings & Merrill LLP / dbox studio.

Figure 15. Concrete base of World Trade Center (partially exposed while under construction) with memorial pool in foreground. Photo by author.

the idea to embed two thousand separate glass panels into the exterior skin. Instead of a brutal thug of a base, it would—as said on the architect's website—"reflect, refract and transmit light in various spectrums to create a dynamic, shimmering glass surface that drapes the tower's base."[31] But ill winds would blow again. After the building was already half built, it turned out the glass prisms were too brittle and subject to shattering. The $10 million already spent on their manufacture was lost. More traditional glass panels, presumably opaque to obscure their lack of function, were specified (see figures 15 and 16). On the SOM website, the project, once considered the commission of the century, is not listed among the firm's "featured" projects.

Even before the glass debacle, criticism was severe. Jeff Speck, then-director of design for the National Endowment of the Arts, called the SOM building "an alienating monument to surrender" and the realiza-

Figure 16. World Trade Center base, as envisioned by architect. © Skidmore, Owings & Merrill LLP / by-encore.

tion of his "most pessimistic imaginings."[32] In only the weakest of ways does the site development conform to any of Jane Jacobs's ideas of city planning (something that Speck, in particular likes to foster). There are no eyes on the street and the heterogeneous streetscape of Radio Row is in no way going to be recapitulated. Nor does it follow premises of sculptural starchitecture of the current or any prior era. It does, in a weirdly nostalgic way, recall the concept of the medieval walled-in for-tresses, but it is in the heart of New York City. Paul Goldberger called it "Fear Tower," and a friend of mine, Bob Killen, names it the "Bomb Me First Building." In functional terms, it would make good prison space, perhaps to replace Guantanamo as suggested by some cynics, thus forcing the alleged terrorists to exist in the structure they helped bring into being. That won't happen, of course, and instead the build-ing will be, in that concrete base and faux jack-up at its top, a reminder of attack and its complexly torqued aftermath. As with other responses to the 9/11 disaster, it taunts and just may act as a darkly self-fulfilling prophecy.

Standing Up Culture

Devoting space to something like arts and culture is an accepted, even necessary, basis of contemporary urban development. If not in the World Trade Center tower itself, plans unfolded for particular cultural institutions to take root elsewhere on the sixteen acres. For some civic leaders, it was a mechanism to have downtown reinforce the city's role, challenged somewhat by the touristic and morale losses of 9/11, as the world's creative hub. For other advocates, the potential for new facilities and subsidies was a way to help arts organizations expand their repertoires—with superior space and a marquee location to attract still more funding and larger audiences. Just having the arts was, by its very nature, an antidote to repressive and anti-democratic regimes, or so said at least a subgroup of arts supporters. It would perform freedom, just through the openness and daring-do that comes with aesthetic expressivity.

Once again, all did not go according to plan. Early choices included the Drawing Center, to be attracted from its SoHo location. The Drawing Center, an eminent institution, had hosted a range of exhibits stretched across the centuries (for example, exhibits on Michelangelo and Albrecht Dürer) and virtually all regions of the world (such as a showing of Rajasthani miniatures). But The Drawing Center's past exhibits have also included a satiric linking of George W. Bush to Osama Bin Laden. The Center showed a hooded Abu Ghraib figure with wires arranged to form the word "Liberty." Opponents, in particular victims' and first-responder families, found such things blasphemous and in no way appropriate at the Ground Zero site. As a result of this exhibition, but perhaps also because of other past displays of aesthetic daring-do, The Drawing Center was not allowed in.

The trail-blazing "Signature Theater" would relocate from the midtown theater district to a new facility designed by Frank Gehry at Ground Zero. But it was a very complex and expensive deal with the new theater budgeted at a very high price of $700 million. It opted out in favor of a Gehry-designed space near its old location in the Theater District, to cost a mere $60 million. And so the theater would not be part of the project either.

Perhaps most problematic of all, there was to be a new institution, a museum devoted to telling the story of freedom—the so-called International Freedom Center. With plans to treat "freedom" in a large sense, by making reference to slavery in the United States and to genocides all over the world (including of U.S. native peoples), the Center was condemned by patriot groups as well as, once again, spokespersons for victims' families. In response, Governor Pataki pulled the plug on having it at Ground Zero. As the governor stated, "We will not tolerate anything on that site that denigrates America, denigrates New York or freedom, or denigrates the sacrifice and courage that the heroes showed on September 11."[33] The Freedom Center's board, which included most famously and perhaps provocatively the philanthropist George Soros, responded by disbanding, saying that the site was intrinsic to the message it was created to bring. A museum of some sort remains in the discourse about future possible projects, but only because it is somehow thought important to "have a museum." The museum solution, aimless in function or purpose, becomes another part of the compulsion to "do something."

The sole remaining occupant of the cultural space, "a lonely Lower Manhattan performance tenant," will be the avant-garde Joyce Dance Theater.[34] God knows what will be made of the full-frontal nudity, gender bending, and erotic stances that occasionally grace its stage. Perhaps dance is sufficiently oblique to elude the oppositional radar. Under the design baton of—once again in the picture Frank Gehry—the Joyce moves forward at Ground Zero while also holding on to its other main theater space in Chelsea and two smaller satellite venues.

Using buildings and urban spaces to shape ideas (as well as to kill them) has long been an aspect of security. Efforts get made, à la Albert Speer (Hitler's starchitect) and Benito Mussolini—never mind the pharaohs laid to rest in the pyramids at Giza—to embalm regime in public constructions. The projects at Ground Zero ultimately show security on the skyline and fear at ground level as they exist in the post-9/11 period. They are centered on the tower of Bush and Giuliani. Like the way airport security contrasts with airline seductions, the market at Ground Zero is (once again) not determinative, subject as it is to a subset of people called "the families," the politicians who curry favor, and the artists of the world who will or will not bend to the powers that be.

What would not happen at Ground Zero was acceptance of defeat as fact—at least in the battle on that day of 9/11. By any reasonable measure, Bin Laden and his troops had certainly won. For about half a million dollars (about what the United States spends to send a single soldier to Iraq or Afghanistan[35]) and a handful of their own lost lives, the attackers killed thousands of people in New York, at the Pentagon, and in the plane over Pennsylvania. They caused billions in direct damage. With the successive wars those costs greatly escalated, according to the 2008 calculations of Linda Bilmes and Joseph Stieglitz, to $3 trillion—more than enough to help explain the country's subsequent fiscal difficulties.[36] And losses to human life, especially in the targeted countries of the Middle East, were many, many times the number of U.S losses. How much better it would have been to respond with deft acumen.

The strongest analysis in the immediate aftermath of 9/11 was by Susan Sontag. She was among the city's ten leading writers invited by *The New Yorker* magazine to provide short pieces on the Twin Towers destruction. She created a storm of denunciation by, in her published text, asking the following question:

> Where is the acknowledgment that this was not a "cowardly" attack on "civilization" or "liberty" or "humanity" or "the free world" but an attack on the world's self-proclaimed superpower, undertaken as a consequence of specific American alliances and actions[37]

She went on to urge,

> Let's by all means grieve together. But let's not be stupid together. A few shreds of historical awareness might help us understand what has just happened, and what may continue to happen.

In subsequent years, Lawrence Wright echoed her provocation in his well-received book *The Looming Tower*, where he speculated, "America's tragedy on September 11 was born in the prisons of Egypt." Wright's words were being invoked by the *New York Times'* conservative columnist Ross Douthat during the 2011 rebellions on the streets of Cairo. As Douthat put it, "History makes fools of us all. We make deals with dictators, and reap the whirlwind of terrorism."[38] Douthat is channeling Sontag, but the new constructions at Ground Zero will hardly reflect anything like this outlook. Thick at the base and void at the top, the new building is the same old bad news.

What to Do?

The U.S. Council on Competitiveness, made up of corporate and university heads, asserts in its major report on the subject that "resilience trumps protection," which means, according to the signatories, that rather than stressing security and protection, the need is to have resilience, which they define as "the capability to anticipate risk, limit impact and bounce back rapidly."[39] The conservative legal scholar Richard Posner backs up the idea that there is ultimately very little a society can do to predict truly novel risks like 9/11. It is best, he argues, to avoid too much front-end planning to prevent such events.[40]

So we're back at Ground Zero resilience. Resilience would mean restoring life to the site, even improving—as people do when they have the chance—on what has been before. Making good on architectural spectacles, along the lines originally conceived, would have provided icons and maybe some aesthetic wonder, as would have dramatic improvements on some other dimension. But there are more ordinary things to do if we consider lessons from the disaster.

• *Honor the stairs.*

The survivors at the World Trade Center were saved not by soldiers, sniffing dogs, or esoteric technologies. Stairwells (and exit signs) saved them—just wide enough, strong enough, and airy enough for them to make their way down and out. Although barely sufficient (if the buildings had been fully occupied at the time, fewer would have gotten out), people could see and hear what they were doing.[41] The structures' architecture was also of help, partly because of the consistent rectilinear modernism of each floor plate. It provided predictable visual cues for people to figure out how to make their way to stairs and exits. For the future, make stairwells better, not just at Ground Zero (where improvements are indeed slated to occur) but for all high-rise buildings. And retrofit, as much as possible, already-existing structures to honor the stairs. Develop pulley systems for wheelchair users to directly hook into and slides for others with special needs—a feature that should be built into the subway stations as well.

• *Help the helpers.*

As we also learned in the case of the subways, escape plans benefit, maybe even require, bystanders to help out—something, which we have learned, happens during disaster. The Port Authority had indeed purchased 125 special evacuation chairs for the towers—devices that work something like a hand truck but for carrying a sitting person rather than a heavy object. It is unknown how many were at hand, but it is doubtful there had been safety drills showing coworkers and companions how to find and guide them down the stairs.[42] Whether through such make-do devices or more ambitious systems of exit, authorities need to be *building in the assumption of common aid, rather than being surprised by it.*

• *Follow market demand.*

However outfitted for egress, whatever is built at Ground Zero might have followed the market and, as Goldberger advocated, provided housing. It might have produced an array of nice buildings and shops—especially if taken as an opportunity for breakthroughs in green building, easily facilitated by density, proximity to the water (ferry service, possible hydropower), and remarkable transit access. Better than the Battery Park City apartment complex built on its fill, the new World Trade Center apartments might truly have been international models of advanced community building. Putting low-income apartments into the mix, as one quite modest goal, would have helped supplant the homogenizing trends of gentrification, something that any rebuilding accelerates.

• *Have real museums.*

The original freedom museum might have worked out fine. As an alternative, and one made poignant by the fact there could be no agreement on what the new museum might be, make the problem itself the solution. The urge to "have a museum" (like its partner cliché, to "have a memorial") could itself be the basis for distinctive institutions. So have a museum about memorials and museums, responding and bringing in to public focus recent debates, including those at Ground Zero but drawing on wider discussions from museology and architecture.[43] How have such places evolved in different places and times? Through what architectural and design techniques? For what social, political, and economic purposes? Such issues were, in effect, already intensely on the agenda after 9/11, so why not incorporate them into the site itself? And if we are going to celebrate heroes, why not give special notice to those who did more than go to work on the fateful day, like the subway worker who decided to open his doors and those who carried others down the stairs? And, yes, of course, the passengers over Pennsylvania who became suicide-*savers* through their spontaneous recognition of what needed to be done? Highlighting such people and events would provoke insight into the way freedom actually works.

Rather as contrast, still another museum option would be devoted to humor—a Location of Laughter (the LOL?). How have people in our own history enjoyed things over the centuries and what's so funny in other cultures and their past times. This would be, so far as I know, a unique contribution to global culture and open up new avenues of thought and insight into how peoples of the world are similar or distinctive. New York already has a Museum of Sex (a quite seriously informative place, by the way). Why not follow up with laughter; something that New York has done a lot to promote, intentionally, in the world?

The list goes on. Supplant the few existing toilet museums that now exist; such a museum in New York would raise issues like those brought up in chapter 2, particularly worldwide sanitation and the toilet's crucial role in building a metropolis. New York's restaurants could also be the basis of a museum, stressing how they translate polyglot culture into genres of food that then spread across the country and back to their originating locations—drawing upon different kinds of foodstuffs and altering agricultural practices near and far. Or maybe we could use a museum of clothing industry, not centered on style or fashion but on the ordinary stuff on people's backs, including how things were made, by whom, and where circulated (at one point 90 percent of all clothing bought in the United States was manufactured in New York). And just how do people choose what to wear, given their cultural location and the specifics of occasion? Maybe we are ready for a "Schmatta Museum," so named to signal the salience of Jews in the industry but also to pull clothing out of the high-fashion atelier and into the streets.

Finally, there is the possibility of building to serve the living. It once was common to memorialize those who fell in wars and other disasters with gyms, libraries, concert halls, schools, stadia, and swimming pools.[44] At Ground Zero, the emphasis—for both the replacement towers and the other edifices—was to stick with a convention of grandiose mourning.

• *Put Islam at Ground Zero.*

A group of prominent American Muslims tried to construct an Islamic Center in downtown Manhattan after 9/11. Although its opponents identified it as "at Ground Zero," the site is in fact several blocks away. Putting aside the fierce resistance it would have faced, the better option would indeed be to build it on the sixteen acres. It could itself be a striking project like the architect Jean Nouvel's greatly admired L'Institut du Monde Arabe, located in central Paris, a short distance from Notre Dame. One of the most elegant modern buildings of the late twentieth century, it celebrates—largely without controversy— Arab contributions to world civilization. Having something similar in New York would be even more useful, given the particular ignorance of Americans about Islam. But it also would be a security device. Muslims visiting from around the world would find a dignified presentation of their religion—in an American context. The U.S. system of beliefs could be seen respecting the intellectual, scientific, and aesthetic contributions of Islam. Islam's tendencies toward violence, like those in

Christianity and Judaism, would be put in context. It would be, in a number of respects, a propaganda piece for peace and would, in that way, recall the memorials at Hiroshima and Berlin.

• *Have creativity up front.*

An uncontested leader of show business, the United States could deploy entertainment. The creative economies are not just a part of the economic system, they are also a living, breathing resource embraced virtually everywhere. As the words from the musical "Rent," proclaim, "The opposite of war is not peace, it's creation!"[45] Turn Ground Zero toward Broadway or even Disney; hand off a piece to Apple and Google or their junior versions coming out of the garages of Brooklyn and Union Square (or wherever else in the world they currently brew). Maybe *South Park* should have a say. Or the stand-up comedians and performance artists. How about pavilions for street performers from New York and all parts of the world. Dictators, fundamentalists, and absolutists can't handle such diversions. As Mick Jagger (once a student at the London School of Economics) well knows, get sex on your side because it won't be on theirs. In Bali and New Orleans, people dance and sing at funerals; Christians in the United States now mark the events brought about by Jesus' death with bonnets, bunnies, and hunts for pastel-colored eggs. Only in some places and under specific conditions does death give rise to grievance, tombstones, and edifice. It may be best to lighten up.

• •

CHAPTER 6

Facing Katrina:
Illusions of Levee and Compulsion to Build

"Floods are an act of God, but flood losses are largely an act of man"—such was the mantra of the pioneer hydrological scholar, Gilbert White. White's analyses, beginning with a 1945 paper, showed that efforts to contain flood damage by building structures like flood walls and dams had the net result of increasing rather than decreasing risk to humans.[1] To "prevent" flood damage, we need to get out of the way of the water—it's as simple as that. The efforts so often made to stop the water with walls and dams—now known, following White, as the "levee effect"—only create risk. At present, a monument is being built to White in Boulder, Colorado, his last home base and still where some of the world's leading hydrologists do their research. But his advice, like theirs, is too often ignored.

This chapter examines how not taking White's advice worked itself out in New Orleans, when Katrina came to call. In the ensuing troubles, almost fifteen hundred people died, billions of dollars were lost in business and residential assets, and hundreds of thousands of lives were disrupted with many individuals never able to return. It is a story of faulty artifacts built out of an equally defective institutional structure, and all with a lot of people in the wrong place. We have a situation where the warning system of an advanced and sophisticated society met up with a response that was, in comparison, primitive—"the worst mishandled disaster I have ever seen in my life," says Enrico Quarantelli, a fifty year veteran of such events.[2] The "mishandling" to which Quarantelli refers was the immediate aftermath, but that was a consequence of a much longer history of error.

Katrina (along with its time-proximate hurricane, Rita) would "have to be," says Oliver Houck of Tulane's Law School, "the most well-predicted and publicized disaster in history."[3] Some of those warnings go back at least to the mid-nineteenth century. I gained my own familiarity with both the warnings and the lack of appropriate response through my research in New Orleans with sociologist Lee Clarke of Rutgers University and with several Ph.D. students from NYU and Rutgers. Our project aimed specifically to reconstruct the warnings and the reactions to them. We interviewed a total of eighty-five Gulf-area scientists and experts, drawn from a wide variety of fields.[4]

BACKGROUND LEVEES

Although in agreement that trouble was ahead, our experts placed different relative weights on specific causes of the disasters in the hurricane aftermath—with a tendency for each specialist to see his or her own discipline as having the most crucial and relevant information. But a master explanation, one I follow here, follows the classic reasoning of White. People were *organized* into vulnerability through political-economic machinations of the region and the federal government. The most fulsome application I know of this thesis has been put forward by a group of environmental sociologists: William Freudenburg, Robert Gramling, Shirley Laska, and Kai Erikson—themselves old hands at disaster research. They combine information from on-site scientists with certain urban theory concepts to describe how New Orleans was made so vulnerable.

Freudenburg and his colleagues push the idea of the "urban growth machine," a concept central to my own thinking over the years. For them it was key to explaining the deaths and destruction. At least in the United States, the argument goes, those who run cities exploit them for profit and power.[5] The key to profits for local and regional growth elites are higher revenues from more intensive and extensive property and industrial development. This dynamic holds back alternative agendas that might be more closely fitted to improving local quality of life or promoting ecological sustainability. While profits, particularly from real estate development, are concentrated in the hands of the few, the public at large bears the costs, including a disproportionate share of disaster risk. At the symbolic level, the city fathers, regardless of their benign contributions to local charities, festivals, and the like, engage in deception to sell their growth goods. If it comes to it, they hold back the scientific knowledge that might interfere. Beyond the usual duplicity of growth interests pushing unwholesome policies, Louisiana and New Orleans are legendary in their histories of corruption and opportunistic manipulations. As a retired congressman, Billy Tauzin, observed in reference not to Katrina troubles but the state's history over a longer period, "Half of Louisiana is under water and the other half is under indictment."[6]

The chicanery shows up virtually from the beginning. In merchandising stock in the Louisiana Company, the American John Law, operating under the patronage of the Duke of Orleans starting about 1716, bilked French investors with false claims of benevolent conditions, including climatic ones. Yellow fever was, in fact, decimating the population at the time, creating not only death but also large financial losses for investors.[7] Levee building also began at an early stage as a way to assure that the city was safe from the river. The French, in 1727, built a three-foot-high earth embankment. It worked, at least more or less, for a good while. New Orleans became the major commercial port on the continent outside of New York and Baltimore and was the fourth-largest city in the United States and its territories by 1840. With continued development of mid-America, it linked the great landmass between the Rockies and Appalachia to the Gulf of Mexico and to the oceans beyond. Investors built warehouses and factories in New Orleans as well as homes for workers and owners. And also, as a matter of course, more levees for protection.

As paving and clearance for farmlands and urbanization went on throughout the Midwest, ever larger volumes of water spilled off surfaces and into the Mississippi. An astonishing 40 percent of the continental United States drains into this single system of waterways, and the channeling anywhere in the system affects the overall flow.[8] The implications were known locally. In an 1850 federally commissioned report charged with making recommendations to prevent floods, author Charles Ellet identified the human-changed regional ecology as key. "The difficulty in protecting the delta from overflow," he wrote, "is produced by the artificial embankments along the borders of the Mississippi, and the cultivation of the praeries."[9]

The Ellet report was a follow-up to reports on floods from the prior year when the raised levees just upriver from the city gave way, submerging two hundred city blocks for weeks. In response, Ellet's findings not withstanding, levees went still higher. By the turn of the nineteenth century, they were above the city's rooftops. There have been nine major floods since 1735 with the last pre-Katrina big one occurring in 1927. The city was to become walled in on all sides, enclosed by what is now part of the larger system of levees along the Mississippi River system. When standing on the ground in New Orleans, neither the Mississippi River on the south nor Lake Pontchartrain on the northern border — the largest lake in the state — is visible; one must go about thirty feet up to see water that is indeed everywhere. It is the reason why ships on the river can appear so oddly gliding above city streets and rooftops of houses.

All this is under the official authority of the U.S. Army Corps of Engineers, which since the 1920s has been the agency responsible for the river system. The city is a barricaded bastion against nature: "Through its interaction with the Corps, the lower Mississippi has become, over the last century at least, something of a military artifact. To say, therefore, that New Orleans in the aftermath of Katrina was a city placed under martial law is rather redundant: the city's landscape has never been under anything *but* martial law," say local environmentalists Geoff Monaugh and Nicola Twilley."[10] The results, after generations of effort, are that the river moves faster and rises higher than it otherwise would and erodes the embankments, where exposed, around it. The river's rise, in a cause and effect relation, is in proportion to the changing levee height.

From fairly early on there were various proposals for levee alternatives such as spillways and reservoirs that would tap into the river during storm season and divert some of the flow to other places. There were schemes to move the levees back to make more "room for the river," a practice recommended by experience in the Netherlands.[11] In contrast to such prescient recommendations, the levee remained king. While so unwise in other regards, a key advantage of levees is that they take minimal amounts of land out of the development process compared to spillways, reservoirs, or simply declaring flood plains uninhabitable. Better to treat "a flood's symptoms, not its cause, which was development throughout the valley," as Ari Kelman summarizes in his history of the river and its city.[12]

The other great problem with the New Orleans levees is that they can serve as walls that trap water *into* the city, something to which New Orleans is especially prone given its very high water table, only two feet below the surface. Big rainstorms mean the water just sits in the bowl that makes up the local topography. The city is kept dry, when the weather is dry and when the flood walls are not leaking, by systems of pumps that hoist the water up and over the levees. Pump failure becomes still another way that the city can drown, as opposed to the levees breaking. This is how the great 1927 storm flooded the city: the pumps depended on electricity and when the electricity went out, the pumps became useless. Furthermore, workers on the job operate each set of pumps, at stations widely dispersed along the river edge. When the Katrina floods happened, the workers had to abandon their stations and the pumps with them (the Corps has now reinforced the pump stations to increase workers' ability to remain on the job).

The setup leads to consequences familiar to observers of other human-nature disaster patterns. By preventing natural cycles of tree and grass burn-off, forest fire prevention means that when fires do occur, they are ferocious and harder to control. Smoky the Bear was wrong on a number of counts: even "you" cannot prevent forest fires and it is not even sensible to try (much less throw the book at the people who forget to stomp out their campfire). The paradox remains that the human ability to reduce over time the consequences of hazards has the effect of increasing their catastrophic potential.[13] Applied to the problem of Mississippi flooding, efforts to enhance security—abetted by technical ignorance and some willful scheming—makes future catastrophe more likely.

What else "caused" Katrina? Destruction of the wetlands is part of the answer. Trees and grasses hold down the force of winds and water from storm surge.[14] As they disappear, protection does too. And the history of the region has been a loss of cypress and marsh plants. In total, since 1932, approximately three hundred thousand acres of the Pontchartrain Basin wetland has been lost to open water[15]—an area one-third larger than the combined five boroughs of New York City; or, to keep the New York-centric focus, a Manhattan Island worth of land lost every year.[16] Translated to the metric of small U.S. states, between 1930 and 2000 the Gulf Coast lost a landmass equal to the size of Delaware.[17] Some of this loss comes from storm surge that would occur with hurricanes no matter what the artificial interventions, but parsing out the specifics becomes impossible since nature and human interference have so dynamically intertwined.

Direct loss of plant material also comes from logging for lumber and tearing up tree roots to harvest for commercial home garden peat consumption, a practice that has drastically declined given how little is now left. But the indirect forces are the most consequential; particularly those that cause salt water from the Gulf of Mexico to make its way into the adjoining wetlands. Canal building is a major culprit, especially from the oil industry. Drilling rigs are portable—they are floated from one site to another where they are then semi-immersed to do their job in place. Once the oil has been tapped and set up for pumping, the rig moves on to a next location ready for drilling. But to move them around, channels need to be dredged. Dredging involves loosening the soil so that it washes away with the tidal action, leaving channels through which the barges and motorized boats can pass through the marsh. The shores of the canals erode over time and thus widen, furthering salt-water intrusion. The scale is huge. Over the forty-year period after 1937, twenty-five thousand wells were drilled in the Louisiana wetlands serviced through four thousand miles of canals. Before the advent of environmental review in the late 1970s, imposed by the National Environmental Protection Act (NEPA), there was virtually no oversight or rules for restoration. About 10 percent of wetland loss comes from these canals.[18] As additional liability, fluid withdrawal for oil and gas production furthers subsidence, with one estimate putting the total loss from oil activities at 43 percent of marsh erosion.[19]

The Takings of Mister Go

Most consequential of all the regional earthworks was the construction of something called the Mississippi River-Gulf Outlet, or "Mister Go" as it is known—MRGO is the acronym. Freudenburg and his colleagues cite this as the primary culprit in causing the Katrina mayhem. Built by the Corps of Engineers beginning in the 1950s, this big ditch, seventy-six miles long and thirty-six feet deep, shortened the route between the city's industrial shoreline and the Gulf of Mexico. To build it, more dirt was excavated than in creating the Panama Canal. Physically linking directly into the Gulf, MRGO was intended as a boon to commercial shipping. But because it also provides wind and water with a straight shot from the Gulf into the heart of the city, some locals called it "Hurricane Highway."

When the Katrina Big One did come, water coursing through MRGO merged with water pouring in through another major canal, the Gulf Intracoastal Waterway (see figure 17 for a map with the details). Storm surge pushed into both of the canals from the adjacent Lake Borgne area (to the city's east), creating a single water expanse in between them. The high outside walls of the two canals thus formed a funnel that drove storm surge toward what became a hypodermic needle into the city's heart. Water then pounded into the major north-south canal, the "Industrial Canal." Floodwalls were not just overtopped but *breached* at various points—catastrophic because unlike overtopping or natural flooding which drains down, breaches require staunching at point of fissure or collapse, a logistical nightmare. There were still other failures, including water pouring in from Lake Pontchartrain (to the north), where despoiled wetlands yielded still another path of destruction. As shown by the map's shaded area, most of the city ended up under water.

This scenario, based on MRGO as a major source of the disaster, had been precisely detailed three months before Katrina by Hassan Mashriqui, research coastal engineer at Louisiana State University. It had also been predicted in a more general way for years before, by Mashriqui and others. Mashriqui was to ruefully remark, "I showed how dangerous that outlet was—there was no ambiguity. And now it's all come true."[20] The major authorities and political leaders had all

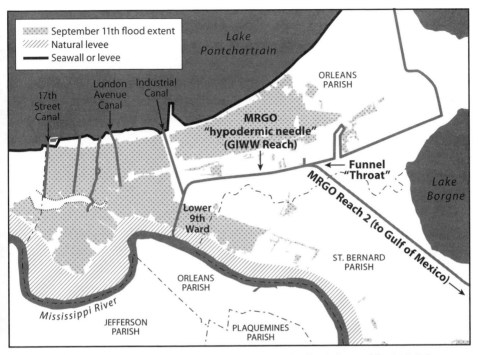

Figure 17. Map of New Orleans showing "funnel effect" formed by MRGO meeting with the Gulf Intracoastal Waterway—the "GIWW Reach." Based on image by Cliff Dupechin originally published in World Watch Magazine (September/October 2007).

worried about the wrong danger—rain and river flow instead of their own contrivances.

Efficient in creating a hurricane highway into the city, MRGO also distributes salinity from the Gulf into the city's lake and internal waterways and wetlands. The Gulf's leading ecology organization calls it "the single greatest man-induced impact to the Pontchartrain Basin estuary system" (the name given to the surrounding locale), one that has "triggered major shifts in habitats and fisheries, caused wetland loss, increased salinity intrusion and created a one-hundred-square-mile dead zone in Lake Pontchartrain."[21] Again, erosion increases the canal's width over time. Originally constructed six hundred and fifty feet wide, it now stretches, in places, to six thousand feet in width.

MRGO was virtually useless at the moment of its completion because it was too shallow to handle the new generation of ships used in ocean transport. It was "obsolete on delivery."[22] The original cost-benefit evaluation from the Army Corps of Engineers, which used what it described as "conservative" assumptions of future use, gave it a strongly net positive economic evaluation. Economic value is what it has certainly failed to deliver to the local economy or any other, despite enormous ongoing subsidies, mostly from the federal government. In 2004, the last year of its operations, MRGO was used for slightly less than twelve round trips, consisting of ships laden with frozen chickens and junk steel. When divided by the annual maintenance dredging cost of just over $19 million during that fiscal year, the subsidy amount was an astonishing $1.5 million per round trip—and this does not include costs associated with original construction or other maintenance expenses over the years.[23]

Despite its uselessness and annual dredging costs, the project could not be turned off. As Freudenburg and his group remark about the growth machine they investigate in New Orleans, and growth machines more generally, "[It] has no internal brakes and no sensors to take note of the damage it is doing as it churns along."[24] And those who manage the growth apparatus, as the authors go on to say, press forward, reshaping the natural world "until the momentum of some venture carries them across the outer line and they come face to face with disaster on the other side."[25] Post-Katrina, plans are finally underway to close MRGO, but not fill it: that would be unfeasible given the huge mountain of soil that would be needed.

One of the pitches used to get the backing to build MRGO, and in particular to get the federal money, was its role in national security.[26] In the Corps' cost-benefit study, the analysts stressed the defense rationale. Because of its relevance to the larger issues raised in this book, I quote part of it here:

> National defense not only involves military installations, but also complete systems of transportation by air, land and water . . . (Item 78) . . . In the recent World War, the port of New Orleans, the Mississippi River, and the system of inland waterways were important factors in deploy-

ment of war supplies, but locks and terminals at New Orleans were greatly overtaxed. With continuing growth of population and development of resources of the Mississippi river, the inland waterways will be used for a still greater extent in another national emergency. . . . Due to the unpredictable nature of future wars, the hazards inherent in industrial concentrations at coastal ports, and the possibility of attack without warning . . . port development plans should include provision for potential sites required by new emergencies.[27]

The report goes on to note "New Orleans riverside wharves, of timber construction on long wood piles, cannot be expected to resist destruction by bombing as practiced in the recent war, and attack by atomic bombs is now possible."[28] Again, MRGO was presented as a positive alternative. And here's the cost-benefit clincher: "Provision of such facilities in time of peace so that they may be available for adaptation to the requirements of any emergency is patently in the national interest."[29] Forward dig.

SINKING AHEAD

Although the French put New Orleans in a sinking place, they had the smarts to put their own settlement at the higher elevations along the river's banks, which is where the celebrated "French Quarter" now sits. But the city rests on about twenty thousand years of deposited silt. Over time, this soft underbelly compacts and now subsides at the rate of about one foot per fifty-year period.[30] River deltas have rich soils and have transportation advantages, being places where rivers join larger bodies of water. The great and vulnerable cities of Shanghai, Mumbai, and Bangkok, like New Orleans, owe their existence to just this pattern. Today, twenty-four out of the world's thirty-three major deltas and the cities built on them are similarly sinking. The natural remedy would be the continued deposit of silt, something complicated by the channeling of rivers and, of course, the subsequent overlay of urbanization. And even if logistically possible, and there are some possibilities at least in the case of New Orleans, the Mississippi River has become less sediment heavy due to dam, canal, and reservoir construction on upper parts of the watercourse. At New Orleans the sediment load is only one-fourth of what it was in the mid-nineteenth century.[31] What sediment there is now, because of the channels and hard surfacing, goes past the city and empties into the Gulf of Mexico, raising the sea bottom in unhelpful ways.

Here again, there had been early warnings. In an 1807 legal dispute sometimes considered the most important in Louisiana history, what today we might term an environmental advocate urged that certain lands at the river edge ("the batture") be held as open space "to repair the losses of the soil which is perpetually falling away, owing to its natural slope, and its situation below the level of the river."[32] Nineteenth-century maps indicate that "the muddy shoal" had almost doubled in one hundred years.[33] The legal case was to drag on, but the net result was development on this very land, albeit with public and quasi-public facilities—the Convention Center and a brewery now made into a shopping mall. It illustrates loss of a natural means of alluvial restoration, in this case one that formed a natural levee in front of the city.

As global warming increases sea level, it enhances direct potential for flood as well as indirect damage through further salt-water intrusion into the wetlands—along with, some experts suspect, subjecting the region to more intense and frequent storms. Solving the global warming problem is obviously not a feasible project for locals, although one might have thought their representatives in Congress would fervently support efforts to ward off climate change. But local authorities and growth elites have not been in the forefront of national debates on these issues—far from it. Both Louisiana's Republican Senator David Vitter and its Democrat Senator Mary Landrieu support oil; Landrieu, for example, was one of the few Democrats to back Arctic drilling. Politics in the state, as in adjacent Mississippi, is strongly on the right and pro-extraction.

Environmental threats tend to have an insidious quality as part of how they work. Atmospheric poisons grow incrementally and are often invisible and without sound or scent. Ulrich Beck posits things would be different if, in his poignant example, radioactivity itched.[34] But we see that New Orleans floods do recur (and as more than an itch), not only in a big way with periodic catastrophes, but also as experienced by residents as minor flooding with every rainy season. It is only the artifice of engineering, such as the pumps that pull the water out and away, and organizational arrangements like flood insurance that keep the reality from intruding—in the same way as the continuous political reassurance of safety sustains the illusion of safety.

This "unpolitics" allows cities and parishes to issue building permits as land becomes officially safe by virtue of levees and related structures. Private insurance companies, if necessary backed up by government guarantees, issue policies. Banks make mortgage loans. In a pattern already familiar to us from the subway and airport cases, the interventions have the advantage of *appearing* to solve the problems, however much the problems are themselves an outcome of the prior interventions. People become sufficiently relaxed to return, rebuild, and expand their presence on the landscape. Between 1978 and 2001 in pre-Katrina days, the Federal Emergency Management Agency (FEMA) paid out $1.08 billion for Louisiana flood claims, the great bulk coming from the New Orleans area. The city has thus, despite its "setbacks," expanded over the years to fill in additional vulnerable land.

BLAMING THE CULPABLE

So all this spells trouble in river city, abetted, thanks again to the routine corruption in the area, as building codes—even weak ones—are ignored. Addressing the tolls to human life and property, Quarantelli puts the blame squarely on those who manipulate government and infrastructure for their own selfish reasons—a refrain he has long sounded. Says Quarantelli, "The violations of building codes and zoning regulations are often carried out by network linkages involving, among others, construction and building companies, elements of the real estate sector, and government inspectors. This kind of criminal behavior almost ensures that disasters and catastrophes will be worse than they would otherwise be. . . . Overall the frequency and significance of disaster/catastrophe-related white-collar and business crimes dwarf by almost any criteria even the worst of those rare mass looting occasions in catastrophes."[35] The term "corporate manslaughter" has been around since about the mid-1980s to describe such modes of criminality and is an official crime, since 2007, in the United Kingdom.

Some local leaders put the case in a still harsher light—albeit without mentioning their own local business and political leaders as at least complicit in the mischief and misjudgments. The president of St Bernard Parish (which adjoins the city of New Orleans), Henry "Junior" Rodriguez, Jr., had this to say in his court testimony in the Katrina aftermath: "I'll be totally honest with you. I think, today, that the corps and the steamboat association should be indicted for murder."[36] The president of nearby Jefferson Parish (which also adjoins the city of New Orleans) used the M word as well, and wept on national television as he fixed the blame: "Bureaucracy has committed murder here in the greater New Orleans area, and bureaucracy has to stand trial before Congress now."[37]

The New Orleans pernicious cycle has at least the pedigree of time: initial development, led by the original and, alas, not altogether candid French locals, leads to artificial intervention that creates additional urbanization, which then yields still more vulnerability. *Apparent* security, part of a security theater of a still different sort than that found at subways, airports, or toilets, is driven by wishful real estate opportunism. It builds insecurity into the future. The process continues post-Katrina, as political scientist Joseph Westphal (himself a former Interior Department official and former Assistant Secretary of the U.S. Army) summarizes, "While it would make sense to rebuild New Orleans in ways to avoid a repetition of the destruction caused by Katrina, the exact opposite is happening. Priorities and resources are flowing to new public works in the very places where Katrina showed us our greatest vulnerability."[38] The new rules generally accept buildings constructed three feet above ground, a height that does not at all deal with historic flood levels. The Corps presumes a security effect from its levees and fixes standards on that basis, but standards insufficiently comprehensive to forestall the kind of failures evident in the Katrina case.

Levees are political. Although its military moniker no doubt helps clear away opposition that may develop, the Army Corps of Engineers is more part of the growth machine than the one that makes wars. It does not respond to the dictates of generals of the military or the U.S. Defense Secretary. Instead, its military officials and civilian employees, the latter of whom make up the vast majority of the Corps workforce (35,000 civilians versus 650 military members[39]), take their orders from Congress. Logs get rolled. Local leaders draw on Congressional representatives—usually from safe seats and hence high in the House and Senate committee structure—to implement schemes hatched at the local level. This results not only in an infrastructural logic that is ecologically misguided, but also in individual projects that follow parochial political goals instead of a master plan evolving from technical overview. So levees rise higher where politicians are strong and remain lower where they are weak. Heights are inconsistent and technical standards unevenly applied. As Westphal remarks, "The corps is often seen as the architect of projects when in fact projects are often hatched by local entities, industry, and support from members of Congress. The Corps then finds itself in the middle of a very intense balancing act between the administration it serves under and the local communities that want a greater share of the economic pie."[40] Add into this the antiregulatory Washington spirit. The Corps has lost almost its entire budget for long-term planning, with only project-specific funding remaining. Ironically, "safety" and "security" are the omnipresent justifications attached to such projects that, if anything, work against the Corps' own professional standards—standards which are higher than those it is allowed to implement.

The New Orleans levees were not, even in the narrow sense of standing up to the anticipated water events, what they were cracked up to be. In some cases, they were constructed on a base of soft clay and peat that was destined to give way as water penetrated *under* their concrete moorings and pressed from the other side. Ivor Van Heerden, a former deputy director of the Hurricane Research Center at Louisiana State University, asserted, with documentation from other sources as well, that construction of the 17th Street levee, one which failed in Katrina, had not sufficiently taken into account underlying soil quality, despite internal warnings to that effect.[41] A still additional contributing factor appears to be, of all things, termites. In constructing levees, the builders placed a mixture of oil and organic waste product from sugar cane production (called "bagasse") between concrete sections to allow for expansion and contraction. Termites eat the bagasse, creating voids below the structures.[42] They are also at work on the roots of large trees near the floodwalls. They eat that wood, leaving caverns of weakened earth. The rush to "protect" fails to consider such insect subtleties.

For its various missteps the federal government, through the Corps, is now the subject of an enormous litigation claim, involving billions in dollars, with the potential for additional billions to follow. The litigation focuses heavily on MRGO, not only because of the scale of damage attributed to it, but also because it is where legal vulnerability may exist. That is because MRGO was built to facilitate commerce. Explicit laws as well as prior court precedents exclude federal flood control projects from damage claims. As part of such the current litigation, the Corps now claims MRGO was always such a flood-protection device. A federal judge has allowed the case to move forward. Whatever the outcome, the Corps strategy shows us how the security label can help insulate an agency.[43]

Pinning down those responsible for calamities can be easy when a driver mows people down or someone releases sarin poison, as the miscreants did in the Tokyo Underground. But those who commit infrastructure mayhem through what appears as part of the development process are not so easily identified as culprits. Present at ribbon-cuttings and with their names on nearby plaques, they disappear when bridges fall or river currents go out of whack. The trouble happens later on when the development villains are gone, or at least gone from the public eye. As Stephen Graham remarks in regard to actions that close off borders and deprive residents of food and clean water, the resulting deaths "are displaced in time and space from the capricious gaze of the mainstream media."[44] Lesser crimes, and Mississippi levee and canal building is indeed lesser than Graham's examples, nevertheless partake of a similar irresponsibility, facilitated by separation of place where the action occurred (like upstream) and the time of its doing (like a previous decade) from place and time of consequence. And all in the face of available information showing that each set of moves was itself a source of the problem and not its remedy.

Still another human-made "cause" of Katrina is the deflection of resources, including national concern, away from natural disaster and toward the threat posed by terror. Again, we need to flash back to New York and the events of 9/11, which themselves were a choice point between "hard" and "soft" reactions. In the wake of the attacks, the Department of Homeland Security (DHS; of which FEMA would soon join with the Transportation Security Administration [TSA] to be a part) was not looking to the kind of soft solutions implied by having more school buses at the ready and cypress trees in the ground. President Bush's appointments process put incompetent leaders in charge at FEMA and caused a huge exit of talent, conclusions drawn not just by outside critics but by the consultants (Mitre International) hired by FEMA's director prior to the Katrina events.[45] The national government was not a likely source of guidance or model of reform before crisis hit or in the aftermath.

There were other useful things to have been doing, like engineering and egress studies of existing buildings—whether in New York or New Orleans—to determine which would make appropriate evacuation centers. As one of our emergency officials informed us in a New Orleans interview, efforts were being launched to inventory the region's public structures for hurricane resistance, something that had not previously been done despite warnings that those previously designated were, in fact, vulnerable. The one and only such structure identified as an official "refuge of last resort" for the City of New Orleans was the Superdome, which in the language of the state's Emergency Operations Plan would allow those taking shelter "to be protected from the high winds and heavy rains from the storm." But the Superdome was to lose part of its roof, exposing the thousands who were using it to the downpours and heat of the Louisiana summer. It was their stranded miseries that became TV fare the world over.

DHS provided New Orleans (and many other U.S. cities) with goods that held little prospect for potential use. One emergency management informant we interviewed in the Gulf area contrasted what officials were getting from the DHS with actual needs:

> I mean, they're buying robots and they're buying Hazmat suits, I mean, and of course we need those things but I don't need every sheriff's deputy in town to have a hazmat suit. I mean, I don't need ten robots, you know, if we got one robot in Metropolitan New Orleans we gotta ro-

bot. . . . So for me now beginning in 2002, late 2002, 2003, 2004 to try to get money locally through the process, through the pipeline for those agencies that I know really need it and are doing work that's necessary for the good . . . but I can't continue to fund these projects because I've gotta buy robots for sheriff's deputies.

Indeed, in the summer just before Katrina, DHS turned down the request of the City of New Orleans for a fleet of aluminum flatboats to transport flood victims. DHS determined that the request did not meet its criteria, which, as we also know from the experience of New York transit, prioritize defense against chemical and bomb attacks, rather than improving on utilitarian bric-a-brac.

Before Katrina, there indeed had been a full-scale eight-day "table-top" exercise, "Hurricane Pam Exercise," held in Baton Rouge in July 2004 to simulate a next big storm and its consequences. It brought together all the relevant emergency-response groups: officials of the state of Louisiana, the cities and parishes (counties) of the Gulf Coast, as well as the federal government. The Corps of Engineers was also well represented to inform about the protections in place, assuring those gathered—in response to explicit questioning—that the levees would hold. Other things that were worked out included exactly who was to do what, when, and where. At the simulation, everyone performed according to procedural script, federal officials included, handling anticipated losses of power and water, shortages of food and medicine, and the reality of mass injury and death. Pam projected fifty thousand fatalities and one hundred thousand casualties compared to a Katrina toll of far less. So the "rehearsal" involved operations of rescue and support well in excess of what was needed to deal with Katrina.

But in the real event, it did not go according to plan, as so many people in the world could see through the eyes of the TV cameras that did manage to be on the scene. One particularly memorable conversation I had was with the former head of Emergency Management of Jefferson Parish, Walter Maestri. His jurisdiction was the area adjacent to the city on the north, a place with (then) a population of about 450,000, the majority of which were white, but by no means a population that was (or is) highly educated or financially well off.

At the Pam exercise, Maestri reports he was skeptical about the timing and type of federal aid that would follow in a real disaster. But still he relied on what he had been told and he consistently enacted the procedures that had been so carefully worked out. The Feds had told him to be ready for forty-eight to sixty hours of isolation, with seventy-two hours the extreme upper limit. He instead prepared for ninety-six hours. In fact, it took eleven and a half days for the first contact from FEMA and the arrival of needed supplies—baby food, diapers, water, ice, medicines, and so forth. So he, along with other emergency managers, had to, like our subway workers, invent as they went along. They abandoned assumptions on which the whole kit and caboodle of security had been built—such as robust engineering, official demarcations of areas supposedly safe from flooding, and expectations of how the disaster would unfold and where jurisdictional authority would reside.

The water was coming from the "wrong" place—due to breaches in the canal levees—not overtopping, as had been a possible concern, but collapse of levees and flood walls. Here from my interview with him, once again is Maestri, now explaining how he learned, from direct report, that the water was not coming from water overflowing levee height but instead was somehow coming into places it should not have been:

> Well, we continued to get the reports and the water does continue to rise in these neighborhoods. So that led [to us thinking]—say, wait a minute, we've gotta go look at those canals, those drainage canals . . . that's where you're getting the water in Jefferson Parish.

Because he realized how the storm surge was entering the city, Maestri wanted to reach his counterpart in the city of New Orleans (the Orleans Parish), where the water was coming in and then flooding his own adjacent jurisdiction:

> Well, the first thing I do is try to find (the official in) New Orleans 'cause it's their, supposedly it's their problem, their jurisdictions, their territory (and) I can't find them. They have, you know, the communications is nil at this time, the powers have come down, we have very little communication. . . . So I gave the order from our perspective to do whatever

you've got to do whether it's in Orleans Parish or not, just to stop the water from flowing through.

And we threw everything we had, I mean abandoned automobiles, whatever, into the hole to try to fill that hole. We had a three-hundred-yard hole where the levee was gone and . . . as much as a million gallons a second was flowing through . . . it was picking up residences that were there off of their foundations, spinning them around as if they were toothpicks in the commode.

At one point, as stated by a different official, Alan Broussard, in his *Meet the Press* testimony (and supported by Maestri in his interview with me), local authorities physically interposed themselves against FEMA. Still, during the immediate mayhem of post-storm recovery, he said on national television,

> Yesterday—yesterday—FEMA comes in and cuts all of our emergency communication lines. They cut them without notice. Our sheriff, Harry Lee, goes back in, he reconnects the line. He posts armed guards on our line and says, "No one is getting near these lines."[46]

These were extreme acts of rule breaking.

At the national level, explaining lack of effective FEMA response, the news media told of official requests that had not been made in the appropriate way and at the right time. Federal authorities apparently considered the local governments' requests as too vague; they needed specific requisition. The forms had to be filled out. Focus of blame moved back and forth between local, state, and national officials. But no one should attribute the inadequacy of response to the catastrophe to "bureaucracy," as did the distraught president of Jefferson Parrish on national television. The emergency management officials quoted earlier were also bureaucrats, as were many others who used common sense to figure out how to proceed in the midst of assumptions being proven—moment by moment—incorrect. The U.S. Coast Guard won rounds of praise for its policy, "Rescue first, ask questions later." They rescued many thousands with a bureaucracy that works "upside down" in emergencies—those closest to the action can change the mission, without fear of recrimination. There were also people, like Sherriff

Lee, who knew better what to do, albeit they were flirting with dangerous vigilantism. Florida's state emergency manager began sending rescue teams into Mississippi before being asked.[47] Real bureaucracies, as opposed to caricatured Weberian models of them, often deal effectively with changing or even unique circumstances. The failure did not stem from a mode of social organization but from the perverse priorities that allowed slavish rule following to persist even under grave circumstance. Given the situation at hand, a pathological bureaucracy was at work here, not a normal one. Seen this way, bureaucracy varies in how it functions. Indeed, it varied in the case of Katrina; rote rule-following was not the universal response even there.

A founding sociological observation, of course, is that organizational actors follow rules—and so they do. Adhering to standard procedures gets a vast amount of routine accomplished, as when the subway workers consistently look for stragglers before pushing the buttons to close their cars' doors. The protocols also rule at the firehouse: the bell rings, firefighters slide down the pole, and jump in the truck. At each scale, there are also specifications on how to fill out paperwork, who will give the clearance, which budget to use, and which agency takes control. But sociologists have also learned that people bend their rules (as we saw in the subways, and at the airports too), responding, for example, to pressures from coworkers and from evolving circumstance of an organization's needs.[48] So there are also, in the sociology lexicon, "informal rules" that affect who does what and at what pace.[49] The organization becomes suppler and more effective. But this still does not go far enough in recognizing the rule ingenuity at play. Bureaucrats, like everyone else, invent as they go, even as they know they will have to figure out how to explain it afterward. Rules, formal or informal, thus operate as a *resource* people use to explain their own and their colleagues' behavior rather than simply determine that behavior in the first place. Instead of merely following through on dictates, individuals have a sense—gestalt-like—of what to do given the context. This frees up their capacity to innovate, to make the rules come alive on the fly.

For good or ill, actors find a way. Receptionists in a welfare agency, sociologist Don Zimmerman showed through ethnographic study, ignore even a simple rule like "first come, first served." They do so when, for example, a screaming child makes it impossible for other workers to be heard by their clients.[50] The family with the child goes first; squeaky wheel gets some grease so that all the other wheels can be kept going. Harried hospital emergency room doctors, whose oath prescribes otherwise, work less hard to save lives of derelicts whose alcoholism they sense will lead to their near-term death anyway.[51] Given what can be harsh pressures of the moment, they set their own priorities and ration care. Sometimes actors discover, from the welter of regulations, another rule, a "better" rule they can declare to be following. They act under the presumption—and this is often a crucial element—that others will later see they did the right thing, no matter what rules they might seem to have ignored. To avoid being dopes, they *must* use such discretion. Otherwise, their mindless rule following appears incompetent, obstreperous, or maybe even insane.[52] And although, as learned by Zimmerman (and his colleagues), 911 emergency call takers can insist on just the facts and in the prescribed order, his research also shows that dispatchers more often adapt and improvise on the script. They follow the common sense that a given situation demands, and they dispatch assistance even if the caller has not enabled them to conform to every aspect of protocol.[53]

Such ad hoc innovation also happens at high levels of organizational life. It was because an official chose to ignore orders coming down from the Prime Minister of Japan that the greatest of the melt down dangers was averted at Reactor Number 1 at the Fukushima Daiichi Power Station in the 2011 nuclear crisis. Masao Yoshida chose to inject seawater to cool down the reactor, and persisted even when told to stop; his decision was later hailed as the only way to have realistically dealt with the disaster.[54] In a very different sort of case, in the aftermath of the Iranian hostage crisis of 1979, the Canadian ambassador in Tehran hid six American diplomats in his living quarters and issued them false Canadian passports for a secret exit—all contrary to Canadian and international law. In retrospect, the Canadian ambassador used an "of course" rhetoric ("a matter of conscience") to explain himself.[55] The ambassador, his wife, and two others on staff were subsequently awarded the Order of Canada, Canada's highest civilian honor. One of the awardees, being a Guyanese-born British subject was technically ineligible, but she got it anyway. For its part, the U.S. Congress awarded the Congressional Gold Medal to the law-breaking Canadian ambassador.

In the Katrina case, similar extraordinary measures were taken, although not much among FEMA officials. The hapless FEMA director Michael Brown (a.k.a "Heck of a Job Brownie") along with others did a poor job of ferreting out which rules to apply and how to apply them. Brown had indeed urged his staff, as they were preparing their Katrina response, to "lean forward and get right to the edge of the envelope." He reassured them, "You're not going to catch any flak from me."[56] But the message does not appear to have sunk in. According to the watch officer on duty at FEMA in Washington as the storm approached—Leo Bosner, a career emergency planner at FEMA—his superiors were almost casual compared to the danger he and others were watching and warning about. He and his colleagues were incredulous at the lack of urgency: "We're saying: 'Oh my God, Why aren't we doing more? Why aren't we getting the orders? Why isn't this being treated like a real emergency?' People were just lost."[57] Preparations were being put in place for only a routine hurricane, not one that was believed to be beyond Category 3 and with impacts that might approach the horrendous conditions envisioned in the Pam exercise. The attitude appears to have been desultory, with a noise level in the main headquarters center described by Bosner as "the sounds of routine."[58]

A big hang-up at FEMA—and all the way up the chain of command—was how to classify the evolving emergency. If the levees had merely been *topped*, it would mean the flooding would end as water drained out of the city. But if the levees had been *breached*, the adjacent waters from canals, the river, and the lake would continue to course through New Orleans and steadily rise. As it turns out, given the role of MRGO, the latter (the breach, and in more than one place) was the case. But early reports of "breach" were either ignored or misheard.[59]

One of the stakes in "topping" versus "breach" is that only the latter type of event, in some of the federal interpretations, would permit a national response called for in a state of *catastrophe*. Only if an event gets the "catastrophe" designation can the president of the United States or the secretary of Homeland Security command all federal assets to deal with a crisis. Otherwise, again in some interpretations, the federal government must await state assistance requests, something that—depending on the retrospective accounts one accepts—did or did not occur in an appropriate way. Deputy Secretary of Homeland Security Michael Jackson held that the catastrophe designation should be reserved "exclusively for terrorist events."[60] Never mind, as the *Wall Street Journal* reporters Christopher Cooper and Robert Block wrote in their reconstruction of Katrina response, that "a large hurricane hitting New Orleans fit the government's very definition of a catastrophic event, as outlined in the fifteen most serious disaster scenarios that Homeland Security had compiled in 2004."[61]

Rules are narrow and constraining if you are without a sufficient contrary motivation, and that is what was apparently absent. Where would such a contrary motivation come from? First, people need a lateral scan that takes in, gestalt-like, the larger context. And part of that context is the suffering of others. The deeper and the more heartfelt the response to the suffering, the more energetic will be the search and rescue for the procedures that can work. Ideally, it is as if oneself or one's own family were in desperate straits. Affect counts.

It also helps to think that one's rule breaking will coordinate with what other people are thinking and doing—a blink of understanding that one is in synch with a community of actors and not alone on a limb of private empathy. Having a sense of the larger world and its arrangement of decencies separates the narrow, of-the-moment vigilante from the actor with a sense of what "everyone" knows to be right in a circumstance of this particular sort. So individuals can be encouraged to think they can get away with commandeering a private bus to pull off a rescue, move funds across budgetary categories to solve a finance problem, and contact people out of the sanctioned communication order. Douglas Doan, a DHS official in the Office of the Private Sector, put generators and massive provisions from Wal-Mart on the government tab with no authorization or contracts. He did know that Wal-Mart actually had capacity to make deliveries from its Gulf area distribution centers. A political appointee and early supporter of George Bush, Doan explained he knew "the President would agree with it."[62] You can throw other people's private property, like their cars, into a hole to try and stem the water's onslaught, as Maestri did.

Sometimes it is a closer call. The subway operator who opened his doors at the World Trade Center was thinking, "I know I'm going to have to hear about this one," as he decided to stop the train. Highly uncertain at the moment, he had it pegged right; he correctly, as it turned out, gauged the relation between his actions and the overall reception they would receive. He was not, in fact, reprimanded but instead appreciated—although no medals from Congress or visits to the White House. Anything that strengthens a sense of social support for initiatives to do the right thing makes people more effective under duress. Another way to put it is that the right politics happens not just at the helm of decision making or even in the protest movements in the streets but in the warp and woof of actors' decisions up and down the hierarchy.

RACISM AND RESCUE

Evacuation in New Orleans did work on a vastly large scale and to such an extent that one set of observers has called it "the most successful rapid evacuation of a major city in human history."[63] But it did not work for everyone equally. According to one set of statistics, there was no racial bias to the mayhem; there were higher rates of death among whites than blacks. But this appears mistaken. The key to the misinterpretation is that so many of the victims were elderly, the group that, conforming to Eric Klinenberg's oft-cited finding, are most vulnerable to disaster.[64] And in New Orleans, the elderly were disproportionately white. If we control for age, as did Patrick Starkey in his detailed analysis of Katrina victims, then the findings reverse themselves: blacks died disproportionately, and it was black neighborhoods that had the highest rates of fatality.[65]

Beyond the death statistics, only ever available *after* a catastrophe, is the issue of who was *evidently* at risk. Television reporting, including that of sympathetic individuals and African American activists, focused on black people in trouble. Helping New Orleans was thus a matter of helping black people. This may not have helped dispatch aid versus the other possible response to disaster, dispatching control.

Indeed, race in the media also portrayed black people as *causing* trouble, and thus putting whites at risk. Much less frequently depicted were black people helping whites survive as well as other black people, which was happening on a massive scale, as Pamela Jenkins has pointed out.[66] Television networks endlessly played the same loops of black people either crying for help or looting. It is not only the public at large that got its information from these TV reports. It was also, given the lack of significant government intelligence on the ground, how Washington was getting information. The twin stereotypes of African American life were brought forward: poverty and lawlessness, even atavistic in flavor. The city's mayor (himself African American), working from media reports of mayhem, characterized conditions in the Superdome as "animalistic."[67] In sharp contrast, the veteran FEMA official who was first on the scene at the Superdome, Marty Bahamonde, was to oppose all such characterizations saying. "They were the most peaceful 25,000 people in horrid conditions I have ever been around."[68] But that word did not get out.

I think that in much of America, poor and black lives are worth less, and this impacts organizational responses to save them. Anything in the "structure of feeling" that inhibits empathy for victims, or weakens the assumption that others share it, undermines the likelihood of effective rescue. Some of the callousness was not very subtle: several days after the storm, a large group of primarily African Americans trying to escape the city across the Crescent City bridge were blocked at gunpoint by police of the neighboring town of Gretna, Louisiana, and kept from crossing in. The Gretna authorities, without internal resources to offer as aid, were evidently also made afraid by the reports of looting and shooting in New Orleans (a Gretna police officer on the scene was said to have remarked, according to an NPR report, "We're not going to have another Superdome down here").[69] More horribly, New Orleans police themselves opened fire on a group of unarmed and innocent individuals on a different bridge, the Danziger Bridge (within the city), who were similarly attempting merely to find shelter. The police killed two and wounded another four. Local courts exonerated the police but the U.S. Department of Justice later indicted them (and others) on charges related to the attacks, including for an alleged subsequent cover-up.

Even a little bit of racism goes a long way in such an environment. It was certainly enough to foster something quite subtle: a default to literalness, to not being able to see a way to take extraordinary action to save others. Such inhumane practice is always available to the irresponsibly prudent, and racial (as well as class) difference helps it come into play. This is another face of institutional racism—the potential to withhold contextually informed ad hoc reasoning when the victims are devalued. And it no doubt helped harm (and kill) some white people as well, such as several Canadian tourists also on the Crescent City Bridge, stranded as they were and associated with the stereotype of who was in trouble (and doing trouble).

In no uncertain terms, the military moved in. A total of seventy-two thousand troops were on the ground about two weeks after the levees failed.[70] It was not, to be sure, a military operation without some restraint. Russell Honoré, the lieutenant general in charge of the operation (and a man who self-identifies as mixed race, part African American) is said—according to some blog sites on post-Katrina issues—to have cautioned a soldier against his threatening display of a weapon, saying, "We're on a rescue mission, damn it!"[71] But the tone of other elements within the military struck a different cord, in particular that of the general in command of the National Guard troops actually on the ground. Here is how an article appearing in the *Army Times* described it:

> NEW ORLEANS - Combat operations are underway on the streets "to take this city back" in the aftermath of Hurricane Katrina.
>
> "This place is going to look like Little Somalia," Brig. Gen. Gary Jones, commander of the Louisiana National Guard's Joint Task Force told *Army Times* Friday as hundreds of armed troops under his charge prepared to launch a massive citywide security mission from a staging area outside the Louisiana Superdome. "We're going to go out and take this city back. This will be a combat operation to get this city under control."[72]

Stories were told of guns being fired at rescue helicopters and troops under assault from civilians. There is no evidence that such incidents actually took place, only a soldier who shot himself in the foot.

One of the largest single DHS contracts after the storm awarded $42 million to Blackwater security to guard FEMA offices against possible confrontational aid applicants.[73] Getting into the FEMA complex in Baton Rouge, according to one of the local experts whom Lee Clarke and I interviewed in our study, "felt like one imagines what would occur in trying to get into a military base in Iraq." "Who was the enemy?" she asks. The various suspicions and reactions of the authorities affect how emergency response can work: who gets help, who resists it, and the way in which particular schemes of remediation can be implemented.

Among other measures taken by the military was the enforcement of curfews—something that, it has been speculated, actually may have hindered families from reuniting and neighbors from helping one another cope. Resources used for policing could have been more directly aimed at rescue and provisioning.[74] The soldiers and other security officials could have, as in my recommendations for guards at the airports (chapter 4), been self-defined as friendly helpers—disarmed for the purpose as a start. A policy put in place that indeed had come from the Iraq war zone was restriction of media access. This further complicated matters by obstructing journalists from seeing conditions on their own.[75] Perhaps the resulting vacuum of first-person observation helped feed the looting reruns and inhibited presentation of more varied coverage. For those watching, the lesson was to get a gun and to support the men in uniform, and—at maybe a practical level—be on guard that marauders would steal your stuff.

We cannot know precisely how much actual crime people perpetrated in the context of Katrina. There were media reports of murder, burglary, and rape at the Superdome and convention center, which also became a gathering location of displaced persons (each vastly overcrowded, with more than 20,000 individuals and many more thousands stranded nearby). There were bodies supposedly stacked in storerooms and violent gangs raping and killing. On the second day after the storm hit, the FEMA deputy coordinator in New Orleans reported in an e-mail message that "it looks like 200 homicide [sic] bodies." In fact, there were a total of four murders in the city during the week after Katrina, which is about the norm for New Orleans. At the Superdome, there were a total of six deaths during the time the building served as refuge: four from natural causes, one was a suicide, and one was from an apparent drug overdose.[76] The misinformation led to further inaction: the National Guard cancelled a plan to deliver supplies to the convention center in the middle of the night, judging it to be too dangerous for troops who would face a thug army reported to have previously fought off eighty-eight police bent on stopping their executions and raping.[77] None of this was plausible.

Rates of arrest for burglary in the city, perhaps a proxy for looting, tell a different story. Official records indicate a vastly higher *rate* of burglary after the hurricane. But this needs to be taken with some reflection.[78] Rates of crime would be biased upward if those unable to exit the city were disproportionately poor and more likely than others, for whatever reason, to commit crime. Some of those "looting" were obviously, seen in another light, harvesting resources like food and diapers from abandoned stores and warehouses. And at least in some cases, those doing the stealing may have been security forces brought in to combat looting; something that police, army, and private security personnel have been known to do. In the case of Katrina, a Cadillac dealership lost much of its stock to police, and others, helping themselves to the inventory.[79]

Whatever the facts on the ground, the larger discourse atmosphere was full of danger and full of blacks; accounts were rife with undeserving types of people acting in indecent ways—abetted perhaps by the appearance of desperate people without access to proper toilet facilities (another egregious failing in a "refuge") as they waited for hours and hours in the hope of boarding buses. The portrayal was not conducive to bureaucratic bravery—taking extraordinary action under the belief that later observers will back you up. Agency officials and political functionaries could not assume their potentially extraordinary actions would be seen as something that was "of course" necessary. They surmised, probably quite accurately, that no parallel decency takeovers would make for coordination across different geographic and administrative spheres. In her ethnography of how emergency responders organized themselves in the Boston area, Kerry Fosher observes that despite whatever careful specification of duties and procedures are made in advance,

> In practice, most locals assume that in some incidents, such as a terrorist attack, . . . the niceties of notification and request would likely be taken care of as time allowed rather than as a precondition for federal involvement.[80]

With Katrina, such expectations could not be taken for granted. The human capacity for overcoming inertia, including formal emergency inertia, was restrained. No one with power reached over, pressed down, or pushed up to make the rescue—or at least not as much as was needed at the time. Let's call it racism by inertia. It draws upon, in effect, prior practices and attitudes among whites toward blacks. Again, as we repeatedly saw in prior chapters, past experience in dealing with trouble becomes the rehearsal space for what will happen at point of emergency.

For their part, the past also informs the worlds of those most dependent—like the poor of New Orleans. Although huge numbers of them did, like others, respond to warnings and leave the city, skepticism made numbers of them less likely to do so. They have reasons to be suspicious of advisories or commands. Ongoing discrimination and police violence enters in, along with the deeply racist history of the region. It makes sense that they might lack confidence they would be cared for outside their home base. How long will the trip take and what will be its conditions? If there are old people in one's retinue, survival itself may be at stake. Children have needs that may or may not be appropriately met, such as specific foods, infant formula, diapers, and refrigerated medications. And what kind of return might there be? What will be an income source while away? Yes, if they stay, they could die, but against this statistically unlikely event, are the very likely costs of leaving.[81] Past warnings, after all, have been wrong, and some took those warnings too seriously, as it turned out. The anxieties of leaving are plausibly stronger for people who have nothing else except the resources in their own home, however modest it may be. Who will watch out for their belongings if *everyone* goes? Besides their material possessions, they rely, as poor people are prone to do, on near-at-hand neighborhood social networks for the aid and comfort that allow them to get by.[82]

Those with routine privilege have personal resources to tide them over; wealth stored up in various hard assets and credit cards in their pockets that are good wherever they go. They are more likely to have family on high ground—whether in Baton Rouge or Phoenix or Chicago—who have largesse to take them in. But they also have some equanimity toward both private and government officials, who will not, they presume, leave them in the lurch. Their own personal encounters with schools, insurers, police, and the courts have tended toward benign. Ironically, given what may be a conservative and antigovernment political rhetoric on the part of many wealthier Americans, they have imbibed media stories of aid coming to those turned out of their homes by earthquakes and forest fires, of agency officials who get people like themselves out of harm's way. The case of a rescue worker racing to save a Malibu woman's horse from a forest fire sticks in my mind. Only some people think that such a level of care would be shown toward them, much less their pets. Also an irony, those of privilege may become less prepared than others, like California homeowners who surround their wood-based houses with fire-prone landscapes. The more help they receive, the less vigilance they maintain, posing what has been called a "samaritan's dilemma" for institutional and public policy.[83] Helping fosters behaviors of dependence, a "moral hazard" in the language of economists. But the putative moral hazards from helping the poor (the "welfare queens" of yore) receive more attention than that of helping the affluent.

Whatever the precise dynamics of coming and going in the near term, whites have made demographic gains through the ways in which social and physical restoration occur. The idea of "ethnic cleansing," a charge made against both local and national agencies in the Katrina aftermath will not seem farfetched. The percent of the city's population that is African American went down by 7 percent (from 67 percent of the population in 2000 to 60 percent in the 2010 U.S. Census).[84] Both whites and Hispanics gained. For those directly affected, it was harsh to return to the city and find one's housing development boarded up with no access to the second floors that contained one's dry belongings—possessions that could never be retrieved. And in replay of the excesses of old-style U.S. urban renewal, most such buildings have now been demolished and replaced by new complexes that house many fewer residents than before—and far fewer who require subsidized housing. It is a case, says New Orleans sociologist Shirley Laska, of "blatant private sector interest supported by the local 'growth machine' in eradicating poor Blacks from N.O."[85] For African Americans and those who labor on their behalf, there appears to be a lackadaisical attitude toward securing the return of those flung to other cities and regions.

Another aspect is post-Katrina housing policy. There is initiative to provide New Orleans with "new, socially and economically integrated neighborhoods."[86] This is, for sure, a laudable goal but less so when the integration is to occur in what previously were all-black areas. As with past efforts to achieve integration in American cities, the going reality always seems to be "however many blacks we now have, that's enough."[87] In this case of the centrally situated Iberville project, as it is known, the housing being demolished is low-rise, brick, and largely intact. From a design perspective, it conforms to currently popular conventions of the New Urbanism, with its pattern of colonial-style structures built around ample and pleasant courtyards. It seems inexplicable to fence it all off to keep prior tenants out and then to tear it down rather than allow those displaced their return. In part due to protest, the current plan is to retain twenty-four of the seventy-four buildings with the remainder replaced by mid-rise apartments and town houses, thus making the project overall oriented to a mixed-income clientele.[88] It still means a loss for those displaced in what, at best, will amount to a decade-long lockout. That people in power would be so unsympathetic feeds suspicion of racist intent.

People in New Orleans may not know the details, but the impression may still linger, of response to the great floods of 1927. African American storm refugees were gathered into camps from which they were hired out by white landowners needing labor to restore damaged farms and facilities. Armed National Guardsmen kept other labor contractors (some from the North) out of the camps and used violence, including murder, to keep blacks from leaving for other purposes or higher pay. Even for white planters coming in, "No man (was) . . . allowed to talk to any other but his own niggers."[89] Whites ruled and skimmed off part of the outside aid as it came in.[90] Some blacks escaped, but for the rest, the camps were essentially prisons. Work crews of African American men were "forced," according to one of the standard histories of the event, into hauling massive amounts of earth to raise levee levels (resembling the way prisoners are now put to work filling sandbags when the Mississippi floods in more upriver zones).[91]

These commandeered persons were not the only victims. To relieve the river's pressure as it streamed into the city, the authorities dynamited a breach in the levee twelve miles south of New Orleans. There were houses, people, and businesses in the adjacent parishes, serving a population of about ten thousand—fishers, trappers, bootleggers, and sugar factory workers—mostly poor people, but I could find no racial breakdown. Some of those dispossessed moved to a shelter set up at the New Orleans' International Trade Exchange, whites on the fifth floor and blacks on the sixth.[92] Approval for the dynamiting had come from both the army and U.S. Secretary of Commerce (and head of flood relief) Herbert Hoover. Despite prior signed pledges from city leaders on behalf of those about to be ruined, only minor compensation followed. Responses to disaster, involving elite dominance and corruption at various levels of authority—and racism—are part and parcel of the very meaning of disaster relief in the region.

This helps us to see how fear intersects stratification. Both whites and blacks live in fear of what they take to be natural disaster, as do both rich and poor. But that fear is assuaged by a sense, among the more generally privileged, that help will be on the way—especially because the troubles came as "acts of God," for which neither they nor their neighbors could be held responsible. Part of the government safety net is the reassurance (and often the reality) that somebody will do something. For African Americans, however, the anxieties interpenetrate. They quite obviously have the same reasons to fear disaster, indeed additional ones given their greater likelihood of living in the lowlands, in houses built less strongly and adjacent to noxious infrastructures that contain poisons and explosives. But in addition, they suffer from the prospect and reality of social risks that exacerbate the impacts of natural events. So they are less likely to get out of the way when disaster strikes. In the aftermath, they see planning schemes that mark their territory off as "green space"—areas to be abandoned in favor of parks and nature preserve—as motivated by nefarious intention, rather than good-sense land-use planning. And their reluctance to be moved prompts still further accusations of them being the source of their own problems.

What to Do?

Various reports and government hearings on Katrina have provided ideas for positive actions, some of which informed the foregoing analysis and the suggestions that follow. I include the small-scale and the most radical of reforms.

• *Keep attending to the mundane.*

Like the stairways at Ground Zero, simple affordances work wonders. In New Orleans, buses at critical spots like the Superdome and convention center would have gotten people out. The presence of flat-bottomed boats solves problems. The larger lesson is to be ready for unlikely events with such likely remedies and the basics: food, ice, medicine, and diapers. Emergency planners know all this; authorities' preoccupation with threats of social disorder disables their expertise and undermines their planning acumen.

• *Shrink the city.*

Far more radical than having supplies on hand, and a source of intense consternation, is the proposal to just let the city go, or at least major parts of it. Some have even dared to voice the unthinkable: abandon New Orleans. Let the tides take the city away. In timed advance sequences, lift away bits and pieces or even whole buildings and relocate them elsewhere as markets, government aid, and philanthropy permit.

New Orleans would, in effect, be a temporary place with uses and users changing as economic and natural conditions evolve.

Less dramatically, abandon only parts of the city—but large parts—that would become the green space of a new, more sustainable metropolis. Such had been the recommendation of the Washington, D.C.-based Urban Land Institute (ULI), a think tank and policy analysis center that operates under sponsorship from the real estate industry. Under this scenario, the French Quarter would remain, along with other parts of the city on higher ground along the river. But substantial zones, including the Lower Ninth Ward, would no longer house people. Such areas would give way to public uses like parks and fair grounds and some transit infrastructure. These are facilities that could be inundated without loss of life or high-value assets.

Part of the solution might involve giving up indefensible parts of the existing landmass below New Orleans; for example, the "foot" of land now at the lower extremity of the delta, in particular, is considered indefensible and worth sacrificing as necessary for a more protective land morphology. It shows the utility of thinking in terms of land trade-offs and what is sometimes called "managed retreat," inevitably threatening to some residents and business interests.

• *Give trust a base.*

To whatever degree ideas of shrinkage or trade-off, like those of the ULI program most especially, may represent a sensible and ecologically appropriate response, many have reasons for suspicion. Reaction was strongly negative, especially from the city's African American citizenry who indeed saw in it a racist scheme to make the city whiter and richer. Experience—lived social and political history—thus intervenes. Instead of removing vulnerable neighborhoods, African American leaders supported the Road Home program—a kind of right-of-return for every person who wished it, and often interpreted as the right to return to the same house or at least the same neighborhood where they once lived. Compared to those dealing with insurance companies or even FEMA (which gave rise to terrible stories of humiliation and delays), those attempting to participate in Road Home reported the experience as stressful.[93]

An obvious background problem is that the United States is not a welfare state, lacking even conventional forms of a safety net found in other industrial countries. So it needs to take special measures to deal with mass suffering, measures for which it does not have a robust preexisting ideological or material infrastructure. Sensing the lack of reliable and benign state welfare, people cling to whatever rights, privileges, or belongings they have "above the net." Fearful of what government might do, they fight city hall. If they sensed a more harmonious world, people might relax and risk such a thing as neighborhood relocation, especially if they believed friends and neighbors would be there too. Once again, as with problems of public restroom access (chapter 2) or comfort in the subways (chapter 3), providing greater social equality would facilitate the provision of a public good, in this case beneficial reorganization of urban space. Cluster housing and commodious parks are good things, but they require trust to make them happen.

• *Restore the wetlands.*

For some ecologically oriented reformers, wetland restoration will make the city safer and maybe even (major optimism required for this) allow rebuilding all parts of the former city to past usage patterns. A collateral benefit would be the sustenance of fisheries and enhanced wildlife stocks and biotic diversity. And indeed, given the wetlands as both a recreational and ecological resource, it would be decent indeed to prevent their further deterioration and even more decent to reverse the losses that have already taken place.

Some actions to take are stroke-of-the-pen simple, but others are politically, financially, and technologically complex. Here are some of both sorts: End any remaining cypress logging and mining for peat. Have no more canal dredging by the oil industry—politically more difficult, especially as evolving technologies make it possible to find new reserves or drill in already explored wetlands. Require restoration to deal with past damage, perhaps through taxes on new Gulf-zone oil extraction. To help calm storm surge, build artificial reefs, using, for example recycled materials, including glass (which is, in essence, sand—a return of a natural material to the ocean floor). Create diversions of the river, potentially both above and below the city that could build up barrier islands out of newly delivered silt from the river. To increase silt load, eliminate dams upstream throughout the Midwest. That may seem crazy ambitious, but many of these dams are well on their way to silting up anyway. Whatever past utility they may have had for flood protection, such utility is coming to an end.

• *Send MoMA to the rescue?*

The design world has come forward with some solutions. The master idea, a conscious part of advanced ecological and planning doctrine, is to abandon the "rigid attempts at resisting the fluid dynamics of an encroaching sea," the "protective muscularity" of striving to efface nature, as phrased by Manaugh and Twilley. Instead, the innovators favor a "maritime urbanism"—which might include building on stilts to let water flow beneath. More ambitiously, encourage floating architecture (some of which is taking shape in New Orleans).[94] As the tide comes in, as the seasons shift, and as historic weather transformations occur, the urban infrastructure more or less floats with it.

Along such lines, New York's Museum of Modern Art (MoMA) in 2010 commissioned five architectural and planning firms to address the problem for New York, a city that although in less dire circumstance than New Orleans, faces some of the same challenges. Under at least a bad-case scenario, New York will face a sea level six feet higher by the time the ice cap melt has run its course. The proposals for the resulting MoMA exhibition, "Rising Currents," are a gorgeous set of accommodations (the show is down but now accessible on the web).[95] All strive to address the coming changes by harnessing natural flows not only to mitigate future flood damage but also to maximize other goals—like improving water quality, aesthetics, and cultural opportunities along the way.

So, we have a proposal for "Oyster-techture," in which oysters become "Man (hattan)'s Best Friend" (the cuteness is theirs). Oysters can do two types of things, according to SCAPE, the name of the design team offering up the plan. One: they cleanse. Oysters take in and release fifty gallons of water per creature per day, and the water, when passed out, is free of pollutants of virtually every kind, organic and inorganic alike (these dirty oysters are, alas, inedible given their filthy job). Filth in, clean out. Two: oysters serve and protect. With some kind of primitive armature put in the water—rope or waste textile or plastic strands—oysters will form reefs that themselves become both habitat for other life forms and also attenuate storm surge.

Other design approaches take aim at the hardedge seawalls, like those at the Mississippi levees but common across the globe. Coastlines of virtually all world cities have been denatured with vertical barriers, sometimes just to increase buildable adjacent land. Typically this was done by dredging the river bottom to fill in what otherwise might be a sloping shore. So the river bottom is dead flat-muck and hence exacerbating the river as a water speedway. Designers at MoMA propose shoreline crenellations, again to slow down surge, for example, with fingers into the bays. These constructions also can provide parkland, recreational boating opportunities, and even (in a project of New York's LTL Architects) amphitheaters facing floating performance stages. The phrases used by several of the designers to describe such projects include "edge porosity," "amphibious landscape," and "blue streets" (water courses through downtowns that allow ocean river in and take rain water out). Another of the design studios (Bunge) calls for a "new Aqueous City." Again, what they all have in common is an acclamation to natural forces rather than trying to command with thoughtless artifice. Nature as friend, not threat.

• *Act globally.*

These design schemes have the seeming advantage, so promoted in this book, of adding delight and pleasure to the world. But here, I'm sad to say, the worry is that it is too good, too cool, for the world's good. Such inventive brilliance may seduce—with fresh ideas, clever wording, and lovely presentations—and inhibit taking the strong and politically complex decisions needed to stave off world effects of climate change. Even if Manhattan can be saved or indeed be made still more lustrous, what will happen to Bangladesh? Where's *their* MoMA? And where are the solutions to the specific problems of such places, given levels of poverty, types of livelihood, and particular meteorological and topographic conditions? Their security is beyond the reach of oysters.

To save the world from Katrinas, we may have to accept the unpleasantness of bold moves that might even risk—worst-case scenario—higher prices for goods and increased taxes. And we may have to link arms, Pete Seeger style, because sea level rise is indeed lapping at everyone's shore: earth in the balance indeed. The fate of New Orleans obviously hinges not just on local solutions, but on global shifts and reassemblage of technique, institutions, and what remains of land and sea. Only the world's power centers of corporate and political authority might stem the tide, but it would be a start if New Orleans and the Gulf region could join island nations and vulnerable Third World places in pressing the agenda. New Orleans is, after all among the most privileged among the world's low-lying zones, and it is culturally iconic for those who matter in the decision-making process. It may be good to understand that just as fire departments are no solution for wildfires, neither FEMA nor MoMA will save the day. We need to do something in advance that is smart and together and for the whole wide world.

• •

CHAPTER 7

Conclusion:
Radical Ambiguity and the Default to Decency

"You never want a serious crisis to go to waste," Rahm Emanuel, then–chief of staff to Barack Obama explained in urging financial reform after the 2008 economic collapse. His boss's predecessor, George W. Bush, understood the principle and used 9/11 as his crisis not to waste—advancing the shock doctrine (Naomi Klein's term)[1] on the world's economic and military fronts. I had called it differently as I watched the towers fall, misreading the catastrophe as clear evidence of the world's interdependence. Everyone had to be given a sense of dignity and belonging to a common community. I wasn't alone, but it was certainly not a consensus.

The debate continues as to whether our aggressive moves abroad (and, on occasion, at home as well) have made the United States safer or only increased its exposure. The case for repression has taken various forms, with the Middle East wars being the massive catastrophic response. At the heart of the ferocious real politick is belief that if we capture, torture, or kill innocents, we will eventually get at the bad guy. Those who survive our wrath will learn the lesson and be less likely to help such people in the future. Anybody thinking of attacking us will respect our power and capacity to get even—more than even. To make this happen, we will go anywhere and do what it takes: the war on terror.

I know no real way to refute such a claim for the wisdom of bellicosity with utter certainty. But surely those who would oppose how I think have at least a modicum of uncertainty for their position—or certainly should have. Put bluntly and at the extreme, I am proposing that *when you don't know what you are doing, the best approach is the more directly humane one.* What will, from the standpoint of basic human empathy and generosity, enhance people's well-being? There should be some kind of affirmative action for that position. Before the application of militarism, one should simply ask what would be most decent? "What would Jesus do?" is not a bad thought experiment. In my secular version, I think of it as *default to decency*. My proclivity, based in part on the kind of evidence put forward in prior chapters, is to go without war, provide aid and support to those who need it, and acknowledge the wisdom of other traditions. While I lack definitive proof that this would work, the "other side" has less evidence that their view of the world works very well at all.

What is "decency"? Who am I, anxiously I ask, to take on the central question in the history of ethics. From a social science perspective, and it is one that I have some privilege to invoke, there are a few ways to pose an answer. One of the empirical lessons taught by studies on disaster response, emphasized again and again in this book, is that people help each other. They see a drowning person, they throw a rope — maybe even jump right in. If a child is in the street, they move the child to safety. It is spontaneous and, unless there are strong reasons to avoid taking the act, they do it. There are, however, well-reasoned systems of thought devoted to overcome this sentiment, both as a theory of human behavior as well as a prescription of how one should behave. Motivation for doing good actually leads, the argument goes, to injurious outcomes — to oneself first of all and probably to most others as well. We hear it in familiar adages: "Give them an inch and they'll take a mile," "Eat or be eaten," or, as put by Machiavelli with characteristic severity, "Before all else, be armed." For some economists, led by the doctrinaire Milton and Rose Friedman, helping behavior disrupts markets by enervating drive to achieve and efficiently produce. Public benevolence is neither empirically common nor ultimately useful and thus, by their lights and over the long run, not even ethical. So people otherwise of good will, who love their children and might as individuals give to charity as even right-wing conservatives do, deny help to those who do not work, health care to those who did not buy insurance, rations to those without food. They have mounted an ideology to disengage what I think of as a basic human instinct to help others. I place my bet with those who think more good in the world comes from giving in to empathy than encouraging its neutralization.

Sometimes empathy means doing nothing at all, akin to the "precautionary principle," which environmentalists use to argue for nonintervention in ecological systems. Very often, however, the need is to be *proactive*, but in a different direction than is ordinarily undertaken in the realm of official security. One should move forward to relax, to assist, and to set up ways for people to make good on their inclination to come to one another's support and rescue. So beyond the wonks and abstract doctrines, we need a massive bias away from remedies of control and punishment. Here are some reasons—mostly derived from the concrete settings and applications of this book—for making the softer path somehow the basis for dealing with threat.

Random Nut Reason

People to whom I indecorously refer as "random nuts," hardly an official psychiatric or criminological category, do exist—if only as a residual after all the other types of explanation have been exhausted. Indiduals perform mayhem that makes no sense, economically or politically; they make no sense whatever. Such people and their behaviors will not be rooted out and certainly not be reigned in by hardening and command. My icon of the random havoc problem was the shooting at the University of Texas in 1966. A former student and ex-Marine, who both failed out of school and was removed from the military, ended up killing sixteen people and wounding another thirty-two. He was shooting from the observation deck of the university's bell tower before killing himself as the final performance of carnage.

A more recent sensational act in the United States was the Tucson shooting of Congresswoman Gabriele Giffords, the wounding of thirteen others, and the killing of six who happened to be in her proximity. As per usual, alternative responses followed according to different theories of violence. Efforts to blame the event on "uncivil discourse" and related excesses of right-wing agitating failed to take off— appropriately enough, I think, given the lack of any real evidence. Predictably, some advocated tighter gun controls. But political leaders in the Arizona legislature, also not wanting to waste a crisis, argued for laws encouraging college students and faculty to bear arms in their own defense. But nobody could really "argue" on any issue with Jared Loughner, the charged assailant; he was not sane enough.

Taking lives (one's own or others') does vary in frequency from one society to another, as the great founder of systematic sociology, Emile Durkheim, went to such great lengths to statistically argue. No doubt, timely interventions can reduce the number of people who commit mayhem "for no good reason." Much debate occurs, including within therapeutic circles, of the connections between rage, violence, and mental illness as well as the kind of social policies that would alleviate the force of private demons.[2] But even peaceable, social-democratic, and culturally homogenous mid-1980s Sweden experienced the assassination of its Prime Minister Olof Palme—who was casually walking to the movies, unguarded as per usual in Stockholm. And we have the much more recent events of the Norway shootings. If for no other reason than growing population density that provides both more targets and individuals with access to them, the one-off crazy grows as a demographic probability. Their vast variety of ailments, resentments, and circumstances of action, however statistically rare, make them supremely difficult to track and stop.

Even the so-called "terrorists" proclaiming ideological motivation come in different mental states. Some form of craziness, if for no other reason than an apparent willingness to so depart from the behavior of the great majority of others of similar background, marks them off as odd—an oddness that disables. How else to explain the almost bizarre incompetence so often exhibited? The attack on the twin towers has become a misleading exemplar, with its display of good planning and precise execution. Even still, enough blunders took place in the plotting (learning only to fly and not take off or land) to have alerted a properly competent system of national intelligence. Other attempts, as previously described in this book, are further off the mark—like wearing shoes too wet to ignite on board a plane or, as in a U.K. case, parking one's bomb-loaded vehicle in a no parking zone.[3] It is this clumsiness of the conspirators—not the guards at the gates or intelligence from the experts (which sometimes does play a role)—that has foiled the plots. Noticing this phenomenon might lead to more counterterrorist strategies that focus on the routine screw-ups, rather than, for example, efforts to ferret out the masterminds. The problem is that routine mucking up lacks the narrative bite of deeds performed by either devils or heroes. It would not serve well as a premise for a *Star Wars* intergalactic battle movie, except if Woody Allen (or Peter Sellers) were in the starring role. This makes it politically useless; you can't have a war on shmucks, or make a big deal out of standing up to them. Further, it provides fewer opportunities, than would a war on a plausibly competent enemy, for private contractors to sign multimillion-dollar contracts.

Not only are terrorists not typically professional terrorists, but they are also not professional criminals at all. Prototypical terrorists lack prior arrests for robbery, rape, or drug offenses—the meat and potatoes of the criminal justice system. So the use of crime records in security clearance is still another error of the binary thinking—and, incidentally, keeps folks with criminal records from getting some decent jobs.

THE SIX DEGREES REASON

One difficulty of pursuing particular individuals is that you alienate those in their network, never mind the innocent people destroyed by bullets and bombs in their neighborhood. The very familiar idea is that anyone on the planet can be connected to any other person on the planet through a chain of acquaintances that has no more than six intermediaries. The actual research shows that far fewer intermediaries, at least in a country like the United States, are needed to link all with all—as few as three.[4] Whatever the precise number, attacking a single individual involves you in the lives of many more—the friends and relatives, the village, the tribe, the ethnic group, and maybe even most of an entire people. This is the demographic undergirding of the "producing more enemies" paradigm that liberals worry about. The numbers are high with estimates of deaths caused by our Middle East wars estimated at one hundred thousand for Iraq alone, with injuries going much higher.[5] The U.S.-based worldwide system of detention reached, according to Mark Danner, nearly the same total—about one hundred thousand individuals.[6] For those who should escape assault or arrest, others offer aid and support, creating additional individuals who have a vested interest in opposing those leading the chase.[7] Mundane social connections thus generate further growth in the numbers lined up on the other side. The sociologist Michael Schwartz, in his mapping of "trouble spots" in the terrain of the Iraq war, thus concluded that where authority goes, trouble follows, rather than the other way around.[8] As Schwartz argues, the particular U.S. strategy of "clear and hold" seems especially tailored to create this dynamic. Destroying houses, businesses, and the local infrastructure creates deprivation generating further insurrection. Schwartz elaborates,

> As the occupation military migrates from locality to locality pacifying "insurgent strongholds," a potentially endless cycle emerges in many communities: initial degradation of local conditions generates initial rebellion; rebellion provokes pacification replete with the heavy hand of . . . (troop) operations; military operations lead to further economic and social degradation . . . subsequent withdrawal by the occupation military unleashes reconstituted rebuilding efforts and perhaps amplified rebellion; with the circle closing when the new round of local organization triggers another round of pacification.[9]

As collateral damage cumulates, one speculates, desire to cooperate erodes and this is costly to those trying to contain insurgency. The most likely source of good intelligence comes from those close in. Friends and family are indispensible informants, and security hinges on them not feeling alienated from a greater good. Of the 120 Muslims suspected of plotting domestic attacks in the ten years after 9/11, fellow Muslims, including the parents of the accused, turned in forty-eight of them.[10] The great majority of Muslims, the sociologist Charles Kurzman reminds us from analyses of worldwide survey data, have little or no sympathy for those who plot and kill in the name of Islam. "Islamist terrorists swim in a sea of possible informers," he says.[11] It is important to keep that sea from changing.

Of course the hunter often gets, even by the military's accounting, the wrong guys, and who knows how many of the 120 suspects were totally misidentified. The whole country of Iraq was misidentified. We know, thanks in part to DNA testing, that U.S. states punish and execute innocent people. This, despite a system of legal protections and exceedingly slow and cumbersome procedures in capital cases within the United States. According to a 2006 report from the U.S. Attorney General (under George Bush), 50 percent of all individual FBI files are inaccurate or out-of-date and, again, this is in a resource-rich and high-public-support policing environment.[12] Police, we additionally know, do plant evidence and authorities fantasize criminal plots where there were none.[13] Imagine the "flaws" in data collection and target selection in, say, Afghanistan. According to two senior commanders operating in that country, as reported by Dana Priest and William Arkin, the success of the elite counter-insurgency Joint Special Operations Command "in targeting the right homes, businesses, and individuals . . . was only about 50 percent."[14] And, again, to continue comparing the two contexts, correcting misidentifications in the United States, even for so simple a matter as a bad credit report, can be complex and infuriating—big brother is a big bungler, as it is sometimes said.[15]

United States officials imagine the country's "enemies" as operating under a command-and-control apparatus, parallel to an idealized vision of the U.S. itself, but with a mastermind in charge. No matter how off the mark this might be, it poses a possible victory, a "win," by killing off the kingpin and decapitating his organization. So we "hunt" for Abu al-Zarqawi in Iraq, whose death in 2006 was supposed to end the insurgency, as Bin Laden's demise would eliminate the insurgencies that followed on. But records from within the military of an inquiry into two hundred U.S.-led assassinations in Afghanistan indicate that deadly attacks on our forces increased, rather than decreased, after successful kills.[16] "The results were damning," writes Andrew Cockburn in his *Harper's* report on the strategy. Indeed, how can such hits possibly succeed? Fuzzy and porous group boundaries mean that new members come in to replace, honor, or celebrate those before them. Again, the common vision of card-carrying members of a well-trained cadre obscures the reality of both geographic as well as social fluidity—a "lightness" of micro-organization as ideas and roles shift across time and place.[17] Individuals may resemble "a bunch of guys,"[18] or series of such bunches, replicating rhizome style, and always with ornery multiplier effects when one of them is killed or captured. The socialness of their lives, their social capital, interacts with bombs and drones to create solidarities, alliances, and resentments that form into, as it has been called from the standpoint of U.S. strategists, "an indecipherable mess."[19]

Part of the mess involves the weapons left behind, available to those on the scene. One liability of weaponry is that it sticks around even when those who brought it in depart. The United States supplies weapons based on its assessments of strategic conditions at a given moment, aiming at the target of the time. But these durables remain in place (more or less) as the real politick shifts along with the sentiments of those we have outfitted and trained. There is little distinction between weapons of defense or offense, for action on our side or the side of some other. The United States can end up catering the whole affair, with assailants later found to have at least training materials, if not the weapons themselves, of the U.S. military.[20] The United States provided much of the armament for both sides in Vietnam due to the enemy's ability to capture arms. The United States prepared, through CIA operatives and other agencies, the emergence of Saddam Hussein to power in Iraq and reinforced his control for a number of years after.[21] Championing Pakistan as a Cold War ally against left-leaning India, starting with Ronald Reagan, the United States financed and continues to finance the wicked and out-of-control Pakistani intelligence service (the ISI). In Iraq and Afghanistan crude corruption siphons off enough of our various aid programs to provision the Taliban with a large proportion of their needs.

Internal Militarization Reason

On the U.S. homefront, increasing the numbers of those deemed enemies means you have to keep raising the numbers of people to watch and catch them as well as the gizmos put at their disposal. It is a militarization of the workforce and its infrastructure. The supposed enemies moving through so many places and spaces, fosters the growth of militarization of such concern to the likes of Chalmers Johnson (see chapter 1).

We can learn from the prisons, because they are always in the business of watchful control. Recognizing the fundamental danger of too much arsenal, prison authorities do not arm the guards. Fighting runs too high a risk of going amiss. One of the lessons of guns at home is that they kill people who live there—in accidents, suicides, and acts of passion, far more than they kill intruders or foreign invaders.[22] Home guns kill home people; the rate of such domestic deaths is twelvefold the number of intruders annually shot; the ratio of shootings for defense compared to domestic violence and suicide attempts is 1:22.[23] Besides also being available for suicide by soldiers (at an increasing rate of incidence),[24] military personnel sometimes use their armaments to settle scores among one another, or just shoot by accident (the only soldier shot in the post-Katrina maneuvers, we should recall, had shot himself).

An analogous danger arises with civilian programs that encourage proactive defense. Thus the Metropolitan Transit Authority (MTA) "See Something . . ." campaign caused people to turn in their personal adversaries to settle private scores. People in Iraq and Afghanistan settle scores by informing U.S. and NATO military that people with whom they have a private grievance (or people toward whom they harbor ethnic resentment, as in Sunnis vs. Shiites) are insurrectionists. This can lead to American and allied soldiers following on with reprisals, "taking sides" in conflicts better avoided.[25] In what is probably the mother of all score-settling, the key informant (codenamed "curveball") who was George W. Bush and Colin Powell's "eye witness" source for Iraq's bio-weapons production facilities had made it all up. As Curveball would later tell the *Guardian*, "I had a chance to fabricate something to topple the regime. I and my sons are proud of that and we are proud that we're the reason to give Iraq the margin of democracy."[26]

In their gathering up of troops into critical mass, commanders create crowds—analogous to those collected by the Transportation Security Administration (TSA) at airport security. Amassing troops and armaments at the borders stimulates a matchup by the other side, readying a pileup for ignition—as in the Europe-wide arms race that was a key lead-up to World War I.[27] More prosaically, the worldwide influenza epidemic of 1918–20 probably had its source among soldiers in the

United States; Fort Riley in Kansas is given as a specific origin site. Its spread was "intimately related to war conditions (including perhaps the weakened bodies of soldiers on the line) and especially the arrival of American troops in France."[28] At the time, it was a crime to utter criticisms against the U.S. government (!), and that included criticism of its handling of public health problems. Local governments routinely denied or minimized the spread of the fatal strains of the disease and in that way inhibited the use of quarantine, or any other method of effective response. Authorities regarded "panic" as dangerous to the public as well as to the war effort. For their part, the press self-censored, holding back on the nature and extent of the danger.[29] In more recent battlefields, thanks in part to antibiotics, survival rates rise but with maiming and life-long disabilities, including posttraumatic stress, drug addiction, and related diseases.

A bastion of modern security, domestic and foreign, is storing digital data on the lives, habits, and capacities of individuals and groups. For both private organizations and public agencies, pressure is on to gather the data and give access to security authorities. But, as per the usual pattern, the twin to the fear of not storing enough data is the potential for an enemy (or just an adventuresome geek) to sabotage entire information systems. By classifying data as "secret," it is nicely bundled as worth the effort to steal. If you build such a database, they will come, packing the algorithms that may also have been developed at government expense to deal with some other threat. With ever-vigilant authorities sniffing various aspects of these possibilities, fantastic scenarios of cyberwar (the new term) now appear on the defense-industry horizon. China in recent times looms as intending nefarious digital activities. And so we will have new rounds of worldwide searches for the culprits, and still another branch of the security-industrial complex to deal with them.[30]

As security expands to new realms, more agencies strive to look like they know what they are doing to deal with the threats assigned as their bailiwicks. Multiplication compounds organizational complexity. A common theme then is to "restructure," an activity for which the mammoth Department of Homeland Security (DHS) is the most prominent example. This adds new intricacies to those already present and probability grows for whole-system failure.[31] All systems tend toward "normal accidents," or—in the long-term eventuality, "worst-case scenarios."[32] Alexis de Tocqueville, according to Robert Darnton's recent commentary, demonstrated how the ancien régime failed because it grew too complex for its authoritarianism and too authoritarian for its complexities: "it married absolutism to bureaucratic intricacy and redundancy."[33] Complexity and authoritarianism combine to threaten whole systems.

Growth in scale and complexity also increases vulnerability for graft and deception, as with the vast budgetary expenditures in Iraq and Afghanistan. Almost $300 billion was spent in a three-year period, says a government report, to fund contractors accused of fraud or wrongdoing in connection with U.S. antiterrorism.[34] For year 2010, Transparency International ranked our two allies, Iraq and Afghanistan, in 175th and 176th position respectively (out of 178 places) on its corruption index. Only Somalia and Myanmar came in under them.[35] Corruption and violence merge as the governing apparatus of security. Secrecy invites irresponsibility and incompetence.

At the level of mundane organizations like the subway system, we get a glimpse of the process, albeit at lower levels of dollar magnitude and of harm to the world. Once it is for a purpose identified as part of "security," the MTA cannot put contracts out for public bid. Agencies have an interest in bringing as many of their expenditures as possible under the security definition so as to gain a funding source otherwise not available. And so construction of floodwall hardening to protect tunnels against bombing that would allow river waters into the subway tunnels cannot go out for competitive bid. In a similar vein, contracts for the system's smart surveillance cameras had to be negotiated privately, with the waste of half a billion on a system that could not be made to work. Release of the technical specs on which bids could be based might, the worry goes, detail system vulnerabilities for an enemy. At the federal level, there were also losses in the hundreds of millions for a technology that would sniff out nuclear materials at the country's ports, but which failed in initial installations to detect even lightly shielded materials—but did set off hundreds of false alarms from Chinese toilets, kitchen countertops, and bananas.[36]

Security also helps straight-out con artists. In one of the cases we know about, a single swindler, Dennis Montgomery, took in the Bush administration to the tune of $20 million. Montgomery was to provide software that could detect terrorist plots supposedly embedded as secret messages in Al Jazeera broadcasts.[37] Other technologies provided by his consultancy caused President Bush, in 2003, to order passenger flights already over the Atlantic to return to the United States. The Bush orders later turned out to have been for no reason, prompting Air France to protest that such ineptitude cost it and its passengers time and money. In the Montgomery instance and in numbers of others, the government chose to keep the case out of court for fear of revealing security secrets, although critics portrayed it as merely another way to shield government incompetence from public view.

As with airlines, where matters of security become an excuse to keep people in their traveling class while in flight (see chapter 4), creation of the DHS excluded, as part of the urgency for secrecy, union membership for the newly reorganized labor force, including the TSA.. We have long-standing precedents for this type of organizational opportunism: Under the guise of fighting communism, J. Edgar Hoover's FBI harassed Martin Luther King and liberal political groups. National and local campaigns against Fred Hampton and the Black Panthers, on the basis of their being an insurrectionary force, led to police killing of the group's militant leaders.

The man chosen by Ronald Reagan to head the Federal Emergency Management Agency (FEMA), Louis Giuffrida, did apparently participate in a larger plan to suspend the U.S. Constitution in case of nuclear attack, and maybe other emergencies. Two *Wall Street Journal* reporters say, in their highly regarded book on disasters, that Giuffrida had developed a plan to imprison twenty-one million American black people as necessary for national survival under states of emergencies.[38] He is also said, although without documentation I could find, to have once written a paper while studying at the U.S. Army War College called "National Survival—Racial Imperative," in which he worked out such thinking.

At least at less draconian levels, those engaging in such "mission creep" may be sincere or at least naive; authorities may come to believe they must expand their purview to deal with danger. Some security officials have thought environmentalists are a threat to the country and must be watched and controlled. In advising U.S. security agencies on strategies against terrorists, RAND Corporation analysts urged vigilance toward environmental groups, warning against "looking in the wrong direction"—in other words, not toward them. "For example," the RAND report notes, "if groups with environmental agendas seek to attack the air transport system, their operatives are unlikely to resemble those of al-Qaeda-associated groups, and security technologies and procedures optimized for the current threat may or may not identify them."[39] In just this vein in March 2001 the FBI named the Earth Liberation Front as the country's "No. 1 domestic terrorist threat." The organization had engaged in many types of nonviolent protest and, in later periods of its short life, destruction to property, like a lumber mill and, in one case, an academic building. One of its operatives, Daniel McGowan, was convicted as a "terrorist" and has been serving out a seven-year term, much of it in isolation to preclude contact with others who might be similarly disposed toward endangering the country.[40]

Besides injustice, militarization is problematic because it is not cool, and cool is now where everyone wants to be. At a time when the so-called creative economy sits at the center of not just urban growth and development, but at the rise of technology itself, countries with intolerant and repressive regimes repel rather than attract those with the right stuff. Wealth is supposed to be one of the things being defended, and wealth also provides the resources to develop appropriate armaments and strategies. Knowledge workers migrate to places of tolerance and expressive liveliness.[41]

The crucial migration of the atomic scientists to the United States was the great case in point. But the subsequent McCarthy era did damage to the country's tolerance profile with a sweep of loyalty oath requirements for academic employees across the country, the most prominent being the 1949 Loyalty Oath imposed by the Regents of the University of California. There were resignations, non-appointments, and the dismissal of thirty-one professors, including some truly distinguished individuals.[42] More recently, scientists and engineers at the Jet

Propulsion Laboratory (JPL) in California protested post-9/11 procedures that allowed routine investigations of workers' political beliefs, sexual tastes, and morality judgments. New employees face mandatory drug testing. In response, some JPL scientists raised the prospect that the national defense will be weakened when those unwilling to put up with such intrusions leave government work. A group of them went to court and, at least in an initial ruling, gained a sympathetic response from the liberally oriented 9th Circuit Court that described the new investigative regime as an "unbounded and standardless inquiry."[43]

Militarization at territorial borders changes not only what happens at the boundaries, but also the quality of life on both sides. The shift is sometimes noted in the case of contemporary Israel, where the contest over borderlands fuels continuing conflict. As put by historian Tony Judt, "That a country with the strongest military in its region, and with an unbroken string of armed victories behind it, should be so obsessed with the security risks of relinquishing a few square miles of land may seem odd indeed."[44] As part of its defense, Israel separates itself from a large segment of what would otherwise be its workforce. This has given rise to imported labor from other parts of the world, like the Philippines, with the result that almost 150,000 "illegals" (people staying past their visa expiration) live in the country.[45] With them has come the dilemma of what to do with their children born in Israel—another threat to the existential survival of a Zionist state.

In the U.S. case, combining the Immigration and Naturalization Service into the DHS further transformed it away from whatever welcoming quality it might have had into an agency whose purpose is scrutiny. One example of this, noticed even by U.S. nationalists, is in the discouragement of "brains" from trying to enter or remain in the country. *New York Times* columnist Thomas Friedman advised stapling a Green Card to every new Ph.D. at U.S. university commencements instead of treating foreign graduates as suspicious characters. In a similar vein, the various machinations of the Israeli security apparatus, some Israeli commentators have warned—although I have not seen any clear data on the subject—may be having counterproductive consequence.[46] The sophisticated, young, and educated of the country leave for other lands where they perceive more opportunity for a placid and joyful life.

THE SECURITY IMPOSTER REASON

While political leaders and their experts really do not know what to do, they act like they do. Deference goes to those least likely to reveal ambivalence. The military and police have appropriate displays, as fitted to the scene, of guns, machines, dogs, and much more. They deploy physical objects that close off spaces in particular ways—jersey barriers, chain link fence, bollards, and commanding signage; these also give off signals of security know-how and the sense that something security-like is going on. Police and military benefit from personal bearing and accoutrements of dress—insignia, medals, and idiosyncratic hanging accessories—all of which cater to what Kerry Fosher calls the "I love a man in uniform" syndrome. They gain obeisance, even when they lack routine knowledge of emergency planning and practices.

Linked into the need for assurance is the rise of the large-scale security industry, spawned by the DHS and its multimillion dollar contracts for the "beltway bandits" of legend. Former Mayor Rudy Giuliani (non beltway in his origin) is the most famous individual recipient, having founded Giuliani-Kerik (an affiliate of his security and management consulting firm) with disgraced former New York City Police Commissioner Bernard Kerik. Kerik, nominated by President George W. Bush to be secretary of the DHS, ended up being sentenced to four years in prison on felony mail fraud and related charges. The surviving Giuliani firm advises foreign governments and private corporations on security matters as well as lobbies Congress and U.S. security agencies. The company had Mexico City as a client; the city signed a million-dollar-plus contract for a one-day consultation visit by Giuliani.

Security firms far larger than his conduct strategic studies and sponsor conferences, meetings, and workshops. They offer confidential consultations on sources of danger and mechanisms for sorting them out. They produce documents of "principles," "strategies," and "priorities," alternatively with vast amounts of verbiage or boilerplate bullet-point tick-offs. Consider this excerpt from a 2002 study commissioned by the State of Louisiana (in league with several other states):

> Was a systematic method used to assess and rank the impact of an attack on critical assets?

Were factors used in the impact assessment relevant and consistently applied?

Were the results of the impact assessment incorporated into the overall risk assessment?[47]

In their review of over four thousand DHS security documents, Priest and Arkin found them frequently "vague, alarmist, and often useless." Hence, a DHS list of vulnerable facilities includes almost everything: "Commercial Facilities, Government Facilities, Banking and Financial, and Transportation."[48] The vague yet comprehensive specifications allow governments, nongovernmental organizations, and corporations to, in effect, outsource the uncertainties, avoiding having to deal with the inevitable holes in the apparatus. On the largest and by now well-known scale, the United States outsourced vast proportions of the Middle East wars—everything from intelligence work to armed patrols—to private contractors whose numbers and costs have, at times, equaled that of maintaining the military itself. In Iraq, in the year 2010, about 80 percent of the eleven thousand or so *armed* private contractors were neither Americans nor Iraqi, but brought in from a third-party country.[49] Armed contractors kill and destroy homes and enterprises, while also yielding up false information to the U.S. military command and State Department. Such activities, according to a Congressional report, "may have undermined U.S. counter-insurgency efforts in Iraq and Afghanistan" as well as helped destabilize the Iraqi government.[50]

In the United States, security firms recruit from the ranks of retired military, intelligence services, and police, as in the Kerik fiasco. Professionals involved with anything like design, as quite clear from airport security, are not at the table; nor are academics from fields like sociology, psychology, or anthropology much in evidence. At the Ground Zero site, as I write, authorities subject tourists to barriers, inspectors, and restrictions in an especially intense way, oblivious to the larger experience of architecture and memorialization. Like those who procure the mundane stuff for the restroom stalls, concern for pleasure and comfort are cast aside by ordering in the standard issue protections.

The security firms do hire people with civilian emergency response backgrounds, tempting them with lucrative salaries. The firms add their names to mastheads and lists of internal experts. To the degree that the firms are successful (recall Walter Maestri, the highly capable Louisiana emergency official, who is a case in point), experienced hands are then lost to public service. Such individuals' real local knowledge of conditions and personnel, according to Fosher, is what provides the greatest resource when trying to coordinate diverse actors under challenging conditions. In creating the private security industry that siphons people off for more bureaucratic but profit-making roles, DHS may thus weaken real competence on the ground.[51]

When it comes to borders with nature, as where rivers and cities meet up (or cities and forests), taking the militarization option generates the unhappy results we have seen, as particularly in the case of New Orleans. Having the Army Corps of Engineers in charge of the Mississippi River—along with their deal-making Congressional enablers— works against long-term ability to defend river-front cities from storm damage and the routines of flood. As part of Zionism, Israeli authorities have removed Palestinian olive groves to make room for the wall, for settlers' houses and schools, and to gain open views of border zones. Where the Israelis want trees, they have preferred pines to the fecundity of the olive groves (pines have symbolic national value for Jews; Palestinians make their livelihoods from olive harvests).[52] In one legal case, involving cutting down a Palestinian olive grove, the court ruled for the government by citing security. As the court reasoned, "Sadly it has been proven that in the last terror attack the olive trees served as a hide-out for the two terrorists."[53] As an ironic twist, it was the pine trees that fueled Israel's greatest "natural disaster," the forest fire of 2010 that killed forty-one people and produced extensive property loss.

Militarization can run deep into the very soul of a citizenry. As Mary Pratt writes, war can be thought of as a mechanism whereby human collectivities renew and revitalize themselves by sacrificing a select number of their own members. Even the equanimous Thomas Jefferson had something like this perhaps in mind when he made his famous remark, "The tree of liberty must be refreshed from time to time, with the blood of patriots and tyrants. It is its natural manure."[54] What counts in war, and I regard this as a usefully provocative thought, to continue with Pratt's commentary, "is not the injury and bloodshed that a group inflicts on its enemy but the bloodshed it undergoes itself."[55] In the war on terror, we do not just send men and women to die through the happenstance of firefight and improvised explosive devices (IEDs), we also create a more routine sacrifice at home, including the expenditure of large sums on security gizmos as well as losses to our own civil liberties and daily affordances. This then becomes still another aspect of the war on terror, the sacrifice of one's time and convenience (and dignity) for the benefit of the cause. Like the enthusiasts in line at airport security, each participant in these intrusions may thus be glad "to do my part." But it is, in this modern U.S. version of privileged war making, "sacrifice lite," and for some, it is highly profitable. This line of analysis helps explain not only the recurrence of bloody conflict on the world stage—revealing as it does the self-perpetuating nature of security apparatuses and the lesser consequences for those calling the shots—but also the more routine forms of civilian self-sacrifice quite regardless of how little sense they may make.

THE EVIL DEMON REASON

A simple way for people to deal with their fear is to identify individuals or groups who are evil—Big Bad Wolf, Chinese, Arabs, or Jews. This generates the search for the so-identified bad ones and their eradication. As certainty grows that such suspect ogres are indeed in our midst, and that midst now includes the entire globe, the lengths to which we will go to demonize similarly scale up.

Some people, domestic or foreign are, or were, up to no good. But the evil demon doctrine presumes a constancy in humans that is naive. Policies based on the idea that certain individuals and groups are permanent enemies are mistaken. From long traditions in social psychological research we know that people change, even their deeply held sense of self, by dint of circumstance. This feature of social life emerged in particular from so-called conformity studies that subject individuals to experimentally manipulated social pressures. Thus from the laboratories of Solomon Asch, and over one hundred replications by others, we see that people will indeed agree to opinions that obviously fly in the face of the facts (like which drawn line in front of them is shorter than adjacent ones).[56] People will change their report of reality to match up to what they perceive everyone else (or most everyone else) reports as perceiving. We also have the famous "prison experiments" of Stanford researcher Philip Zimbardo, who randomly assigned half a group of undergraduates to act as "guards" over the other half of randomly assigned students who would be "prisoners." Over the course of only a few days of confinement in a simulated jail on the Stanford campus (and then a "real" one at the Palo Alto police department), the two groups readily acted out their roles, so much so that Zimbardo had to end the experiments rather than continue the sadism, victimization, and pathetic supplication that so dramatically set in. And most everyone knows of Stanley Milgram's experiments at Yale, replicated at many other places and under differing conditions, in which ordinary people are—in the majority—induced to inflict pain, and even apparent death, on innocent individuals merely because they appeared to be slow at an ersatz "learning" task. Normal and ordinary people, decent people, conform and take on behaviors that bespeak brutality, even wanton brutality.

We always must keep in mind normal life and the way each of us compromises in daily interactions and "go along to get along," or even enthusiastically show solidarity with people and positions with which we do not, in some other times and places, identify. Who among us has not been two-faced? When we are with party x, we assent and go along with the positions they expound, through our body gestures and positive agreements, to the extent that we can. But then, when we are with the adversary of x, we adjust toward the criticisms from the opposition—deferring at least in small ways to the critic's point of view. Children behave horribly at home but are model citizens at school, or vice versa.

Patty Hearst did not become a different human being when she joined in with the radical gang that kidnapped her ("brainwashed" as some media reported), nor a different person again when she rejoined the society of her elite family after she got out of jail. She switched around as conditions changed. There are undercover police who come to change sides and then turn up at legal proceedings to testify for the defense, as happened in one London trial of environmentalists

charged with plotting to shut down one of Britain's largest power stations.[57] Again, people do not come in neat ideological packages, and
this helps explain how a given individual can shift allegiances and how,
in a normal sort of way, whole groups can (re)align with circumstance.
In some cases only the passage of time dissolves a foe's rigid stance; the
system is dynamic as a matter of course, and so it may be that patience
along the way can be beneficial.

All this makes it easier to understand the double agent as a per-
sonality subtype. The double agent may not be selling out one side
to serve the other through some careful plot. He or she may be, as
we might say, especially impressionable. Individuals do vary by per-
sonality in this regard. It may not hurt that besides praise, there may
be rewards of money that come from both directions in return for
conforming to expectations. And, of course, there may be the added
"seduction of crime," as Jack Katz refers to the gratification of taking
on an outlaw role, even for a teenager out on a shoplifting spree.[58]
Plotting to do mayhem, and the double agent role in particular, must
have its own frisson.

A person can also be a double agent because of the substantive issues at hand— serving one master in regard to one good and the other
master to advance a different one. A crime boss can be arranging the
death of a competitor while at the same time supporting the hospital
for crippled children. In various parts of the world, certainly regions of
Mexico where the drug trade predominates, criminals are significant
elements of local social welfare. A different operative can side with the
United States in regard to its drug war but not with its foreign policy
toward a particular country. So we have the case of one David Headley,
a key plotter of the Mumbai attacks of March 1993, which killed 257
persons and injured seven hundred others, including four Americans.[59]
He was on the U.S. payroll as an informant on the drug trade. Two of
his ex-wives independently came forward to warn that he was (also) a
terrorist. One wife, an American, went to investigators in New York to
report on the guy; the other went to the U.S. embassy in Islamabad.
Both women provided concrete information, including details of his
alleged terrorist training in Pakistan. But when the U.S. antiterrorist
authorities went to pursue their investigation, the antidrug authorities

warned them off. One of the women had told officials, according to her report, that "either he is a terrorist or he works for you."[60] In a way and apparently beyond her imaginings, Headley was both. U.S. officials had not even placed him on a no-fly list, and indeed he was able to move unimpeded between the United States and Pakistan.[61] Dividing the world into "good guys" and "bad guys" once again messes things up, because people can be "split"—divided in the allegiances they hold and the substantive goals they pursue. This is *normal*.

The existence of these multiple orientations facilitates entrapment. Entrapment is not just a civil liberties issue in some abstract sense; its on-the-ground procedures operate as a seducer. Many of us have had evil in our heart, and a skilled interlocutor can lure us into expressing it. We have mentally plotted or at least given due consideration to abetting the death of a parent, sibling, or boss. There is thus an ambiguous state between being a violent lawbreaker and entertaining everyday fantasies of doing horrible things to others. And entrapment can bring out the potential in many if not most or even all of us, certainly to the point of plotting. The practice of entrapment increases the population of those made visible as ready to do others in.

All this takes on additional importance as the threshold goes lower for opening focused surveillance of a given individual by authorities. With very little to show for its efforts, the Bush and Obama administrations have opened thousands of what the FBI terms "assessments" of particular individuals, along with sending confidential informers to infiltrate an organization and attend political and religious meetings. There is no legal requirement to show "cause," gain court approval, or even to have concrete evidence of wrongdoing.[62] Imagine how this might work when the person doing the entrapment is better educated, resourced, and more articulate than the individual under surveillance. The trapper knows the score in special ways, probably with training in how to source and deploy illicit materials as well as the laws and habits of authorities. A supportive and information-rich companion can intensify sympathies toward, for example, Arab nationalism or Islamic radicalism. We have mountains of relevant research to document that young men will do a lot to fit into to a masculinist hierarchy. Who knows the proportion of people who can be engaged in idiosyncratic behavior through well-matched enablers?

Here indeed is the account of a New York Muslim leader, Zein Rimawi of the Queens Islamic Society, as he speaks of one of the two young co-conspirators in the plot to blow up the Herald Square subway station, James Elshafay. Elshafay's participation was certainly facilitated by the police informant who nursed him along (see chapter 3). When a reporter raises the point that Elshafay has apparently pleaded guilty, Rimawi responds,

> Innocent or not is not the point. . . . If you take a young man like that and tell him you are religious and you are experienced and clever, and you work him for a year and you keep talking to him and telling him "We have to do this," it's easy for that young man to say, "Yes, let's do it." Of course that would happen. Doing this, they could arrest most young Muslim people.[63]

Elshafay was eventually given a reduced sentence of five years in exchange for testimony against his co-conspirator Shahawar Siraj, who got thirty.

We do not know how many terrorist plots there have been against the homeland since 9/11. A Heritage Foundation report says that in the ten years since 9/11, authorities were able to thwart forty-one "Islamist-inspired terrorist plots."[64] In many of these, entrapment played an obvious role—with the most recent event involving a single individual's plot (working with two FBI informants) to outfit a miniature plane with cell-phone explosion devices meant to do in the Pentagon and U.S. Capitol.[65] However calculated, the volume has been low; we don't have much to show for all the defenses put in place.

Could it be, we might ask, that beyond the reported cases, there are numbers of others that never reach the media, or even the Heritage Foundation analysts? I doubt it. Authorities are avid publicists of threats and especially of thwarted ones—recall the media event sponsored by Mayor Bloomberg and his police chief in the Jose Pimentel case (mentioned in chapter 3). It was a showpiece press conference. The FBI did not itself have a high bar for announcing suspicions; in early 2003, the agency director told Congress there were "militant Islamics [sic] in the US." He suspected, he said, "that several hundred of these extremists are linked to al-Qaeda." But according to the Justice Department itself, in the five years after 9/11, about a dozen people were convicted for links with al-Qaeda and, through a different tally by academic researchers, "fewer than 40 Muslim-Americans planned or carried out acts of domestic terrorism."[66] We need to keep in mind the weak basis of many such charges as well as shaky bases of convictions, and the peculiar etiology of their origins.

Might it be possible, to further press the idea that our bastions accomplish something significant, that the various security bric-a-brac deter just by their existence? Maybe it discourages miscreants from the outset. This stretches credulity, given what we see the captured and accused plotters to be like. Where they are not simple saps of entrapment, they are half-sane or bewildered. Or, as rightly feared, they are suicidal—whatever the other qualities of mind they may possess, they don't care what happens to them. Deterrence would not count for much among such individuals. Surely, they would have at least *tried* to storm the barricades; it is what committed people do in the face of efforts to thwart them.

Plotters do exist, to be sure—always have, and always will. Some will prepare new assaults. But we have lost our ability to know what a "plot" might existentially be. Conspiracies are full of our own law-enforcement people aligning with fantasists, incompetents, and the more simply malevolent, goading them on, paying their air fares, buying them equipment, and helping form their ideas. This is not intelligence, but another way we can manage to provide for all sides, stirring up a sense of self-congratulatory effectiveness while risking organizational sanity.

The Real Order and Ways to Build on It

I return to the thinking with which this book began—how people make life. The system of mundane order is a system of security and needs to be the basis of any security system whatever. As Noah McClain concludes from our subway research, as well as from reviewing the disaster literature, "The evidence is in the everyday, not just in the rubble."[67] Any deliberate security system, as with—again—any other social contrivance, needs to work with the ongoing procedures as they exist and, most profoundly, with the means that people use to manage their lives together. To paraphrase Donald Rumsfeld's quote about the U.S. Army in its Middle East wars, we must secure ourselves with the kind of human nature we have, not the kind of human nature we might wish to have. But that is good news if we look closely at how our order works.

There are two key characteristics of this ordinariness: tacit and mutual, themselves working together.

Tacit: when we ride a bike, we do not articulate how we do it, and thinking too hard makes it impossible to carry on. We get the "hang" of it, including how to adjust with change in terrain and other circumstance. We don't need, as a prima facie condition, to be told—and indeed such instruction, inappropriately deployed, interferes with accomplishment. *Nothing* goes a long way.

Mutual: Following again from the likes of Goffman, we know we have hyper-awareness of one another's actions—their sighs and utterances as well as the organizational context in which all of it occurs. We sense and we align. We ignore the ways people's behavior shows incompleteness, including their use of ambiguous words that, as an essential aspect, make up all the conversations in which we participate ("kill" can mean many different things, as you may recall from chapter 4). So, as a practical matter, we "let it pass" in the words of sociologist Harold Garfinkel.[68] And this "do nothing" attitude lets life go forward to a next iteration. "Don't just do something, stand there," can be as applicable to security preparedness as everyday interaction. That is why when police and other authorities are helpful, it comes from the fact that, as scholar Alice Hills explains after a worldwide scan of civil war and natural disaster responses, they "are better at reproducing order than producing it."[69] Best to replicate or at least build on people's complexly tacit and mutual means of doing the world rather than trying to invent a world that does not exist.

Too often the temptation is to reform through rules and official procedures that can sidestep those usual ways of doing things. But mundane life contains fantastic human capacity for mutuality; it should be interfered with only on pain of screwing things up in a big way. To create apparent order, you kill the actual order. You "clean up" more than dirt; you efface the tacit mechanisms and social work-arounds that people use to get things done together. If it requires breaking some eggs—*these eggs*—so the authorities reason, that is just the route to the security omelets. They bypass the radically local nature of predicaments and the first-hand ability of actors to solve them. As state agents follow one another's "best practices," error is systematically replicated. Authorities, as we say, "step in" and then foul it up.

The mothers of all modern U.S. security catastrophes are, of course, the wars in the Middle East. Their creators pulled levers that could unleash planes, missiles, bombs, and battalions. The war in Iraq, we know, was based on clear deception told by those in the highest reaches of power. Some holding to conspiratorial theories think the whole thing was masterminded by a segment of the U.S. right, maybe with connivance of the oil companies. For me, the result could not have been planned: vast waste of national wealth, deaths to U.S. soldiers, and continued thug-driven civil mayhem in our imagined model client state—and almost no oil. I cannot muster that level of cynicism. So, as in explaining the irrationalities at the airport, the subways, and New Orleans floods, I see the culprit to be the myopic urge to control and its narrowed sense of the world. If this be theater, it is theatrically awful.

The problem was not in knowing how to push the buttons of war but in dealing with life. Blinded by power and ignorance, no notice was taken of order on the ground. Whatever other motivations may have been in play—ideological commitment to a capitalist-democratic Middle East, some nice opportunities for big oil and little Israel, or avenging the president's father's humiliation—there was a profound sociological mistake, and this lay in the glaring lack of consideration of the social basis for any system of security. Those of us with experience in moving an academic department from one building to another think through matters such as who will get what space, or where will the copy machine go, and consider the precise circumlocutions needed to tamp brewing resentment (why is her office bigger than mine?). No less should occur with a military invasion.

So Now: What to Do?

Security entails thinking *critically* and in a comprehensive manner about present strategies and questioning them—at general levels as well as in specific detail. We need to deal with security just as we do with any other realm of individual stance or public policy. We need considered judgment based on empirical evidence cleansed of the deep anxieties of fear and vengeance that so feed the reflex to command and control.

At the same time, we cannot be utopian about what publics will or will not accept. Some evil is out there and some wars are worth fighting. And quite regardless of how reasonable they may or may not be in any given context, the people, their politicians, and the surrounding media have their fears. Things must be done in response—machinery put in place, policies enacted, flags unfurled. To sound the refrain again, like it or not, something must be done. As shown by the chapters that have come before, however, these things can be different from what they have been. There are ways to move forward under the gun of some inevitable real trouble and the gun of political necessity to take more positive action. Here's the list.

• *Go with the flow.*

Fight fire with fire, not firemen, and fire happens all on its own if we let it. As Mike Davis famously wrote, we should "Let Malibu Burn," and that also means letting Bambi die. That thin strip of glamorous land stretched between the Pacific and the Santa Monica mountains is too expensive and dangerous to protect from the "ravages of nature," as they are ideologically called. Put in geographer Gilbert White's gentler dictum, Davis is telling us not to build houses in fire-prone areas and if you are close to such areas, build them in a fireproof way. Don't celebrate those who vow, after a fire or flood, to return and rebuild.

There are routines in the subway, like routines of the forest. Learn them and go with them. Commanding the Mississippi does not protect. Real security comes from the assemblage of artifacts, habits, and procedures, which mostly are already there. Find ways for people to access solutions they often utilize: give them stairways literally and figuratively. Work with people's ordinary sense making that, in Karl Wick's term, must not be pressed into "collapse."[70]

• *Make nice.*

As we have noticed before, the attacker is thin tailed and hard to hit. As a security analyst says, "There are an infinite number of disruption scenarios," but only a finite number of possible protections.[71] The way to deal with the problem of thin tails is swamping all in kindness. Choose interventions that have a positive impact no matter what. Mechanisms that flush out stale air in buildings, subways, tunnels, or within aircraft defeats attackers by having fewer people getting sick, whether by poison or each other's germs. Official measures interfering with organic modes of provisioning and being together can in fact create vacuums that come to be filled by shysters, thugs, and political opportunists. Like a bad turnstile or weapons cache, the damage continues to shape outcomes, social and physical, long after the disaster subsides.

People will indeed come together if given half a chance. One concrete application of this idea is for planners to engineer in the time to get it together, time for mutual regard to take hold. Disaster preparation should strive to create holding places—spatial as well as temporal—not primarily for authorities, but for ordinary people. Try to make it like the *Titanic*, where the bases of social order can play a role (giving advantage to at least some of the women and children), rather than the *Lusitania*, where utter crisis overwhelms anything like altruism. In concrete ways, plan for the catastrophe to be at least *slowed down*, sometimes by providing rest stops and way stations.

• *Leverage redesign.*

Demands for "more security" and apparent willingness to pay for it could invite an examination of everything an organization does, not just to harden it but to improve it on all fronts. Security is, in effect, a design problem. Whether in the toilet or a war, how do you array diverse elements to maximize solutions for as many difficulties as possible?

Problems in any sphere always come in batches and are interconnected. Some of them need attending because they are, like the HEET turnstiles, inadvertent effects of solutions to prior troubles. Since no instrument or organizational setup is ever independent, nothing done to solve one problem is without impacts. This sets up the need for continuous change and refinement—with no end ever. Security too often presumes finality—armor in place, bad guys dead or behind bars, instead of ongoing attentiveness to ranges of interacting opportunities and constraints.

Designers—architects, landscape architects, and product designers—have the experience of being forced to rework their plans and the prior stuff that they have collectively done. The client is not happy, the government imposes a new regulation, or aesthetic taste makes its inevitable shift. The good designer uses the change to produce an even better outcome, reexamining aspects of the design not directly incriminated. Creating a sturdier toilet stall (with good sound insulation) may invite a do-dad for needle exchange. Airline security gates could serve to guide passengers to the right flight or to distribute facemasks for those who will be sneezing on board. The subway platform can have special places for street entertainers available also for gurneys if the need should arise. It's all about dual-use, triple-use, n-use, and the inclusion of bespoke advantages along the way. This puts it beyond the "all hazards" planning that is now part of the disaster preparedness canon. The point is to go beyond disaster, period.

Good design always means a focus on overall goals. So while perhaps asked to design a toothbrush, the designer can see the problem as really oral hygiene and that may mean no toothbrush at all. Toilet paper holders might best go extinct with a water rinse replacing it and its associated products. Translated into security concerns, it means trying to figure out the system that leads into a particular danger and that then leads out from it, and then design every element at every scale to accomplish reform. Architects have spoken of this approach as design from "spoon to city," but too often that results only in a consistent set of motifs—or "design vocabulary." The more ambitious goal is to work through the ways spoon and city interconnect (artifact to waste, for example), and design accordingly.

In his thinking about urban infrastructure, the sociologist and safety expert Charles Perrow pushes for minimizing the presence of hazardous materials where populations aggregate. Storage of incendiaries at urban production sites is a clear offense against this principle. Much of the material is there as residue from a time when the land was cheap and before more benign material substitutes existed. Changing things might be a net good for lowering production costs as well as enhancing public safety.[72] Vast leakage from what had been, before the Gulf oil spill of 2010, the largest oil leak in U.S. history—at San Luis Obispo County in California—harmed the local environment as well as costing the oil company money in lost revenue.[73] Having sensors, photo images, and magnetic resonance systems wherever chemicals are stored, including refineries and pipelines, averts leaks and pollution. If properly engineered and installed, they can do more than detect the plot of the proverbial terrorist.[74]

• *Be inclusive.*

Applied to the security apparatus, universal design translates as spreading knowledge and utility to the larger population and not restricting understanding to those with special knowledge, keys, or tools. That means anyone can join in the rescue or escape because they see and comprehend the infrastructure around them and have been given the straight dope about the nature of threat and not some poppycock about "See Something." There used to be a slogan about the AIDS epidemic, "Silence = Death." Yes, and so does bullshit.

Knowledge tends to be a distributed good; making it effective means finding a way for those who have pieces of it to come together. So setting up people's wireless communication devices, and making them more secure, speeds up and widens the circle of interaction. It enhances the self-organizing capacity and its durability. Rescue volunteers as well as those trapped in their attics benefit. And meanwhile, on a day-to-day basis, everyone is better off.

The larger goal, across the board and in whatever ways possible, is to equip people's Jacobean eyes and enhance their agile willingness to intervene. Build on such intervention rather than noting it after the fact, as I did in regard to how subway passengers aid MTA employees or how office workers helped one another down the stairs on 9/11. Individuals figure out what to do ad hoc. Let them do their thing and set them up to know together; it is at least as likely to turn out right as the alternative and it is democratically rich.

• *Add in some equality.*

Systems of sharing, prevention, and resilience work best in a benign social environment, one that makes people less desperate or resentful. They become more likely to warn one another and alert authorities. They take care of hazards like holes in the ground and do not plug up toilets or vandalize the public sphere. They do not have to steal the toilet paper for home use or gum up the MetroCard vending machine so they can sell their swipes. They do not mug other human beings. Museums with only suggested admissions prices experience high rates of full-fare payment among visitors; the good will and I presume lack of abject poverty in the clientele makes it unnecessary to pursue free-riders through the galleries. For their part, authorities can let it be.

• *Accept loss.*

T. S. Eliot wrote of a humankind that "cannot bear very much reality."[75] We need to accept bad outcomes, most importantly, death. Lack of acceptance makes us sitting ducks for any program, policy, or action that can be spoken of as adding "security"—regardless of how little sense it makes.

Take falling off a cliff. There are places in the United States, and indeed across the world, where high cliffs meet up with oceans, where mountain precipices overlook valleys, where bridges span deep crevasses. Often, they are *wonderful*. But there is continuous effort by those made anxious to put up fences to block bodies from going over.

Should the protections be built? The downside is that these locations inspire and add to the sum of happiness in the world. Perhaps because they exist, they give some a reason to take care of themselves, or at least to not do themselves in. Maybe they become iconic suicide locations precisely because of their grandeur. If you try to end the suicides, you may kill the wonder—for all—but not lower the death rate. So death may shift from the Golden Gate to the home garage. The suicide is deprived of the sublime. Political debates swirl about what to do: stop the suicides no matter what or honor the intent to end life if that is someone's will. There are, of course, positions in between. Aesthetes, environmentalists, and architectural commentators engage with social agencies, religion officials, and victims' families to debate which side to be on or whether there are compromises in between. It is another case of radical, moral, and empirical ambiguity. Going with the flow, defaulting to decency means—albeit in an ethically complex way—allowing self-destruction, on the spot and in the here and at the now.

Accepting such death follows the bias of this book toward the embrace of life. We have seen, in various settings, the limits of command—including, to continue with the last example, "Thou shalt not jump." Walling off the edge is another instance of depriving the collectivity out of anxiety for what one individual might do. We worry about toilets and what can happen in them, so everyone goes without. Authorities at the subway impose restrictions and insert instructions ("If you see something . . .") that have little relevance to anything except making people feel still more anxiety. They set up ways to block fare-beaters that then create other ways to beat the fare, and in the process produce barriers for emergency exit. In the airport, as in the subway, interventions mount up to yield almost nothing of value. They are a pain in the ass. In the most dramatic of displays, the airport security gate gathers up a target itself. At Ground Zero, bomb fear builds a bizarrely bombastic structure that defeats both market logic and the prospect of global appreciation.

The alternative—the default to decency advocated in the chapters of this book—is only a lead-in for further political and moral debate, because, to sound still another refrain from previous chapters, nothing is certain. A lot of ambiguity—it is the nature of life—will remain.

We each have our way of trying to see past trouble. In this book I have aligned with the many others whose sympathies accord with, and indeed have shaped, my own—sympathies I take to be positive, trusting, and informed. Out of it all I press the central point that I believe reaches into the beings of people and can be the basis for effective reform: the best antidote to fear is an activist search for beauty and delight. Join in the "love train," like it says in the song.[76]

Notes

•••

CHAPTER 1

1. Susan Leigh Star, "The Ethnography of Infrastructure." *American Behavioral Scientist* 43, no. 3 (November/December 1999): 377–91.

2. Donald Norman, *The Design of Everyday Things* (New York: Basic Books, 2002).

3. Alfred Gell, *The Anthropology of Art: Essays and Diagrams* (London: Berg, 1999).

4. On nuclear plants, see Charles Perrow, *Normal Accidents: Living with High-Risk Technologies* (New York: Basic Books, 1984). On space exploration disaster, see Dianne Vaughan, *The Challenger Launch Decision: Risky Technology, Culture, and Deviance at NASA* (Chicago: University of Chicago Press 1996).

5. Vitrine text for a Bis Pole, Metropolitan Museum of Art, New York, http://www.metmuseum.org/Collections/search-the-collections/50004299.

6. Christopher Lane. "Living Well Is the Best Revenge: Outing Privacy and Psychoanalysis," in *Public Sex/Gay Space*, ed. William Leap (New York: Columbia University Press, 1966), 266.

7. Bridget M. Hutter and Michael Power, "Organizational Encounters with Risk: An Introduction," in *Organizational Encounters with Risk*, ed. Bridget M. Hutter and Michael Power (Cambridge, England: Cambridge University Press, 2006), 10; see also Tom Baker and Jonathan Simon, "Embracing Risk," pp. 1–26 in *Embracing Risk*, ed. Tom Baker and Jonathan Simon (Chicago: University of Chicago Press, 2002); Richard Ericson and Aaron Doyle, "Risk and Morality," pp. 1–11 in Richard Ericson and Aaron Doyle (eds.), *Risk and Morality*, ed. Richard Ericson and Aaron Doyle (Toronto: University of Toronto Press, 2003). For data on the *Titanic*, see Bruno S. Frey, David A. Savage, and Benno Torgler "Interaction of natural survival instincts and internalized social norms exploring the *Titanic* and *Lusitania* disasters," *Proceedings of the National Academy of Science* 107, no. 11 (March 16, 2010): 4862–65, http://www.pnas.org/content/early/2010/02/17/0911303107.full.pdf.

8. Edward Shils, *The Torment of Secrecy: The Background and Consequences of American Security Policies* (Chicago: Ivan R. Dee, 1956).

9. Here is the language, verbatim:

> A. TSA does not prohibit the public, passengers, or press from photographing, videotaping, or filming screening locations unless the activity interferes with a TSO's ability to perform his or her duties or prevents the orderly flow of individuals through the screening location. Requests by commercial entities

to photograph an airport screening location must be forwarded to TSA's Office of Strategic Communications and Public Affairs Photographing EDS or ETD monitor screens or emitted images is not permitted.

B. TSA must not confiscate or destroy the photographic equipment or film of any person photographing the screening location.

10. David Dunlap, "A Bus Depot and a Continuing Fight to Photograph New York," *New York Times*, February 8, 2012, A24.

11. Melvin Pollner, *Mundane Reason: Reality in Everyday and Sociological Discourse* (Cambridge, England: Cambridge University Press, 2010).

12. Anthony Giddens, *Modernity and Self Identity: Self and Society in the Late Modern Age* (Cambridge, England: Polity), 92.

13. The Tomlin quote owes to Eugene A. Rosa and Lee Clarke, "A Collective Hunch? Risk as the Real and the Elusive," *Journal of the Association for Environmental Studies and Science*, forthcoming.

14. Pollner, *Mundane Reason*, 123.

15. Kai Ericson, *A New Species of Trouble: Explorations in Disaster, Trauma, and Community* (New York: W.W. Norton, 1994), 144.

16. Ibid., note title of book.

17. This formulation comes from Kerry Fosher. See Fosher, *Under Construction: Making Homeland Security at the Local Level* (Chicago: University of Chicago Press, 2009), 73.

18. James Short, "Introduction" to James Short and Lee Clarke, eds., *Organizations, Uncertainties, and Risk* (Boulder, Colo.: Westview, 1992), 7, as cited in Hutter and Power, *Organizational Encounters with Risk*, 21.

19. Fosher, *Under Construction*, 227.

20. Ulrich Beck, "From Industrial Society to the Risk Society: Questions of Survival, Social Structure and Ecological Enlightenment," *Theory Culture and Society* 9, no.1 (1992): 105.

21. Newsmax.com Wires, "Bush: 'Smoke Them Out,'" September 26, 2001," http://archive.newsmax.com/archives/articles/2001/9/25/211541.shtml. See also Brian Knowlton, "Terror in America / 'We're Going to Smoke Them Out': President Airs His Anger," *New York Times*, September 19, 2001, http://www.nytimes.com/2001/09/19/news/19iht-t4_30.html.

22. John Mueller, *Overblown: How Politicians and the Terrorism Industry Inflate National Security Threats, and Why We Believe Them* (New York: Free Press, 2009).

23. Ibid., 135.

24. Quoted in Kari Norgaard, *Living in Denial: Climate Change, Emotions, and Everyday Life.* (Cambridge, Mass.: MIT Press, 2011), 186. This point owes to her formulation. See also Peter Schwartz and Doug Randall's report "An Abrupt Climate Change Scenario and Its Implications for United States National Security" (Pasadena: Jet Propulsion Laboratory, October 2003).

25. Chauncey Starr, "Social Benefits versus Technological Risks," *Science* 165, no. 3899 (September 1969): 1232–38

26. Robin Gregory and Robert Mendelsohn. "Perceived Risk, Dread, and Benefits," *Risk Analysis* 13, no. 3 (1993): 259–64; Paul Slovic, Baruch Fischhoff, and Sarah Lichtenstein, "Why Study Risk Perception?" *Risk Analysis* 2, no. 2 (1982): 83–93.

27. Mary Douglas, *How Institutions Think* (Syracuse, N.Y.: Syracuse University Press, 1986). See also Pat Caplan, "Terror, Witchcraft and Risk," *AnthroGlobe Journal*, first posted January 19, 2006, http://www.anthroglobe.info/docs/caplanp_witchcraft_060119.htm.

28. Fosher, *Under Construction*, 107.

29. Ibid., 73.

30. Enrico Quarantelli, "Disasters: Recipes and Remedies," *Social Research* 75, no. 3 (Fall 2008): 896.

31. Jason D. Averill, Dennis S. Mileti, Richard D. Peacock, Erica D. Kuligowski, Norman Groner, Guylene Proulx, Paul A. Reneke, and Harold E. Nelson, "Federal Building and Fire Safety Investigation of the World Trade Center Disaster, Occupant Behavior, Egress, and Emergency Communications," NIST NCSTAR 1-7 (Washington, D.C.: U.S. Department of Commerce, September 2005).

32. Ibid., 107.

33. Ibid., 149.

34. Ibid., 168.

35. Bruno S. Frey, David A. Savage, and Benno Torgler, "Interaction of Natural Survival Instincts and Internalized Social Norms Exploring the *Titanic* and *Lusitania* Disasters," *Proceedings of the National Academy of Science*, 107, no. 11 (March 16, 2010): 4862–65.

36. Joy Parr, "Working Knowledge of the Insensible: An Embodied History of Radiation Protection in Canadian Nuclear Power Stations, 1962–1992," *Comparative Studies in Society and History* 48, no.4 (2006): 851.

37. Jörg Potthast, "Sense and Security: A Comparative View on Access Control at Airports," *Technology and Innovation Studies* 7 no. 1 (2011): 89.

38. Gary Marx, "Ironies of Social Control: Authorities as Contributors to Deviance through Escalation, Nonenforcement and Covert Facilitation," *Social Problems* 28, no. 3 (February 1981): 221–46.

39. Chalmers Johnson, *The Sorrows of Empire* (New York: Holt, 2004).

40. Eric Klinenberg, *Heat Wave* (Chicago: University of Chicago Press, 2003).

41. Kathleen Nolan, *Police in the Hallways: Discipline in an Urban High School* (Minneapolis: University of Minnesota Press, 2011).

42. Alice Goffman, "On the Run: Wanted Men in a Philadelphia Ghetto," *American Sociological Review* 74, no.3 (2009): 339–357; see also Bruce Western, *Punishment and Inequality in America* (New York: Russell Sage Foundation, 2006).

43. Loic Waquant, *Punishing the Poor* (Durham, N.C.: Duke University Press, 2009).

44. Jimmy Carter, "Call Off the Global Drug War" *New York Times*, June 16, 2011.

45. Ian Hacking, "Making Up People," in *Historical Ontology* (Cambridge, Mass.: Harvard, 2002), http://www.lrb.co.uk/v28/n16/ian-hacking/making-up-people.

46. These data exclude minor cases not directly linked to terror allegations (such as making financial contributions to suspect charities). See this report: "Terrorist Trial Report Card, September 11, 2001–September 11, 2010," with an introduction by Karen J. Greenberg (New York: Center on Law and Security, New York University School of Law, http://www.lawandsecurity.org/Portals/0/Documents/01_TTRC2010Final1.pdf

47. Dianne Hagaman, *How I Learned Not to Be a Photojournalist*, (Lexington: University Press of Kentucky, 1996).

48. Douglas, *How Institutions Think*, 102.

49. William James, "What Pragmatism Means," in *Pragmatism and Other Writings*, ed. G. Gunn (reprint: New York: Penguin Classics, 2000; first published in 1907).

50. Gregory Squires and Chester Hartman, *There is No Such Thing as a Natural Disaster: Race, Class, and Katrina* (New York: Routledge, 2006).

51. Hutter and Power, "Organizational Encounters with Risk: An Introduction."

CHAPTER 2

1. Playwright John Guare's quotation can be found in John Lahr, "Wild at Heart," *New Yorker*, May 9, 2011.

2. A group of toilet scholars is represented in Harvey Molotch and Laura Norén, eds., *Toilet: Public Restrooms and the Politics of Sharing* (New York: New York University Press, 2010). See also Olga Gershenson and Barbara Penner, eds., *Ladies and Gents: Public Toilets and Gender* (Philadelphia: Temple University Press, 2009); Dominique LaPorte, *History of Shit* (Cambridge, Mass.: MIT Press, 2002); Rose George, *The Big Necessity: The Unmentionable World of Human Waste and Why It Matters* (New York: Metropolitan Books, 2008).

3. WebMD, "What Can You Catch in Bathrooms?" http://www.webmd.com/balance/features/what-can-you-catch-in-restrooms.

4. Charles P. Gerba, "Application of Quantitative Risk Assessment for Formulating Hygiene Policy in the Domestic Setting," *Journal of Infection* 43 (2001): 95. Cited in Ruth Barcan, "Dirty Spaces: Separation, Concealment, and Shame in the Public Toilet," in *Toilet*, 36.

5. Mary Douglas, *Purity and Danger* (London: Routledge, 1978).

6. Norbert Elias, *The Civilizing Process* (Oxford: Blackwell, 1939).

7. My use of the term differs from both Nigel Thrift's meaning and from that of his source, Giorgio Agamben. See Nigel Thrift, *Non-Representational Theory: Space, Politics, Affect* (London: Routledge, 2007): 60; Giorgio Agamben, *State of Exception* (Chicago: University of Chicago Press, 2005).

8. G. William Domhoff, *The Scientific Study of Dreams: Neural Networks, Cognitive Development, and Content Analysis* (New York: New York Psychological Association, 2002).

9. Personal communication (e-mail), December 19, 2008. See the Domhoff dream collection on his website, dreambank.net.

10. George, *The Big Necessity*.

11. International Year of Sanitation 2008, "Sanitation Is Vital for Human Health," http://esa.un.org/iys/health.shtml.

12. This point derives from observations by Tamar Remz, whose NYU senior project involved a comparative census of an affluent New York City neighborhood with a poor one. Tamar Remz, "Counting the Spots," senior project, Metropolitan Studies, New York University, May 2008.

13. Haegi Kwon, "Public Toilets in New York City: A Plan Flushed with Success?" Master's thesis, Department of Urban Planning, Columbia University, New York, 2005.

14. See Mitchell Duneier, *Sidewalk* (New York: Farrar, Straus and Giroux, 1999).

15. Philippe Bourgois and Jeff Schoenberg, *Righteous Dopefiend* (Berkeley: University of California Press, 2009).

16. See Barcan, "Dirty Spaces," where she includes this note about the "prewarmed seat":

> I'm using this example from Nicholson Baker's delightful novella *The Mezzanine*, in which he describes the protagonist Howie's awkwardness about the enforced sociality of the office toilets: "I used the stalls as little as possible, never really at ease reading the sports section left there by an earlier occupant, not happy about the prewarmed seat." *The Mezzanine: A Novel* (New York: Vintage Books, 1986), 83.

17. "A Modest Proposal," Opinion, *New York Times*, November 5, 1990, http://www.nytimes.com/1990/11/05/opinion/a-modest-proposal.html.

18. Mathis-Lilley, Ben, "Dead Heads," *New York Magazine*, March 5, 2006, http://nymag.com/news/intelligencer/16393/.

19. Laura Norén, "Only Dogs Are Free to Pee: New York Cabbies Search for Civility," in *Toilet*.

20. Schaller Consulting, *Taxicab Handbook*, vol. 3 (New York: B. Schaller, 2006). See also: Schaller Consulting, *The Changing Face of Taxi and Limousine Drivers: U.S., Large States and Metro Areas and New City* (New York: B. Schaller, 2004).

21. Norén, "Only Dogs Are Free to Pee."

22. Duneier, *Sidewalk*.

23. Malise Ruthven, "Excremental India," *New York Review*, May 13, 2010, 46.

24. Reports such as this are contained in the documentary film *Q2P* by Paromita Vohra. See www.planetinfocus.org/festival/q2p.

25. Monica Krause, "Boundaries of the Universal: How Humanitarians Make Decisions about Relief," Ph.D. diss., New York University, 2009.

26. P. 54, Spencer Cahill, William Distler, Cynthia Lachowetz, Andrea Meaney, Robyn Tarallo, Teena Willard, "Meanwhile Backstage: Public Bathrooms and the Interaction Order" *Journal of Contemporary Ethnography* 14, no. 1 (April 1985): 54.

27. Terry Kogan, "Sex Separation: The Cure-All for Victorian Social Anxiety," in *Toilet*.

28. Betsy Foxman, Robin Barlow, Hannah D'Arcy, Brenda Gillespie, and Jack Sobel, "Urinary Tract Infection" *Annals of Epidemiology* 10, no. 8 (November 2000): 509–15; Norén, "Only Dogs Are Free to Pee"; National Kidney and Urologic Disease Information Clearinghouse, National Institute of Health.

29. Besides thousands of articles in women's magazines, we have more serious reports like those of Nora Ephron's *I Feel Bad About My Neck and Other Thoughts on Being a Woman* (New York: Vintage, 2008). Recognizing the phenomenon, but taking a more critical attitude, are authors like Susie Orbach. See for example her book *Bodies* (New York: Picador, 2009).

30. Harvey Molotch, "The Rest Room and Equal Opportunity," *Sociological Forum* 3, no. 1 (1988): 128–32.

31. For a fuller discussion, see Barbara Penner, "Female toilets: (Re) Designing the 'unmentionable,'" in *Ladies and Gents*.

32. Sheila L. Cavanagh, *Queering Bathrooms: Gender, Sexuality, and the Hygienic Imagination* (Toronto: University of Toronto Press, 2010), 178.

33. Ibid.

34. Mary Anne Case, "Why Not Abolish the 'Laws of Urinary Segregation'?" in *Toilet*. The phrase "urinary segregation" comes from Jacques Lacan, "The Instance of the Letter in the Unconscious, or Reason since Freud," in *Écrits: A Selection*, trans. B. Fink (New York and London: W. W. Norton, 2002).

35. Ibid., 221.

36. National Association for Continence, "What Is Incontinence," http://www.nafc.org/bladder-bowel-health/; George, *The Big Necessity*, 142, was the original source.

37. Kerri Berson took to NYU campus buildings in a wheel chair to simulate the difficulties facing those with disability. Kerri Berson, "A Half-Ass Job?" senior project, Metropolitan Studies, New York University, May 5, 2008.

38. This is a repeated observation, perhaps first mentioned by Erving Goffman, *Relations in Public: Microstudies of the Public Order*; (New York: Basic Books, 1971), 59; see also, Lee Edelman, "Men's Room," in *Stud: Architectures of Masculinity*, ed. Joel Sanders (New York: Princeton Architectural Press, 1966), 153.

39. Howard S. Becker, *Outsiders: Studies in the Sociology of Deviance* (New York: Free Press, 1963), 147–53.

40. On the Harvard Science Center case, see Bryan Reynolds, "Rest Stop: Erotics at Harvard," in *Toilet*.

41. S. Parkin and R. Coomber, "Fluorescent Blue Lights, Injecting Drug Use and Related Health Risk in Public Conveniences: Findings from a Qualitative Study of Micro-injecting Environments," *Health & Place* 16, no. 4 (2010): 629–37.

42. Laud Humphries, *Tearoom Trade: Impersonal Sex in Public Places* (New York: Aldine, 1970).

43. See George Chauncey, *Gay New York* (New York: Basic Books, 1995), 215.

44. Ibid., 198.

45. Sulabh International Service Organisation, "Aims and Objectives," accessed February 15, 2010, http://www.sulabhinternational.org/ngo/aims_objective.php.

46. David McDonald, "ACT Syringe Vending Machines Trial 2004–2006: Progress Report No. 3, August to December 2005, and Preliminary Evaluation Findings" (Canberra: Siggins Miller in association with Social Research & Evaluation Pty Ltd, 2006).

47. Denise Scott Brown, "Planning the Powder Room" *AIA Journal* (April 1967): 81–83.

48. See the schematic proposal for a large-scale public restroom (figure 12.1) in "On Not Making History," in *Toilet*, 266.

49. Clark Sorensen's catalogue of urinal structures, http://www.clarkmade.com/urinals.html.

CHAPTER 3

1. Noah McClain, "The Institutions of Urban Anxiety: Work, Organizational Process and Security Practices in the New York Subway," Ph.D. diss., Sociology Department, New York University, 2010. See also Harvey Molotch and Noah McClain,

"Things at Work: Informal Social-Material Mechanisms for Getting the Job Done," *Journal of Consumer Culture* 8, no. 1 (March 2008): 35–67.

2. "Lawsuit Targets Racial Profiling at Subway Checkpoints," *NYCLU News* 60, no. 2 (n.d.): 6.

3. "DiNapoli Report Finds MTA Security Program in Disarray Completion of Electronic Security Uncertain as MTA, Lockheed in Costly Litigation," January 26, 2010, http://www.osc.state.ny.us/press/releases/jan10/012610.htm. See also "Progress Report: The MTA Capital Security Program (Report 19-2010)" (Albany: Office of the New York State Comptroller, January 2010).

4. Michael M. Grynbaum, "M.T.A. Is Short on Money For Transit Security System," *New York Times*, January 27, 2010.

5. Noah McClain, "Institutions of Urban Anxiety."

6. Manny Fernandez, "A Phrase for Safety after 9/11 Goes Global," *New York Times*, May 11, 2010, A17. One New York woman has provocatively tattooed the slogan in correct typeface (including its Spanish version) on her leg (as photographed in the *Times* story).

7. Mike Frassinelli "NJ Transit riders can send text messages about suspicious activity to authorities" *Star-Ledger*, June 08, 2011, http://www.nj.com/news/index.ssf/2011/06/nj_transit_can_send_text_messa.html.

8. The information contained in this paragraph and the next comes from William Neuman, "In Response to M.T.A.'s 'Say Something' Ads, a Glimpse of Modern Fears," *New York Times*, January 7, 2008.

9. Michael Luo, "M.T.A. Sharpens a Get-Suspicious Campaign," *New York Times*, June 24, 2004, B3.

10. Al Baker, "Unexploded Car Bomb Left Trove of Evidence," *New York Times*, May 3, 2010.

11. "British spies help prevent al Qaeda-inspired attack on New York subway," *The Telegraph*, December 9, 2009.

12. Christopher Dickey, *Securing the City* (New York: Simon and Schuster, 2010).

13. Ethan Brown, *Snitch: Informantsas, Cooperators, and the Corruption of Justice* (New York: Public Affairs, 2007).

14. Associated Press, "Lawyer Argues Entrapment in Bomb Plot," *New York Times*, December 13, 2010, http://www.nytimes.com/2010/12/14/us/14bomb.html.

15. William Rashbaum and Joseph Goldstein, "Informer's Role in Terror Case Is Said to Have Deterred F.B.I," *New York Times*, November 22, 2011, A1, A26.

16. Michael Brick, "Officer Charged in Bomb Blast at Subway" *New York Times*, August 1, 2004. See also, William Rashbaum, "Forced from Job, Officer Is a Focus in Pipe Bomb Case," *New York Times*, July 21, 2004.

17. I am uncertain of the bona fide of the term as a psychological syndrome, but see, for example, Robert A. Hershbarger and Ronald K. Miller, "The Impact of Economic Conditions on the Incidence of Arson," *Journal of Risk and Insurance* 45, no. 2 (June 1978): 275–90.

18. In the year 2000, there were officially 5.6 crimes per day in the New York subway system compared to the 1990 average of forty-eight crimes a day. In 1998 New York Police Commissioner Howard Safir acknowledged that subway crime had been undercounted by 20 percent for "many years." David Kocieniewski, "Safir Is Said to Seek to

Punish a Chief over False Crime Data," *New York Times*, February 28, 1998, http://www.nytimes.com/1998/02/28/nyregion/safir-is-said-to-seek-to-punish-a-chief-over-false-crime-data.html. Among the very reasonable classificatory ambiguities: a brawl that begins above ground can be continued below; a crime on a platform can continue above ground. The decision affects crime rates "in the city" versus in the subways.

19. Harvey Hornstein, *Cruelty and Kindness: A New Look at Aggression and Altruism* (Englewood Cliffs, N.J.: Prentice Hall 1976).

20. James Barron, "Pushed to Tracks, Woman Is Killed by F Train" *New York Times*, January 5, 1995.

21. Enrico Quarantelli, "Disasters: Recipes and Remedies"; see also Erik Auf der Heide, "Common Misconceptions about Disasters: Panic, the 'Disaster Syndrome,' and Looting," in M. O'Leary (ed.) *The First 72 Hours: A Community Approach to Disaster Preparedness*, ed. M. O'Leary (New York: iUniverse Publishing, 2004), http://www.iuniverse.com/bookstore/book_detail.asp?&isbn=0-595-31084-2.

22. See the report prepared by Nandi Dill and Jennifer Telesca, "Imagining Emergency," NYU Institute for Public Knowledge, New York, 2011, pages 42, 56.

23. Kareem Fahim and Mathew Sweeny, "Postal Worker Sliced by Saw-Wielding Attacker," *New York Times*, July 7, 2006.

24. McClain, "Institutions of Urban Anxiety."

25. Rule 9.01(r) states "Conductors must observe the doors of their trains from their operating positions until the train has moved 75 feet. Failure to comply with this division constitutes, of itself, a reason for charges of misconduct and incompetence" Metropolitan Transportation Authority,"Rules and Regulations Governing Employees of MTA New York City Transit, Manhattan and Bronx" (2003): 174.

26. While lacking data on precise locations of incidents, MTA data indicate sixty-nine spitting cases in the year 2009; about half of workers involved took days off (sometimes a significant number of days) after the event. See Jim Dwyer, "Transits Ills are Worse than Accounts of Spitting," *New York Times*, May 26, 2010, A20.

27. See McClain, "Institutions of Urban Anxiety," 117–19.

28. Workers use this term interchangeably with "shoe slipper"; MTA documents refer to it as "wooden paddle."

29. Horn volume is significantly higher than the already high noise level on subway platforms, which is an average of 86 ± 4 dBA (decibel A-weighting). For details, see Robyn R. M. Gershon, Richard Neitzel, Marissa A. Barrera, and Muhammad Akram, "Pilot Survey of Subway and Bus Stop Noise Levels," *Journal of Urban Health* 83, no. 5 (September 2006): 802–12.

30. Track workers are an exception; they operate in crews that can vary in size but tend to include about a half dozen people.

31. In the context of the London Tube, authors Heath, Hindmarsh, and Luff use this term to describe communication between supervisors and train operators. C. Heath, J. Hindmarsh, and P. Luff, *Video in Qualitative Research* (London: Sage, 2010).

32. Pete Donohue, "MTA Token Booth Clerks Call in 400+ Emergencies a Day," *New York Daily News*, March 26, 2010.

33. Jack Whalen and Don Zimmerman, "Observations on the Display and Management of Emotions in Naturally Occurring Activities: The Case of 'Hysteria' in Calls

to 9-1-1," *Social Psychology Quarterly* 61, no. 2 (1998): 141–59. See also Marilyn Whalen and Don Zimmerman, "Sequential and Institutional Contexts in Calls for Help," *Social Psychology Quarterly* 50 (1987): 172–85.

34. Jack Whalen, Don H. Zimmerman, and Marilyn R. Whalen, "When Words Fail: A Single Case Analysis," *Social Problems* 35, no. 4 (October 1988): 335–62.

35. Geoffrey Raymond and Don H. Zimmerman, "Rights and Responsibilities in Calls for Help: The Case of the Mountain Glade Fire" *Research on Language and Social Interaction* 40, no. 1 (2007): 33–61.

36. Robert Jackall as cited by Bridget Hutter, in "Ways of Seeing: Understandings of Risk in Organizational Settings," in *Organizational Encounters with Risk*, 86.

37. Robert Jackall, *Moral Mazes: The World of Corporate Managers* (New York: Oxford University Press, 1998).

38. Scott Sagan, *The Limits Of Safety: Organizations, Accidents And Nuclear Weapons.* (Princeton: Princeton University Press, 1993), as cited in Diane Vaughan, "Organizational Rituals of Risk and Error," in *Organizational Encounters with Risk*.

39. Harold Garfinkel, *Studies in Ethnomethodology* (New York: Prentice Hall, 1967).

40. McClain, "Institutions of Urban Anxiety," 274.

41. This illustration owes to Noah McClain.

42. See McClain, "Institutions of Urban Anxiety," 375.

43. Martin Golden, "Golden: Assembly Inaction Allows MetroCard Swipe Scam to Continue in New York," press release from legislator's office, 2008.

44. See Noah McClain, "Hardware Mechanisms: Infrastructural Change and the Distribution of Social Consequence in the New York Subway System," working paper, Institute for Public Knowledge, New York University, January 2011.

45. Pete Donohue, "Cheaters Cost MTA Millions," *New York Daily News*, March 16, 2010.

46. McClain, "Hardware Mechanisms," working paper, Institute for Public Knowledge, New York University, 2011, 30.

47. Karl Weick, *Sensemaking in Organizations* (Thousand Oaks, Calif.: Sage Publications, 1995).

48. For a summary of Aronson's views as well as kindred scholars, see Elliot Aronson, "Fear, Denial, and Sensible Action in the Face of Disasters" *Social Research* 75, no.3 (2008): 855–72.

49. Ibid., 860.

50. Faye Steiner, "Optimal Pricing of Museum Admitions," *Journal of Cultural Economics* 21, no. 4 (1997): 307–33. See also Gypsy McFelter, "The Cost of 'Free': Admission Fees at American Art Museums," *American Association of Museums*, http://www.aam-us.org/pubs/mn/MN_JF07_cost-free.cfm.

51. Bloomberg News, http://www.bloomberg.com/apps/news?pid=newsarchive&s id=aK4TfewPa37M.

52. "Railroad Accident Brief, CSX Freight Train Derailment and Subsequent Fire in the Howard Street Tunnel in Baltimore, Maryland, on July 18, 2001," (Washington D.C.: National Transportation Safety Board, 2001). http://www.ntsb.gov/publictn/2004/RAB0408.htm (accessed June 11, 2009).

53. G.H. Frederickson and T. R. LaPorte, "Airport Security, High Reliability, and the Problem of Rationality," *Public Administration Review* 62 (2002): 36.

54. Timothy Crowe, *Crime Prevention through Environmental Design: Applications of Architectural Design and Space Management Concepts* (Oxford: Butterworth-Heinemann, 1991).

CHAPTER 4

1. Kim Hopper, *Reckoning with Homelessness* (Cornell: Cornell University Press, 2003).

2. John Braithwaite and Peter Drahos, *Global Business Regulation* (Cambridge, England: Cambridge University Press, 2000).

3. James Scott, *Seeing Like a State* (New Haven: Yale University Press, 1998).

4. Mark B. Salter, "Heterotopia and Confession," *International Political Sociology* 1 (2007): 49–66. See also Kevin D. Haggerty and Richard V. Ericson, "The Surveillant Assemblage," *British Journal of Sociology* 51 (2000): 605–22. Haggerty and Ericson argue that "this assemblage operates by abstracting human bodies from their territorial settings and separating them into a series of discrete flows. These flows are then reassembled into distinct "data doubles" which can be scrutinized and targeted for intervention" (p. 606).

5. Scott Shane and Eric Schmitt, "Officials Detain Two Airline Passengers, Fearing a Test of a Terrorist Plot," *New York Times*, August 31, 2010, A10.

6. Lee Clarke, *Worst Cases: Terror and Catastrophe in the Popular Imagination* (Chicago: University of Chicago Press, 2005).

7. flyertalk, "Airport Check-In Security Questions," accessed July 27, 2010, http://www.flyertalk.com/forum/travelbuzz/289797-airport-check-security-questions.html.

8. Rob Kitchin and Martin Dodge, "Airport Code/Spaces., pp. 96–114 in *Aeromobilities*, ed. C. Saulo, S., Kesselring, and J. Urry (New York: Routledge, 2009).

9. Erving Goffman, *Asylums: Essays on the Social Situation of Mental Patients and Other Inmates* (Garden City: Anchor Books, 1961).

10. Ole Pütz, "From Non-places to Non-events: The Airport Security Checkpoint," *Journal of Contemporary Ethnography* 41, no. 2 (January 2011): 154–88.

11. Ibid.

12. Marcus Warren, "Shoe Bomb Joke Causes Man To Miss Wedding, Pilot Faces Jail over Shoe Bomb Joke" *Daily Telegraph*, August 11, 2003.

13. Potthast observes signs at various airports that warn passengers against making jokes; here is one of them: "Making *any* [emphasis added] jokes or statements during the screening process may be grounds for both criminal and civil penalties. All such matters will be taken seriously." See Jörg Potthast, "Sense and Security: A Comparative View on Access Control at Airports," *Technology and Innovation Studies* (forthcoming).

14. "Man Who Threatened to Blow Airport 'Sky High' Could Face Jail" *Daily Telegraph*, June 11, 2011.

15. Aaron Cicourel, *The Social Organiation of Juvenile Justice* (New Brunswick, N.J.: Transaction books, 1995).

16. Sarah Lyall, "A Wee Tweet Blows Up into a Cause Célèbre" *Herald Tribune*, November 13, 2010.

17. As this book goes to press, technologies are under development that would blot out physiological details while still revealing extraneous contraband.

18. Gary Armstrong and Clive Norris, *The Maximum Surveillance Society: The Rise of CCTV* (London: Berg, 1999).

19. CBS News, video, "Airport Body Scans Debated," November 15, 2010, http://www.cbsnews.com/video/watch/?id=7057978n&tag=related;photovideo.

20. CBS News, poll on airport security, November 15, 2010, http://www.cbsnews.com/stories/2010/11/15/politics/main7057902.shtml?tag=contentMain.

21. Nate Silver, "New Poll Suggests Shift in Public Views on T.S.A. Procedures," *New York Times*, November 22, 2010.

22. Daily Mail Reporter, " 'They were staring me up and down': Woman claimed TSA security staff singled her out for her breasts," *Daily Mail*, November 26, 2010.

23. For a National Public Radio summary, see http://www.npr.org/templates/story/story.php?storyId=126833083.

24. Leon Kaufman and Joseph W. Carlson, "An Evaluation of Airport X-ray Backscatter Units Based on Image Characteristics," *Journal of Transportation Security* 4, no. 1 (2010): 73–94.

25. The Intel Hub, "DHS Bomb Implant Threat Debunked, New Step in Ongoing Terror Hype," July 7, 2011, http://theintelhub.com/2011/07/08/dhs-bomb-implant-threat-debunked-new-step-in-ongoing-terror-hype/.

26. For news coverage as well as video interview with the passenger, see http://www.nydailynews.com/news/national/2011/07/25/2011-07-25_tsa_agent_squeezed_my_urostomy_bag_got_urine_all_over_me_cancer_survivor.html.

27. Christena Nippert-Eng, *Islands of Privacy* (Chicago: University of Chicago Press, 2010).

28. msnbc.com, Travel News, "TSA Responds to Nipple Ring Complaint," updated March 31, 2008, http://www.msnbc.msn.com/id/23830845/#storyContinued.

29. Jeffry Mallow, "Airport Insecurity," *Jewish Daily Forward*, December 31, 2004.

30. The full aphorism reads like this: "The law, in its majestic equality, forbids the rich as well as the poor to sleep under bridges, to beg in the streets, and to steal bread." See Anatole France, *The Red Lily*, chapter 7 (1894), and http://www.quotationspage.com/quote/805.html.

31. Jeffrey Goldberg, "Private Plane, Public Menace," *Atlantic Monthly*, January/February 2011, 20.

32. Associated Press, nbc4i.com, "Bathroom Emergency Leads to Felony Charge," nbc4i.com, published April, 29, 2009, http://www.nbc4i.com/cmh/news/crime/article/bathroom_emergency_leads_to_felony_charge/14621/.

33. Daniel Prendergast and Michael Straw, "TSA's 'Trusted Traveler' Program May Mean Fewer Headaches for Some Airline Passengers," NYDailyNews.com, August 14, 2011, http://articles.nydailynews.com/2011-08-14/news/29902791_1_tsa-administrator-kip-hawley-traveler-program-airline-passengers.

34. Robert W. Poole Jr., "A Risk-Based Airport Security Policy," Policy Study #308, (Los Angeles: Reason Foundation, 2003), 23.

35. Steven Greenhouse, "Unions Woo Airport Security Screeners," *New York Times*, April 16, 2011, B1, 7.

36. Richard J. Lundman and Robert L. Kaufman, "Driving While Black: Effects of Race, Ethnicity, and Gender on Citizen Self Reports of Traffic Stops and Police Action," *Criminology* 41, no. 1 (2003): 195–220. See also David A. Harris, "The Stories, the Statistics and the Law: Why 'Driving While Black' Matters," *University of Minnesota Law Review* 84, no. 2 (1999).

37. See Matthew DeLong, "'Flying While Muslim,' the New 'Driving While Black,'" *Washington Independent*, January 2, 2009, http://washingtonindependent. com/23578/flying-while-muslim-the-new-driving-while-black. We also have evidence from the subways (see prior chapter) of complaints that being Arab-looking generates a vast number of stops.

38. Bruce Schneier, "Profiling Makes Us Less Safe," *New York Times*, January 4, 2010.

39. See Hutter and Powell, *Organizational Encounters with Risk*, for the larger concept of organizational shaping of security precaution.

40. Brian A. Jackson, "Marrying Prevention and Resiliency Balancing Approaches to an Uncertain Terrorist Threat," RAND occasional paper (Santa Monica, Calif.: RAND Corporation, 2008).

41. William Freudenburg, "Institutional Failure and the Organizational Amplification of Risk: The Need for a Closer Look," in *The Social Amplification of Risk*, ed. Nick Pidgeon, Roger E. Kasperson, and Paul Slovic (Cambridge, England: University of Cambridge Press 2003), 115.

42. Lisa Parks, "Points of Departure: The Culture of U.S. Airport Screening," *Journal of Visual Culture* 6, no.1 (2007): 183–200.

43. Charles Rumford Walker, Robert H. Guest, and W. Powell, *Man on the Assembly Line* (Cambridge, Mass.: Harvard University Press, 1959).

44. Josiah McC. Heyman, "Putting Power in the Anthropology of Bureaucracy: The Immigration and Naturalization Service at the Mexico-United States Border," *Current Anthropology* 36, no. 2 (1995).

45. Poole, "A Risk-Based Airport Security Policy," 11.

46. David Muir, "Newark Airport Security Breach Called a 'Management Failure,'" ABC World News, January 6, 2010, http://abcnews.go.com/WN/ security-breach-newark-airport-management-failure/story?id=9496125.

47. For passenger airport comments experiences, go to http://www.airlinequality. com/main/forum.htm. For Schneier's blog, go to http://www.schneier.com/blog/archives/2006/03/airport_passeng.html.

48. Meredith Jessup, "Security Fail: Loaded Gun Passes through TSA Screening," posted December 17, 2010, http://www.theblaze.com/stories/ security-fail-loaded-gun-passes-through-tsa-screening/.

49. For a first-person video from the passenger, see http://www.youtube.com/ watch?v=RosjJtyIjYA.

50. Fox Butterfield, "Threats and Responses: The Shoe Bomb Case; Qaeda Man Pleads Guilty Flying With Shoe Bomb," *New York Times*, October 5, 2002, http://www. nytimes.com/2002/10/05/us/threats-responses-shoe-bomb-case-qaeda-man-pleads-guilty-flying-with-shoe-bomb.html?ref=richardcreid (accessed Jan 31, 2011).

51. Post by MK to Greg Laden's blog, "Overheard at Airport," July 30, 2009, http:// scienceblogs.com/gregladen/2009/07/overheard_at_airport.php.

52. Flying with Fish blog, "TSA Enhanced Pat-Downs: The Screeners' Point of View," Boarding Area, November 18, 2010, http://boardingarea.com/blogs/flyingwithfish/2010/11/18/tsa-enhanced-pat-downs-the-screeners-point-of-view/.

53. Doreen Carvajal, "Reporter Breaches Amsterdam Airport's Security," *New York Times*, March 10, 2010.

54. Samidh Chakrabarti and Aaron Strauss, "Carnival Booth: An Algorithm for Defeating the Computer-Assisted Passenger Screening System," *First Monday* 7, no. 10 (2002), http://www.uic.edu/htbin/cgiwrap/bin/ojs/index.php/fm/article/view/992/913.

55. Interview with TSA officials.

56. Matthew L. Wald, "Senators Criticize Decision to Allow Scissors on Planes" *New York Times*, December 13, 2005.

57. Department of Homeland Security Office of Inspector General, "Review of Allegations Regarding San Francisco International Airport, OIG-07-04," October 2006, http://www.dhs.gov/xoig/assets/mgmtrpts/OIG_07-04_Oct06.pdf.

58. Jim Doyle, "San Francisco International Airport screening tests were sabotaged; Security workers were warned when undercover agent arrived," SFGate, November 17, 2006, http://articles.sfgate.com/2006-11-17/bay-area/17322570_1_security-breach-tsa-officials-screeners.

59. A. G. Sulzberger, "2 Men Convicted in Kennedy Airport Plot," *New York Times*. August 2, 2010.

60. Deirdre Boden, *The Business of Talk* (Oxford: Blackwell, 1995).

61. Cathy Booth Thomas "11 Lives—The Flight Attendants," *Time*, September 1, 2002, http://www.time.com/time/covers/1101020909/aattendants.html.

62. U.S. District Court, United States of America v. Richard C. Reid, criminal complaint (filed December 22, 2001), retrieved from NEFA [Nine Eleven Finding Answers] Foundation and Wikipedia, accessed July 30, 2010, http://nefafoundation.org/miscellaneous/FeaturedDocs/U.S._v_Reid_Complaint.pdf Monday (2005-07-25). See also Pam Belluck, "Threats and Responses: The Bomb Plot; Unrepetant Shoe Bomber Is Given a Life Sentence for Trying to Blow Up Jet," http://www.nytimes.com/2003/01/31/us/threats-responses-bomb-plot-unrepentant-shoe-bomber-given-life-sentence-for.html?pagewanted=all&src=pm.

63. Scott Shane and Eric Lipton, "Passengers Took Plane's Survival into Own Hands," *New York Times*, December 26, 2009, http://www.nytimes.com/2009/12/27/us/27plane.html?_r=1&hp.

64. See Garrick Blalock, Vrinda Kadiyali, and Daniel H. Simon, "The Impact of Post-9/11 Airport Security Measures on the Demand for Air Travel" forthcoming *Journal of Law and Economics*, http://dyson.cornell.edu/faculty_sites/gb78/wp/JLE_6301.pdf.

65. See the 2002 study by the Air Transport Association (Washington, D.C.): "State of the Airline Industry One Year After 9/11," p. 13. See also Don Phillips, "Airlines' Representative Deplores Security 'Mess,'" *International Herald Tribune*, December 10, 2004. See also Barbara De Lollis, "'Trusted-Traveler' Card Could Speed Security Check," *USA Today*, July 1, 2002.

66. Blalock et al., "The Impact of Post-9/11 Airport Security Measures."

67. Michael Mecham, "Flying Less, Irritated More—Biz Travelers Sound Off," *Aviation Week and Space Technology*, April 29, 2002, 64.

68. Garrick Blalock, Vrinda Kadiyali, and Daniel H. Simon, "Driving Fatalities after 9/11: A Hidden Cost of Terrorism," *Applied Economics* 41, no. 14: 1717–29.

69. Nate Silver, "The Hidden Costs of Extra Security," *New York Times*, November 11, 2010, http://fivethirtyeight.blogs.nytimes.com/2010/11/18/the-hidden-costs-of-extra-airport-security/?partner=rss&emc=rss.

70. Blalock et al., "Driving Fatalities after 9/11," 1728.

71. Air Canada, Travel Update, accessed March 2, 2002, http://www.aircanada.com/en/news/trav_adv/091226.html.

72. Susan Stellin, "A Long Wait Gets Longer," *New York Times*, Aug. 23, 2011, B4.

73. Pilita Clark and Jeremy Lemer, "Broughton releases pent-up industry tension," *Financial Times*, October 27 2010. http://www.ft.com/cms/s/0/25c69348-e201-11df-a064-00144feabdc0.html#axzz1KMlz9odR Accessed April 23, 2011.

74. Ibid.

75. Ibid.

76. This is the International Civil Agency Organization (ICAO). For access to this unit's security branch, go to: http://www.icao.int/atb/avsec/index.asp

77. The term now circulates widely but is often associated with Bruce Schneier, *Beyond Fear* (New York: Copernicus, 2006).

78. "TSA + NGC + IDEO: TSA Checkpoint Vision" *Phase 2 Review*, June 29, 2007, IDEO publication, no date or location given.

79. See Richard Thaler and Cass Sunstein, *Nudge* (New Haven: Yale University Press, 2008).

80. Glenn Wharton and Harvey Molotch, "The Chanllenge of Installation Art," pp. 210–222 in (eds.), *Conservation: Principles, Dilemmas, and Uncomfortable Truths*, ed. A. Bracker and A. Richmond (London: Elvsevier 2009).

81. Terry L. Schell, Brian G. Chow, and Clifford Grammich, "2003 Designing Airports for Security," RAND Issue Paper (Santa Monica, Calif.: RAND Corporation, 2003): 6.

82. G.H. Frederickson and T. R. LaPorte "Airport security, high reliability, and the problem of rationality," *Public Administration Review* 62 (2002): 33–43.

83. Poole, Jr., "A Risk-Based Airport Security Policy."

CHAPTER 5

1. Video of Bush at ground zero site, http://www.youtube.com/watch?v=f4BkzuV0LYE.

2. Eric Pooley, "Mayor of the World," *Time*, December 31, 2001.

3. David W. Dunlap and Julie V. Iovine, "Reaching the Sky, and Finding a Limit; Tall Buildings Face New Doubt as Symbols of Vulnerability," *New York Times*, September 19, 2001.

4. Kevin Rozario, "Making Progress: Disaster Narratives and the Art of Optimism in America," in *The Resilient City: How Modern Cities Recover From Disaster*, ed. Lawrence J. Vale and Thomas J. Campenella (Oxford: Oxford University Press, 2005), 33.

5. William Langewiesche, "American Ground: Unbuilding the World Trade Center," *Atlantic Monthly*, July–August 2002, 47.

6. Carl S. Smith, *Urban Disorder and the Shape of Belief: The Great Chicago Fire, the Haymarket Bomb, and the Model Town of Pullman* (Chicago: University of Chicago Press, 1995).

7. Anita Gates, "America Rebuilds II: Return to Ground Zero," *New York Times*, September 11, 2006.

8. Ibid.

9. Denise Grady, "Lung function of 9/11 Rescuers Fell, Study Finds," *New York Times*, April 7, 2010. A listing of 250 articles on health impacts of 9/11 can be found at Centers for Disease Control and Prevention, "World Trade Center Health Programs," last updated November 23, 2011, http://www.cdc.gov/niosh/topics/wtc/SciSumAllBy-Year.html.

10. M. P. Mauer, K. R. Cummings, R. Hoen, "Long-term Respiratory Symptoms in World Trade Center responders," *Occupational Medicine* 60, no. 2 (March 2010): 145–51.

11. S. Lin, R. Jones, J. Reibman, D. Morse, and S. A. Hwang, "Lower Respiratory Symptoms among Residents Living near the World Trade Center, Two and Four Years after 9/11," *International Journal of Occupational and Environmental Health* 16, no. 1 (January–March 2010): 44–52.

12. Anthony M Szema, Meera Khedkar, Patrick F. Maloney, Patricia A. Takach, Michael S. Nickels, Harshit Patel, Francesmary Modugno, Alan Y. Tso, and Deborah H. Lin, "Clinical Deterioration in Pediatric Asthmatic Patients after September 11, 2001," *Journal of Allergy and Clinical Immunology* 113, no. 3 (March 2004): 420–26.

13. Anthony DePalma, "EPA Whistle-Blower Says U.S. Hid 9/11 Dust Danger," *New York Times*, August 25, 2006.

14. Andrew Stephen, "The Poisonous Legacy of 9/11," *New Statesman*, June 4, 2007.

15. Office of Inspector General, U.S. Environmental Protection Agency, Evaluation Report, "EPA's Response to the World Trade Center Collapse: Challenges, Successes, and Areas for Improvement," report no. 2003-P-00012, August 21, 2003. See also DePalma, "EPA Whistle-Blower."

16. James M. Klatell, "Insider: EPA Lied about WTC Air," CBS News, video, September 10, 2009, http://www.cbsnews.com/stories/2006/09/08/earlyshow/main1985804_page2.shtml?tag=contentMain;contentBody.

17. Paul Betts, *The Authority of Everyday Objects: A Cultural History of West German Industrial Design* (Berkeley: University of California Press, 2007).

18. Paul Goldberger, "Why We Should Build Apartments at Ground Zero," *New Yorker*. May 30, 2005.

19. Kathryn S. Wylde, "The Old Downtown Economy Won't Return," *New York Times*, March 29, 2002.

20. Fosher, *Under Construction*, 181.

21. Civic Alliance to Rebuild Downtown New York, http://www.rpa.org/civicalliance/.

22. Philip Nobel, *Sixteen Acres: Architecture and the Outrageous Struggle for the Future of Ground Zero* (New York: Metropolitan Books, 2005), 115.

23. Associated Press, "NY Gov. Pataki Says NO to Commercial Building at WTC Site," Firehouse Forum, July 2002, last accessed May 2, 2011, http://www.firehouse.com/forums/showthread.php?t=38437.

24. Nobel, *Sixteen Acres*, 196.

25. Transcript of Donald Trump interview with Chris Mathews, "Trump Calls Freedom Tower 'Disgusting' and a Pile of Junk,'" MSNBC TV, last updated May 13, 2005, accessed October 27, 2010, http://www.msnbc.msn.com/id/7832944/#slice-2.

26. "The World Trade Centre Slow Building," *The Economist*, April 23, 2009.

27. Dunlap and Iovine, "Reaching the Sky."

28. Ibid.

29. Theresa Agovino, "Condé Nast Deal at 1 WTC Now Official" *Crain's New York Business Daily*, May 25, 2011, http://www.crainsnewyork.com/article/20110525/REAL_ESTATE/110529932#ixzz1XawWMHPh; see also Joe Nocera, "9/11's White Elephant," *New York Times*, August 20, 2011, A17.

30. David W. Dunlap, "A New World Trade Center that Wasn't to Be," *New York Times*, October 2, 2008, http://cityroom.blogs.nytimes.com/2008/10/02/a-new-world-trade-center-that-wasnt-to-be/.

31. Website of Skidmore, Owings, and Merrill, accessed October 27, 2010, http://www.som.com/content.cfm/one_world_trade_center.

32. Jeff Speck, "The Freedom Tower: An Alienating Monument to Surrender," *Metropolis Magazine*, July 5, 2005.

33. Patrick D. Healy, "Pataki Warns Cultural Groups for Museum at Ground Zero" *New York Times*, June 25, 2005, http://www.nytimes.com/2005/06/25/nyregion/25rebuild.html?pagewanted=print.

34. According to the arts blog "Hyperallergenic," http://hyperallergic.com/10201/frank-gehrys-latest-development-tango-the-joyce-theaters-new-lower-manhattan-home/.

35. Timothy Noah, "Why No More 9/11s?" *Slate Magazine*, March 5, 2009.

36. Linda J. Bilmes and Joseph E. Stiglitz, "The Iraq War Will Cost Us $3 Trillion, and Much More," *Washington Post*, March 9, 2008. A later *New York Times* data source put the figure at $3.3 trillion. See Amanda Cox, "A 9/11 Tally: $3.3 Trillion" *New York Times*, September 11, 2011, 13.

37. *New Yorker*, "Talk of the Town," September 24, 2001, http://www.newyorker.com/archive/2001/09/24/010924ta_talk_wtc#ixzz1CfbLQsiI.

38. Ross Douthat, "The Devil We Know," *New York Times*, January 30, 2011.

39. Council on Competitiveness, "Resilient Enterprise Paradigm," U.S. Department of Commerce, accessed June 21, 2011, www.ntis.gov/pdf/Report-ResilientEconomyParadigm.pdf.

40. Richard Posner, *Catastrophe: Risk and Response* (New York: Oxford, 2004).

41. Jason D. Averill, Dennis S. Mileti, Richard D. Peacock, Erica D. Kuligowski, Norman Groner, Guylene Proulx, Paul A. Reneke, and Harold E. Nelson, "Federal Building and Fire Safety Investigation of the World Trade Center Disaster, Occupant Behavior, Egress, and Emergency Communications," NIST NCSTAR 1-7, U.S. Department of Commerce, Washington, D.C., September 2005.

42. Josie Byzek and Tim Gilmer, "Unsafe Refuge: Why Did So Many Wheelchair Users Die on Sept. 11?" *New Mobility Magazine*, December 2001, accessed August 2, 2011, http://www.newmobility.com/articleView.cfm?id=476&action=browse.

43. David Lowenthal, *The Heritage Crusade and the Spoils of History* (Cambridge, England: Cambridge University Press, 1996).

44. Max Page, "Rethink the Type of Memorial We Want," *Gotham Gazette*, November 29, 2003, accessed November 29, 2011, http://www.gothamgazette.com/article/iotw/20031124/200/768.

45. Max Page provided this quote; see his "On Edge, Again," *New York Times*, October 21, 2001, accessed November 29, 2011, http://www.nytimes.com/2001/10/21/nyregion/on-edge-again.html?pagewanted=all.

CHAPTER 6

1. See, for example: G. F. White (with the Committee), *Integrated River Basin Development* (New York: U.N. Department of Economic and Social Affairs, 1958). See also, J. L. Wescoat, "Gilbert Fowler White (1911–2006), Wisdom in Environmental Geography," *Geographical Review* 96, no. 4 (2006): 700–710.

2. Quarantelli as quoted William R. Freudenburg, Robert Gramling, Shirley Laska, and Kai Erikson, *Catastrophe in the Making: The Engineering of Katrina and the Disasters of Tomorrow* (San Francisco: Island Press, 2009), 27.

3. Oliver Houck, "Can We Save New Orleans?" *Tulane Environmental Law Journal* 19 (2006): 30.

4. This work was carried out under the auspices of the Social Science Research Council and funded by the Gates Foundation, under the coordinating leadership of Kai Ericson. A series of volumes is being published by the University of Texas Press based on these studies.

5. John Logan and Harvey Molotch, *Urban Fortunes* (Berkeley: University of California Press, 1987).

6. Bret Schulte, "A Troubling Bayou Tradition: Louisiana's History of Corruption Bodes Ill for the Relief Money Headed Its Way," *U.S. News and World Report*, October 2, 2005, http://www.usnews.com/usnews/news/articles/051010/10louisiana.htm.

7. Ari Kelman, *A River and Its City: The Nature of Landscape in New Orleans* (Berkeley: University of California Press, 2003).

8. Committee on the Restoration and Protection of Coastal Louisiana Ocean Studies Board, Division on Earth and Life Studies, National Research Council of the National Academies, "Drawing Louisiana's New Map: Addressing Land Loss in Coastal Louisiana" (Washington, D.C.: National Academies Press, 2009).

9. Charles Ellet, "Report on the Overflows of the Delta of the Mississippi," in Senate, Ex. Doc. 20, 32nd Congress, 1st session, as quoted in Kelman, *A River and Its City*, 163.

10. Geoff Manaugh and Nicola Twilley, "On Flexible Urbanism," in *What Is a City?* ed. Phil Steinberg and Rob Shields (Athens: University of Georgia Press, 2008), 63, emphasis in original.

11. W. Silva, F. Klijn, and J. Dijkman, "Room for the Rhine Branches in the Netherlands, Lelystad" (Netherlands: Rijksinstituut voor Integraal Zoetwaterbeheer en Afvalwaterbehandeling, 2003), as cited in Freudenburg et al., *Catastrophe in the Making*, 153.

12. Kelman, *A River and Its City*, 195.

13. R. W. Kates, C. E. Colten, S. Laska, and S. P. Leatherman, "Reconstruction of New Orleans after Hurricane Katrina: A Research Perspective," *Proceedings of the National Academy of Sciences* 103, no. 40 (2006): 14653–60. The concept owes to Gilbert White's early formulation.

14. John Bohannon and Martin Enserink, "Scientists Weigh Options for Rebuilding New Orleans," *Science* 309 (2005): 1808–9. This role of wetlands in dampening storm surge was repeated to others and myself in our post-Katrina interviews with Gulf-area scientists.

15. S. Penland, A. Beall, D. Britsch, and J. Williams, "Pontchartrain Basin Land Loss – Process Classification," in *Environmental Atlas of the Lake Pontchartrain Basin*, ed. Shea Penland, Andrew Beall, and Jack Kindinger, U.S. Geological Survey, Open Report 02-206, (Reston, Va.: U.S. Geological Survey, 2002).

16. Freudenburg et al., *Catastrophe in the Making*, 117.

17. Steinberg and Shields, *What Is a City?* 72.

18. See R. E. Turner, "Wetland loss in the Northern Gulf of Mexico: Multiple Working Hypotheses," *Estuaries* 20 (1997) 1–13. In contrast, one group claims that the influence of dredging on wetland loss varies spatially, and only 9 percent of the nondirect loss is due to altered hydrology and saltwater intrusion (as quoted from Committee on the Restoration and Protection of Coastal Louisiana Ocean Studies Board, "Drawing Louisiana's New Map," 38); see J. W. Day, G. P. Shaffer, L. D. Britsch, D. J. Reed, S. R. Hawes, and D. Cahoon, "Pattern and Process of Land Loss in the Mississippi Delta: A Spatial and Temporal Analysis of Wetland Habitat Change," *Estuaries* 23 no. 4 (2000): 425–38.

19. Committee on the Restoration and Protection of Coastal Louisiana Ocean Studies Board, "Drawing Louisiana's New Map," 39.

20. Michael Grunwald, "Canal May Have Worsened City's Flooding," *Washington Post*, September 14, 2005, http://www.washingtonpost.com/wp-dyn/content/article/2005/09/13/AR2005091302196.html. See also the UC Berkeley–led report from the National Academy of Science, "Investigation of the Performance of the New Orleans Flood Protection Systems in Hurricane Katrina on August 29, 2005," July 31, 2006. Christopher Cooper and Robert Block also incriminate MRGO as a cause of New Orleans flooding; see Cooper and Block, *Disaster: Hurricane Katrina and the Failure of Homeland Security* (New York: Henry Holt: 2006), 26–28.

21. *Comprehensive Habitat Management Plan for the Lake Pontchartrain Basin* (New Orleans: Lake Pontchartrain Basin Foundation, 2006).

22. Freudenburg et al., *Catastrophe in the Making*, 64.

23. Robert Gramling, William R. Freudenburg, Shirley Laska, and Kai T. Erikson. 2011. "Obsolete and Irreversible: Technology, Local Economic Development and the Environment" *Society and Natural Resources* 24 (2011): 521–34. The $19 million maintenance cost comes from Charles Camillo of the U.S. Army Corp of Engineers,

as personal communication to Robert Gramling (September 19, 2008). See chapter 8, endnote 15, Freudenburg et al., *Catastrophe in the Making*, 179.

24. Freudenburg et al., *Catastrophe in the Making*, 10.

25. Ibid., 10. Or, as Erikson has put it, there is a "technological Peter principle" at work that causes things to be built up to the very edge of capacity, such that artifacts and systems cannot deal with even a slight stress beyond. See Kai Ericson, *Everything in Its Path: The Destruction of Community in the Buffalo Creek Flood* (New York: Simon & Schuster, 1976).

26. Freudenburg et al., *Catastrophe in the Making*, 79.

27. U.S. House of Representatives, "Mississippi River-Gulf Outlet," 82nd Congress, 1st Session, House of Representatives Document No. 245, (Washington, D.C., 1951). Quoted material comes from the UCSB microfiche collection, "MISSISSIPPI RIVER-GULF OUTLET," provided to me by William Freudenburg, University of California, Santa Barbara

28. U.S. House of Representatives, "Mississippi River-Gulf Outlet," item 76, p. 42.

29. Ibid., item 79, p. 42.

30. Committee on the Restoration and Protection of Coastal Louisiana Ocean Studies Board, "Drawing Louisiana's New Map," 36.

31. R. H. Kesel, "The Decline in Suspended Load of the Lower Mississippi River and Its Influence on Adjacent Wetlands," *Environmental Geology and Water Sciences* 11 (1988): 271–81, as cited in Committee on the Restoration and Protection of Coastal Louisiana Ocean Studies Board, "Drawing Louisiana's New Map."

32. Pierre Derbigny, "Case Laid Before Counsel for Their Opinion on the Claim to the Batture, Situated in Front of the Suburb St. Mary" (New Orleans: n.p., 1807): xvii, as cited in Kelman, *A River and Its City*, 38.

33. Kelman, *A River and Its City*, 44. The forced surface drainage is also part of the problem, because it lowers the water table, hence creating a vacuum. See Committee on the Restoration and Protection of Coastal Louisiana Ocean Studies Board, "Drawing Louisiana's New Map," 38.

34. Ulrich Beck, *Risk Society: Toward a New Modernity* (Thousand Oaks, Calif.: Sage Publications, 1992), 120.

35. Enrico Quarantelli, "Conventional Beliefs and Counterintuitive Realities," *Social Research* 75, no. 3 (2008): 886.

36. "Plaintiffs Wrap Up Their Case in MRGO Trial," *The Picayune Item*, May 2, 2009.

37. Quote is from the transcript of *Meet the Press*, NBC News, September 4, 2005, cited also in Ivor Van Heerden, *The Storm: What Went Wrong and Why During Hurricane Katrina—The Inside Story from One Louisiana Scientist* (New York: Penguin, 2006).

38. Joseph W. Westphal, "The Politics of Infrastructure," *Social Research* 75, no. 3 (2008): 802.

39. Ibid, 795.

40. Ibid, 801.

41. Van Heerden, *The Storm*, 232–33, 247. For full documentation, based on the NSF/UC Berkeley study of the Katrina engineering failures, see http://www.ce.berkeley.edu/projects/neworleans/.

42. Matt Palmquist, "Did Termites Help Flood New Orleans?" *Miller-McCune*, January–February, 2009, 22–25.

43. C.A.5, 1971, *Graci v. United States*, 456 F.2d 20, 2 ERC 1591, 1971 A.M.C. 2296.

44. Stephen Graham, "Disruption by Design: Urban Infrastructure and Political Violence," in *Disrupted Cities: When Infrastructure Fails* (New York and London: Routledge, 2010), 126.

45. Mitre Corp., "A Vision for the Future," EP&R/FEMA Study, March 7, 2005. See also, "Highlights of Two FEMA Disaster Reports," Associated Press, April 3, 2006.

46. Aaron Broussard on *Meet the Press*, NBC News, September 4, 2005; see transcript, http://www.msnbc.msn.com/id/9179790/ns/meet_the_press/.

47. Cooper and Block, *Disaster*, 190.

48. C. R. Walker and R. H. Guest, *The Man on the Assembly Line* (Cambridge, Mass.: Harvard University Press, 1952).

49. Peter Blau, *The Dynamics of Bureaucracy; A Study of Interpersonal Relations in Two Government Agencies* (Chicago: University of Chicago Press, 1973).

50. Don Zimmerman, "Tasks and troubles: The Practical Bases of Work Activities in a Public Assistance Agency," in *Explorations in Sociology and Counseling*, ed. D. Hansen (New York: Houghton-Mifflin 1969); Don Zimmerman, "The Practicalities of Rule Use," pp. 285–95 in *Understanding Everyday Life*, ed. J. Douglas (Chicago: Aldine, 1970).

51. David Sudnow, *Passing On: The Social Organization of Dying* (Englewood Cliffs, N.J.: Prentice Hall, 1967).

52. Garfinkel, *Studies in Ethnomethodology*.

53. Marilyn Whalen and Don Zimmerman, "Sequential and Institutional Contexts in Calls for Help," *Social Psychology Quarterly* 30 (1987): 172–85.

54. Norimitsu Onishi and Martin Fackler, "In Nuclear Crisis, Crippling Mistrust," *New York Times*, June 13, 2011, A1, A9.

55. Jean Pelletier, *The Canadian Caper* (New York: William Morrow, 1981). See also CBC Archives, "Canadian Caper Helps Americans Escape Tehran," broadcast January 29, 1980, http://archives.cbc.ca/war_conflict/terrorism/clips/12843/.

56. Cooper and Block, *Disaster*.

57. PBS Frontline, interview with Leo Bosner, "The Storm," http://www.pbs.org/wgbh/pages/frontline/storm/interviews/bosner.html.

58. Cooper and Block, *Disaster*.

59. One of the mishearings may have resulted from the fact that the technical term for what are commonly referred to as "levees" are, in some cases, "floodwalls." So one internal alert stated, "Floodwalls were overtopped. . . . Sections of wall failed in each area" (ibid., 142).

60. Ibid., 131.

61. Ibid, 132.

62. Ibid, 265.

63. Freudenburg et al., *Catastrophe in the Making*, 19.

64. Eric Klinenberg, *Heat Wave: A Social Autopsy of Disaster in Chicago* (Chicago: University of Chicago Press, 2002).

65. Patrick Sharkey, "Survival and Death in New Orleans: An Empirical Look at the Human Impact of Katrina," *Journal of Black Studies* 37, no. 4 (March 2007): 482–501.

66. Pamela Jenkins, "Before and after Katrina: Gender and the Landscape of Community Work," in *The Women of Katrina: How Gender, Race, and Class Matter in an American Disaster*, ed. Emmanuel David and Elaine Enarson (Nashville: Vanderilt University Press, forthcoming).

67. Nagin's quote comes from an interview on *The Oprah Winfrey Show*, which aired September 5, 2005. See also, Cooper and Block, *Disaster*, 193.

68. Cooper and Block, *Disaster*, 197.

69. National Public Radio, transcript, "Evacuees Were Turned Away at Gretna, La.," September 20, 2005, http://www.npr.org/templates/story/story.php?storyId=4855611.

70. Kathleen Tierney, Christine Bevc, and Erica Kuligowski, "Metaphors Matter: Disaster Myths, Media Frames, and Their Consequences," *Annals of the American Academy of Political and Social Science* 604, no. 1 (2006): 57–81.

71. Altlhough this is an oft-reported quote, but I could find no original source.

72. Joseph R. Chenelly, "Troops Begin Combat Operations in New Orleans," *Army Times* September 2, 2005.

73. P. W. Singer, "Strange Brew: Private Military Contractors and Humanitarians," in *Disaster and the Politics of Intervention*, ed. Andrew Lakoff (New York: Columbia University Press, 2010), 89.

74. Tierney et al., "Metaphors Matter."

75. Ibid, 72.

76. Cooper and Block, *Disaster*, 223.

77. Ibid., 206.

78. Kelly Frailing and Dee Wood Harper, "Crime and Hurricanes in New Orleans," *The Sociology of Katrina*, ed. David L. Brunsma, David Overfelt, and Steven Picou (Lanham, England: Rowman & Littlefield, 2010).

79. Anna Mulrine, "When the Cops Turn Into the Bad Guys the New Orleans Police Department Hits Its Nadir," *U.S. News and World Report*, October 2, 2005.

80. Fosher, *Under Construction*, 39.

81. Thanks to Wesley Shrum (Sociology Department, Louisiana State University) for bringing these plausible calculations to my attention through his "Video-Ethnography of the Army Corps of Engineers," Meetings of the Southern Sociological Society, New Orleans, April 2, 2009.

82. Carol B. Stack, *All Our Kin: Strategies for Survival in a Black Community* (New York: Harper, 1974).

83. For elaboration of the idea and rebuttal to it, see Deborah A. Stone, *The Samaritan's Dilemma: Should Government Help Your Neighbor?* (New York: Nation Books, 2008).

84. For 2010 census quick facts on New Orleans, see http://quickfacts.census.gov/qfd/states/22/2255000.html.

85. Personal e-mail communication to author, July 4, 2011.

86. This is the way HUD officials defended the action in public debates as well as in litigation. See Comments from Left Field, "Razing the Project to Save it," posted January 28, 2009, http://commentsfromleftfield.com/2009/01/razing-the-project-to-save-it.

87. See Harvey Molotch, *Managed Integration* (Berkeley: University of California Press, 1973).

88. Nicolai Ouroussoff, "To Renovate, and Surpass, City's Legacy," *New York Times*, April 7, 2011.

89. Robyn, Spencer, "Contested Terrain: The Mississippi Flood of 1927 and the Struggle to Control Black Labor," *Journal of Negro History* 79, no. 2 (1994): 173.

90. Ibid. See also Michael P. Powers, "A Matter of Choice," pp. 13–36 in *There Is No Such Thing as a Natural Disaster*, ed. Chester Hartman and Gregory Squires (New York: Routledge, 2006); John M. Barry, *Rising Tide: The Great Mississippi Flood of 1927 and How It Changed America* (New York: Simon and Schuster, 1997).

91. Kelman, *A River and Its City*, 176.

92. Barry, *Rising Tide*, 255.

93. Christine Bevc, Keith Nicholls, and J. Steven Picou, "Community Recovery from Hurricane Katrina: Storm Experiences, Property Damage, and the Human Condition," in *Sociology of Katrina*, 135–56.

94. Manaugh and Twilley "On Flexible Urbanism," 75.

95. See the MoMA "Rising Currents" website, http://www.moma.org/explore/inside_out/2009/12/01/rising-currents-two-weeks-deep/.

Chapter 7

1. Naomi Klien, *The Shock Doctrine*, (New York: Knopf, 2007).

2. Thomas Scheff, personal correspondence.

3. NBC News, "Three Sought after Second Car Bomb in London," updated June 29, 2007, http://www.msnbc.msn.com/id/19495826/ns/world_news-europe/. For a listing of bungled efforts over recent years, see Carol Bengle Gilbert, "Biggest Bunglers Associated with Osama bin Laden," Yahoo Voices, May 2, 2011, http://www.associated-content.com/article/8023405/biggest_bumblers_associated_with_osama.html.

4. Ithiel de Sola Pool and Manfred Kochen, "Contacts and influence," *Social Networks* 1 no. 1 (1978[?]): 42.

5. Sabrina Tavernise and Andrew W. Lehren, "A Grim Portrait of Civilian Deaths in Iraq," *New York Times*, October 22, 2010.

6. Mark Danner, "Our State of Exception," *New York Review of Books*, October 13, 2011, 44–48. See also Jeffrey Travers and Stanley Milgram, "An Experimental Study of the Small World Problem," *Sociometry* 32 (December 4, 1969): 425–43.

7. Alice Goffman, "On the Run: Wanted Men in a Philadelphia Ghetto," *American Sociological Review* 74, no. 3 (2009): 339–57.

8. Michael Schwartz, "Military Neoliberalism: Endless War and Humanitarian Crisis in the 21st century," *Societies Without Borders* 6, no. 3 (2011): 190–303.

9. Ibid.

10. Data comes from the Triangle Center on Terrorism and Homeland Security, linked to the Research Triangle at Duke University and University of North Carolina. See Laurie Goodstein, "Muslims To Be Hearings' Main Focus," *New York Times*, February 8, 2011.

11. Charles Kurzman, *The Missing Martyrs* (London and New York: Oxford University Press, 2011).

12. "Injustice in the Name of Security," *New York Times*, July 13, 2009.

13. Initially charged with "conspiracy to riot in furtherance of terrorism," the yippee-like "Welcoming Committee" for the 2008 Republican Convention in New York City included video clips that the group had made showing, according to the charges, "a figure dressed in black using a Molotov cocktail to ignite a backyard grill." See Colin Moynihan, "Charges Dropped for 3 Accused of Planning to Riot," *New York Times*, September 17, 2010.

14. Dana Priest and William M. Arkin, *Top Secret America* (New York: Little Brown, 2011), 229.

15. Jean-Paul Brodeur and Stéphane Leman-Langlois, "Surveillance Fiction or Higher
Policing?" in *The New Politics of Surveillance and Visibility*, ed. Edward D. Haggerty and Richard V. Ericson (Toronto: University of Toronto Press, 2006).

16. Andrew Cockburn, "Search and Destroy: The Pentagon's Losing Battle Against IEDs," *Harper's*, November 2011, 71–77, quote is from page 76.

17. I take the idea of "lightness" from Karin Knorr Cetina, "Complex Global Microstructures: The New Terrorist Societies," *Theory, Culture & Society* 22, no. 5 (2005): 213–34.

18. The quote is from Marc Sageman, a forensic psychiatrist and former CIA officer. See Terry McDermott, "The Mastermind: Khalid Sheikh Mohammed and the Making of 9/11," *New Yorker*, September 13, 2010, 50.

19. Ibid.

20. The man convicted in 1991 of a "terrorist" crime accomplice to the murder of zealous Zionist Meir Kahane (El Sayyid Nosair) had training manuals from the American Special Warfare School at Fort Bragg in his apartment. From Mark S. Hamm, *Terrorism as Crime: From Oklahoma City to Al-Qaeda and Beyond* (New York: New York University Press, 2007), 30.

21. Juan Cole, *Engaging the Muslim World* (New York: Palgrave Macmillan, 2010).

22. Arthur L. Kellermann et al. "Gun Ownership as a Risk Factor for Homicide in the Home," *New England Journal of Medicine* 329 (1993): 1084–91.

23. A. L. Kellerman, G. Somes, F. P. Rivara, R. K. Lee, and J. G. Banton, "Injuries and Deaths Due to Firearms in the Home," *Journal of Trauma* 45 (1998): 263–67.

24. Bridget M. Kuehn, "Soldier Suicide Rates Continue to Rise," *Journal of the American Medical Association* 301, no. 11 (2009): 1111–13.

25. For this and related information, I thank sociologist Michael Schwartz and his IraqViews postings. See also Michael Schwartz, *War without End: The Iraq War in Context* (Chicago: Haymarket Books, 2008).

26. Priest and Arkin, *Top Secret America*, 23–24.

27. Niall Ferguson, *The Pity of War* (New York: Basic Books, 1999), 82, as quoted in David Stevenson, *Cataclysm: The First World War as Political Tragedy* (New York: Basic Books, 2004).

28. F. Burnet and E. Clark, *Influenza: A Survey of the Last 50 Years in the Light of Modern Work on the Virus of Epidemic Influenza* (Melbourne, Australia: Macmillan, 1942).

29. Paul Ewald. *Evolution of Infectious Disease* (New York: Oxford University Press, 1994). See also *The Threat of Pandemic Influenza: Are We Ready? Workshop Summary, Institute of Medicine (U.S.) Forum on Microbial Threats*, ed. S. L. Knobler, A. Mack, A. Mahmoud et al., editors (Washington, D.C.: National Academies Press, 2005).

30. Seymour Hersh, "The Online Threat: Should We Be Worried about a Cyber War?" *New Yorker*, November 1, 2010, http://www.newyorker.com/reporting/2010/11/01/101101fa_fact_hersh#ixzz1QPi0zAn9.

31. Perrow, *Normal Accidents*. See also Scott Sagan, *The Limits of Safety: Organizations, Accidents, and Nuclear Weapons* (Princeton: Princeton University Press, 1993).

32. Lee Clarke, *Worst Cases: Terror and Catastrophe in the Popular Imagination* (Chicago: University of Chicago Press, 2005).

33. Quote is from Peter Brooks writing about Robert Darnton's *Poetry and the Police*, in *New York Review of Books*, January 13, 2011, 30; the Tocqueville book in discussion is *The Old Regime and the Revolution*.

34. N. M., "Contracted National Security Software May Be a 'Complete Fraud'" *National Security Law Brief* (Washington, D.C.: American University-Washington College of Law, 2011), http://nationalsecuritylawbrief.com/2011/02/19/contracted-national-security-software-may-be-a-complete-fraud/.

35. Transparency International, "Corruption Perceptions Index 2010 Results," http://www.transparency.org/policy_research/surveys_indices/cpi/2010/results. See also Dexter Filkins, "The Afghan Bank Heist," *New Yorker*, February 14, 2011.

36. Martin Matishak, "Homeland Security Cancels Troubled Radiation Detector Effort," *Global Security Newswire*, July 26, 2011, http://www.govexec.com/dailyfed/0711/072611-radiation-detector.htm. See also David, Sanger, "Nuclear-Detection Effort Is Halted as Ineffective," July 29, 2011, http://www.nytimes.com/2011/07/30/us/30nuke.html.

37. For details of the Montgomery case, see Eric Lichtblau and James Risen, "Hiding Details of Dubious Deal, U.S. Invokes National Security," *New York Times*, February 20, 2011.

38. Cooper and Block, *Disaster*, 51. I could not find corroboration.

39. Brian A. Jackson, "Marrying Prevention and Resiliency: Balancing Approaches to an Uncertain Terrorist Threat," RAND Homeland Security Occasional Paper (Santa Monica, Calif.: RAND Corporation, 2008), 17.

40. For some relevant information, see Daniel McGowan, "Tales from inside the U.S. Gitmo," *Huffington Post*, June 8, 2009, http://www.huffingtonpost.com/daniel-mcgowan/tales-from-inside-the-us_b_212632.html.

41. See Michael Storper, *The Regional World: Territorial Development in a Global Economy* (New York: Guilford Press, 1997); Elizabeth Currid, *Warhol Economy* (Princeton: Princeton University Press, 2008); Richard Florida, *The Rise of the Creative Class* (New York: Basic Books, 2003).

42. University of California History Digital Archives, "The Loyalty Oath Controversy, University of California, 1949–1951," last updated September 29, 2006, http://sunsite.berkeley.edu/~ucalhist/archives_exhibits/loyaltyoath/.

43. HSPD12 case, *Nelson et al. v. NASA et al.*, accessed June 21, 2011, http://hspd12jpl.org.

44. Tony Judt, "Amos Elon (1926–2009)," *New York Review of Books* 66, no. 11, July 2, 2009.

45. Dan Erlich, "Illegal Immigrants the Aspect of Success Israel Doesn't Want," *Huffington Post* (UK), accessed March 7, 2012, http://www.huffingtonpost.co.uk/dan-ehrlich/israel-illegal-immigrants_b_1184898.html.

46. Jeffrey Goldberg, "The Point of No Return," *Atlantic Magazine* 306, no. 2 (2010): 56–69.

47. "Principles for a Comprehensive Security Strategy: An Evaluation Guide for the Transportation Industry" (Baton Rouge: Legislative Auditor, State of Louisiana, 2002). The guide was developed in conjunction with the Arkansas Division of Legislative Audit, Connecticut Auditors of Public Accounts, Office of the New York State Comptroller, Rhode Island Office of the Auditor General, and the U.S. General Accounting Office.

48. Priest and Arkin, *Top Secret America*, 153.

49. Moshe Schwartz, "The Department of Defense's Use of Private Security Contractors in Iraq and Afghanistan: Background, Analysis, and Options for Congress," Congressional Research Service, Library of Congress, June 22, 2010.

50. Ibid., 1. See also Bobby A. Towery, "Phasing Out Private Security Contractors in Iraq," master's thesis, U.S. Army War College, Carlisle Barracks, Pennsylvania, March 15, 2006.

51. This conclusion is at least implicit in Kerry Fosher's arguments. See her book *Under Construction*.

52. Irus Braverman, *Planted Flags: Trees, Land, and the Law in Israel/Palestine* (Cambridge, England: Cambridge University Press, 2009).

53. Ibid., 141.

54. Thomas Jefferson, letter to William S. Smith, November 13, 1787, quoted in Saul Kussiel Padover, *Thomas Jefferson on Democracy* (New York: New American Library, 1939); see also *Memoirs, Correspondence, and Private Papers of Thomas Jefferson*, vol. 2, ed. Thomas Jefferson Randolph (London: Henry Colburn and Richard Bentley, 1829), http://books.google.com/books?id=imMmIlv1G7MC&pg=PA268&q=&f=false#v=onepage&q=&f=false.

55. Mary Louise Pratt, "Harm's Way: Language and the Contemporary Arts of War," *PMLA* 124, no.5 (2009): 1521. See also Carolyn Marvin and David Ingle, *Blood Sacrifice and the Nation: Totem Rituals and the American Flag* (Cambridge, England: Cambridge University Press, 1999).

56. Rod Bond and Peter B. Smith, "Culture and Conformity: A Meta-analysis of Studies Using Asch's Line Judgment Task," *Psychological Bulletin* 119, no. 1 (January 1996): 111–37.

57. Rob Evans and Paul Lewis "Mark Kennedy Case: CPS Accused of Suppressing Key Evidence," guardian.co.uk, June 7, 2011.

58. Jack Katz, *Seductions of Crime: Moral and Sensual Attractions in Doing Evil* (Chicago: University of Chicago Press, 1988).

59. Jane Perlez, Eric Schmitt, and Ginger Thompson, "U.S. Received Warnings on Man Behind Mumbai Plot," *International Herald Tribune*, October 18, 2010.

60. Ibid.

61. Sebastian Rotella, "Feds Confirm Mumbai Plotter Trained with Terrorists while Working for DEA," ProPublica, October 16, 2010, http://www.propublica.org/article/feds-confirm-mumbai-plotter-trained-with-terrorists-while-working-for-dea.

62. Charlie Savage, "F.B.I. Casts Wide Net under Relaxed Rules for Terror Inquiries, Data Show," *New York Times*, March 27, 2011.

63. Craig Horowitz, "Anatomy of a Foiled Plot," *New York Magazine*, May 21, 2005.

64. James Jay Carafano, Matt Mayer, and Jessica Zuckerman, "Forty-First Terror Plot Foiled: Homegrown Threat Thwarted by Local Law Enforcement and Intelligence," The Heritage Foundation, Webmemo 3376, September 29, 2011, http://www.heritage.org/research/reports/2011/09/forty-first-terror-plot-foiled-homegrown-threat-thwarted-by-local-law-enforcement-and-intelligence.

65. The most recent case (forty-first on the Heritage Foundation list) is that of Rezwan Ferdaus, which involved, among other peculiar aspects, the shipping of large numbers of rigged-up cell phones for use by terrorists in the Middle East on the apparent assumption of cell-phone unavailability in such locations.

66. These quotes owe to Kurzman, *The Missing Martyrs*, 13.

67. McClain, "Institutions of Urban Anxiety."

68. Garfinkel, *Studies in Ethnomethodology*, 216.

69. Alice Hills, *Policing Post-Conflict Cities* (London: Zed Books, 2009), 208. Hills cites Otwin Marenin, "Policing Change, Changing Police," in *Policing Change, Changing Police: International Perspectives*, ed. Otwin Marenin (New York: Garland Press, 1996).

70. Weick, *Sensemaking in Organizations*.

71. Debra van Opstal, *Transform. The Resilient Economy: Integrating Competitiveness and Security* (Washington, D.C.: Council on Competitiveness, 2007).

72. Charles Perrow, *The Next Catastrophe* (Princeton: Princeton University Press, 2011).

73. Thomas Beamish, *Silent Spill: The Organization of an Industrial Crisis* (Cambridge, Mass.: MIT Press, 2002).

74. van Opstal, *Transform*, 40.

75. T. S. Eliot, "Burnt Norton," in *Four Quartets* (New York: Harcourt, 1943).

76. Check it out: The O'Jays, "Love Train," video version edited by Infinite Green 28, YouTube, September 9, 2009, http://www.youtube.com/watch?v=9w6p4gYHd-E.

Index